THE BASQUE COUNTRY

Landscapes of the Imagination

Landscapes

THE BASQUE COUNTRY

A Cultural History

PADDY WOODWORTH

Signal Books
Oxford

First published in 2007 by
Signal Books Limited
36 Minster Road
Oxford OX4 1LY
www.signalbooks.co.uk

A catalogue record for this book is available from the British Library

ISBN 978-1-904955-31-3 Paper

Cover Design: Baseline Arts
Cover Images: Lurrak/Manuel Díaz de Rada, Paddy Woodworth, Luis Alberto García
Photographs:
    Lurrak/Manuel Díaz de Rada pp.i, xvii, 2, 12, 64, 69, 94, 97, 136, 140, 214, 238;
    Paddy Woodworth pp.xxi, 53, 74, 82, 131, 142, 160, 169, 190, 233, 246, 263, 270;
    Lurrak/Jon Benito p.7; Courtesy Sogecine p.30; Luis Alberto García pp.38, 104, 172,
    178; Lurrak/Jaqoba Zenon p.48; Courtesy Bernardo Atxaga p.147; Lurrak/Josu Zulaika
    p.205; Lurrak/Javier Arizabalo p.242; Jaime Roset/istockphoto p.257
Printed in India

CONTENTS

To my late parents,
Phyllis and Dudley Woodworth,
with love and happy memories

Acknowledgements

Frank advice is a very rare thing, and should be acknowledged first. A meticulous historian, Selma Huxley, was working on a TV documentary in the Basque County in the spring of 1979. One day she needed an urgent film delivery, and a friend and I agreed to help out. But it so happened that this was the day of a general strike, in response to a killing by the Guardia Civil. Political strikes were a serious business in those days. The main roads had been blocked by protesters, and there were police checkpoints everywhere. But she needed the film badly so, feeling alternately like strike breakers and subversives, we took dozens of back roads and made our delivery, with a scare or two along the way. High on adrenalin, and getting higher on the excellent wine she offered us, I blurted out that I wanted to write a book about the Basque Country. I had barely published two articles at that stage, and she looked at me coolly but not unkindly. Her advice was succinct: "Perhaps you should give it another ten years." I took the point, and ended up giving it nearly three decades. I am grateful that she stopped me then in my over-eager tracks. I am not at all sure now that I don't need another lifetime to get it half-way right, so I still await her judgement with trepidation.

All of the people who have helped and informed me so generously since I first went to the Basque Country in 1975 have made a contribution to these pages. To list them all is beyond both my memory and the space available, and I must beg the forgiveness of those who are omitted, and thank them for their essential if anonymous assistance.

There are several people without whom this book would not have happened, at least in its current form, and to whom I would like to give special mention. Stephen Hayward kindly recommended me to Signal, and for good or ill Michael Dwyer and James Ferguson took his advice. I am deeply grateful to them for the opportunity to write this kind of book about a country I love so much. Not many publishers, especially in these mean and mercenary times, tell a writer to "follow your own obsessions", as James did. That's a brave—and scary—instruction, and I hope it, and all his subsequent patience, have been fruitful. And, by way of a Stop Press, many thanks to Devdan Sen for his fine production work, and Kathleen May and, very especially, Kate Bowe, for their work on publicity.

Txomin Artola has been an invaluable friend and informal guide in matters Basque since we met in 1979. Joseba Zulaika's books have long offered me a most fruitful and provocative analysis of Basque culture. I am very lucky that he has also offered me tremendous encouragement (a writer's greatest external need), as well as unstinting assistance with endless queries, over the last two years. Bernardo Atxaga's novels and essays have nourished me for many years with a different register of insights, and in the few months since we have met he has also been extraordinarily generous with his time, his library and his insights.

Txema Montero and Irune Zuluaga of the Fundación Sabino Arana were unstintingly helpful in providing invaluable local contacts for my research on fiestas (a not altogether painful task, as you may gather). Txema and his wife Marivi Larrauri offered me generous hospitality besides, and Txema took me on a remarkable walk around the summit of Amboto with his hill-walking *cuadrilla*.

There was a welcoming glass, a full table and a warm bed at the home of Joe Linehan, his wife Cristina Martín, and their daughter Sinéad in Hernani, whenever I buckled before the open road. Joe, Alan Griffin, Toni Strubell and Alberto Letona were kind enough to share their own very rich experience of the Basque Country with me. José Ignacio and María Pilar, who are too modest to let me use their surnames, also offered me an open house, and took me into corners of Euskal Herria I would never have found on my own.

Pello Elzaburu brought me on a most fruitful drive from one end of Navarre to the other at very short notice. Kepa Aulestia and Teresa Casanovas gave me privileged access to the Vizcayan mining villages. My brother-in-law, Pa Duhig, read several chapters with perspicacity at a difficult time. Jesús Albores gave me invaluable help from the archives of *El País*. Igone, Carlos, Carmen and all the staff at the delightful Iturrienea Ostatu in Bilbao always gave me the warmest of welcomes.

And here I would also like to acknowledge some very old debts: Mertxe Etxebeste and Txanan Álvarez took a young journalist off the streets and into their home in Irún nearly thirty years ago. My career in the Basque Country might well have been stillborn without the welcome sanctuary they provided over several years. Iñigo Ciriquain and Margarita Echeverria were unfailingly kind neighbours to me in this period also.

I would like to express my warm thanks to the many people who speak to me in the pages that follow. Their generosity with their time and knowledge was invaluable. Other individuals not mentioned the text also made helpful contributions in various ways: Pello Andonegi; Iñaki Antigüedad; Bixente Arozena; Idoia Arrizabalaga; Jaione Arrasate; Maribel Benito; José Luis de la Granja; Gustavo de Arístegui; Lisa Doherty; Mike Eaude; Anton Erkoreka; Peio Etcheberry-Ainchart; Mertxe Ezeiza; Genoveva Gastaminza; Aitor Guenaga; José Luis Goikoetxea and his colleague Fernando; Txaro Goñi; Aitor Guenaga; Iñigo Gurruchaga; Andreas Hess; John Holmwood; Helen Jones; Kontxi Irizar; José María Kazalis Eiguren; Javier Landa; Ander Landaburu; Gorka Landaburu; Xabier Lapitz; Alex Longhurst; Maud McKee; José Luis Mendoza; Juan Fermín Michelena; Ángel Luis de Miguel; Sagrario Morán; Pedro Oiarzabal; Xabier Olaizola; Pablo Otaola; Begoña Sagasti; Francisca Segura; Aurora Sotelo; Rob Stone; Sue Tucker; Cyril Peyramond; Eamonn Rodgers; Laura Yanci; Mertxe Zabala Odiaga.

Luis Alberto García was exceptionally generous in supplying excellent photographs, and I would also like to thank Manuel Díaz de la Rada, Jesús Uriarte and the other photographers at www.lurrak.com for their fine images. Likewise Sebastian Ballard for his work on the map.

No-one who helped me bears any responsibility for any views expressed by me in this book, nor for how their own views are presented, nor for any errors which may arise. Most of them will disagree with some things I say, and some of them will disagree with almost everything. I can only fall back on William Blake's bracing aphorism: "Opposition is true friendship."

My thanks to my late parents, Phyllis and Dudley Woodworth, to whom this book is dedicated, who always encouraged me to write "a travel book". I wish they had lived to hold it in their hands. Finally, no words can express my gratitude to my wife, Trish Long, whose love and support are the kind of bedrock all writers need, and very lucky writers find.

Paddy Woodworth
Stoneybatter
Dublin
May 2007

Preface

The Basque Country has had more than its fair share of stereotypes thrust upon it. The Basques have sometimes resisted this typecasting, but they have not been shy about making their own contributions, some as extravagant as any foreigner's, to stock images of their homeland.

Even before Victor Hugo described the Basques as "the people who sing and dance at the foot of the Pyrenees"—a cliché which makes many Basques apoplectic today—the region had become a magnet for professional and amateur seekers after exotic folklore and unique customs. As "Europe's aboriginals", all things Basque were seized upon as ancient and original. Basque nationalism, a relatively recent invention, has avidly cultivated some of these stereotypes, stressing those aspects of culture which made the Basques distinct from the Spanish and the French.

However, archaeologists, anthropologists, folklorists and nationalists have not flourished here by accident. The Basque cultural landscape is fertile ground for their enterprises. The Basques are, indeed, one of the oldest, if not *the* oldest, European people. They have probably lived in their home place longer than other ethnic group on the continent. Their language, Euskera, is not only non-Indo-European, but it has no clear family relationship with any other tongue. And Basques, on both sides of the Pyrenees, have kept alive a vibrant tradition of folk costumes, folk dances, folk sports and folk music which few other European peoples can match. But some things which appear old turn out to be relatively recent innovations, and some things which appear to be quintessentially Basque have their origins elsewhere.

What makes the Basque Country really fascinating is that a traditional culture persists in a heterogeneous society which today exudes a dynamic, if confusing and sometimes dangerous, post-modern energy. The reinvention of Bilbao—a project led by Basque nationalists—has become a cosmopolitan model for the twenty-first-century city of cultural services and information technologies. The "Guggenheim effect" has sent ripples into the remotest Basque villages.

In fact, the Basques have long been at the cutting edge of Iberian history, culture and commerce: Basque kings were prominent in the wars against (and in alliances with) the Islamic caliphates; the Basque Juan Sebastián de Elcano was the first captain to circumnavigate the globe; Basque iron mines kick-started the Spanish industrial revolution. Bilbao is not only the womb of Basque nationalism; it was also a midwife to Spanish socialism, and the mother of an industrial and financial oligarchy. Several of the leading writers of Spain's literary "Generation of Ninety-Eight", including Pío Baroja and Miguel de Unamuno, were Basques. The Basques have made less impact on France, though Henry III of Navarre, in becoming Henry IV of France, bequeathed the mixed legacy of religious peace and the Bourbon dynasty to the French nation.

Yet many Basques today feel no identity with either Spain or France, and want independence, or something close to it. Many other Basques are content to be French or Spanish citizens, and some of them feel deeply threatened by Basque nationalism.

The physical landscape offers similar contrasts: it ranges from moist green valleys to semi-desert badlands, from frozen sierras to warm sandy beaches and tortuous coastal cliffs, from harsh industrial landscapes to bucolic beech woods and alpine meadows.

In this book I have sought to offer a variety of points of entry to this diverse and plural culture; to explore its enigmas and contradictions, and to suggest something of the rich and complex enchantment it can weave over half a life-time. There are many kinds of Basqueness, and I have made no attempt here to be comprehensive or chronological. Some big and delightful cities like San Sebastián, worthy of full-length studies in themselves, are only mentioned in passing. One small village, Asteasu, gets most of a chapter.

Some writers and artists are treated in detail, others are omitted. Rather than an overall survey, I have sought to offer a series of intimate portraits, ranging from cultural, political and historical analysis to personal anecdotes. I hope that this approach, inevitably more than a little idiosyncratic, will reflect some of the pleasure, and a little of the heartbreak, that any close encounter with the Basque Country engenders. The chapters do not have to be read in sequence, though information in the early chapters is usually taken as given in the later ones.

A note on Basque orthography: it is difficult to completely standardize the form of Basque words in an English text, partly because the Basques themselves are often inconsistent when writing in Spanish and French contexts. The plural in Euskera usually ends in –k. Yet some (but not all, that would be far too simple) familiar Basque words are commonly written in a Spanish language context with plurals ending in –s. I have followed common practice, as I understand it. So we will say *euskaldunak* for "Basque speakers", and *baserriak* for "farmhouses", but *ikurriñas* for "Basque flags" and *arranzales* for "fishermen".

Introduction

Land of Stone, Iron and Glass: Land of the Basques

The dolmen of El Sotillo, "the little thicket", lies in a grove of evergreen oak trees. Heavy grey sandstone slabs indicate the outline of a burial chamber and passageway, mostly below ground level. The rocky face of the Sierra de Cantabria stands a few miles to the north. The Ebro, Spain's longest river, is about the same distance to the south, where it traces the southern boundary of Euskal Herria, the Land of the Basques.

The slope up to the sierra is striated with vineyards—not a typical sight in Euskadi, another of the names the Basques give their country. The province of Álava includes a small patch of the Rioja region and has produced excellent wine for centuries, certainly back to the time when the Romans cultivated vines here. The Rioja Alavesa forms part of a fertile alluvial plain which extends into the Ribera region of the neighbouring Basque province of Navarre, and of course into the province of La Rioja itself, across the river.

The cluster of dolmens that studs this geographical enclave bears witness to a long history of human habitation. Only a few miles to the east, you can find the foundations of an entire Bronze-Age town, La Hoya. Within walking distance of La Hoya is another dolmen, La Chabola de la Hechicera, "the hut of the sorceress". Seen from the slope below, it stands proud of the horizon. Its capstone, still in place, seems to echo the jagged outline of the sierra in its rough, dramatic profile.

We know very little about the Stone-Age people who were buried in these dolmens except that they were capable of making the flint knives, polished axes, ceramic bowls and obscure objects of devotion which were interred with them. We know that they lived about 5,000 years ago, and we can probably assume that they built dolmens because they wanted to be remembered. Standing in El Sotillo's oak grove alone at sunset, the temptation to inhale a faint scent of antiquity is seductive. But the scent can be misleading, even dangerous. Archaeology is politics in this corner of the world.

Baserri in the mist: the traditional Basque farmhouse is the spiritual home of Basque nationalism, but farmers struggle to find a place in the modern Basque economy.

Remembering the past, including the Paleolithic and Neolithic past, has an extraordinary significance in the Basque Country. In the nineteenth and twentieth centuries a school of anthropologists and ethnologists sought to establish links between the region's Stone-Age inhabitants and its contemporary residents. The tenuous evidence they uncovered was seized upon by Basque nationalists as proof that the Basque "race" had evolved *in situ* from the Cro-Magnon period. The myth of the Basques as Europe's living primitives has been remarkably resilient, and can still enter conversations today in surprising ways.

While researching this book, I met a Navarran photographer with an encyclopaedic experience of his country. I mentioned to him that I was consulting a woman from Bilbao about the Basque version of handball, known as pelota or *jai alai*. He was outraged. "What could a woman from Bilbao know about pelota?" he demanded. "This is a shepherd's sport from Navarre and Iparralde [the French Basque Country]. Its origins go back to the Stone Age, when they played with rocks against the sides of dolmens. Its magic elements are stone, air, and human flesh." It was late at night, and some drink had been taken, but he insisted he was serious.

There is not much evidence either way about Neolithic handball. But it has a certain imaginative reality. The full title of Julio Medem's monumental and illuminating film documentary about the contemporary Basque conflict is *Euskal Pilota: Larrua Harriaren Kontra* (The Basque Ball: Skin against the Stone). The most influential collection of poetry published in the Basque language in the last century is *Harri eta Herri* (Stone and People) by Gabriel Aresti. The last verse of his best-known poem, *Nire Aitaren Etxea*, The House of My Father, runs like this:

Ni hilen naiz,
nire arima galduko da,
nire askazia galduko da,
baina nire aitaren etxeak
iraunen du
zutik.

I shall die,
My soul will be lost,

My descendants will be lost,
But the house of my father
Will remain
Standing.

Aresti was thinking of the roof tree of the classic Basque farmhouse, the *baserri*, but his words could surely apply equally well to the dolmen-makers. Aresti's poems toughened the will of several generations of ETA militants; indeed, the last word in this poem became, and remains, the title of ETA's internal bulletin. Here it is expressed as a kind of command: *Zutik!* Translated slightly differently from the poem, the word echoes a phrase in the signature Spanish Civil War exhortation of the great Basque revolutionary from an earlier period, Dolores Ibárruri, *La Pasionaria*: "It is better to die *on our feet* than to live on our knees. They shall not pass."

Ibárruri was born in Gallarta, a mining town near Bilbao where many of the workers were immigrants. They were driven to desert their hungry villages in Castile, Andalusia, Extremadura and Galicia to seek harsh work on starvation wages, strangers in a strange damp land, extracting iron from Basque stone. Unable to speak Basque and with very different traditions from those of the Basque countryside and small towns, they nonetheless became an essential part of the history of Euskal Herria, and of Spain, in the twentieth century. Their arrival inadvertently stimulated the rise of Basque nationalism, as the indigenous middle classes reacted to the rise of a largely immigrant proletariat and a native oligarchy that were both equally indifferent to Basque customs.

The mines made the Basque oligarchy one of the wealthiest and most powerful groups in Spain. Their energetic and ruthless capitalism also made the Basque Country the richest region in the state. And it was from these mines that some of the first members of the Spanish Socialist Workers' Party (PSOE) and of the Communist Party (PCE) would be elected to parliament. Bilbao became a stronghold of the General Workers' Union, the UGT, which fought numerous street battles with ELA, a union set up to represent Basque nationalist workers in the 1930s. Then the Spanish Civil War forged new alliances. Socialist and Basque nationalist battalions fought side by side against the Basque financiers and Spanish nationalists who supported General Franco's uprising. But this was always to be an uneasy union. Despite the best efforts of leftist nationalists in the ETA of the 1960s and 1970s, many descendants of immigrants still feel excluded from the Basque nation which is being built so energetically in the twenty-first century. So, however, do many native Basques. As we will see, the fracture which distorts Basque civil society today is not ethnic—it is primarily an ideological fault line.

Ibárruri, who was herself a native Basque, spoke for the immigrants in her autobiography. She understood their nostalgia for a Spain they could recognize, expressed as a lack of significant monuments from the past: "In Vizcaya there are neither Giraldas, nor Mezquitas, nor Hanging Houses, nor aqueducts nor Gothic cathedrals, and this is a matter for regret."

Taken literally, this is not quite accurate. Some of the best Gothic architecture in the Iberian Peninsula is to be found in the Vizcayan fishing port of Lekeitio, for example. But her point is well taken, nevertheless: the monuments of the Basque Country do not, by and large, bear the imprint of the great Moorish and Roman cultures that dominated the rest of the peninsula for so long. Yet nowhere else is the significance of relics of the past so passionately disputed. Simultaneously, the new monuments of the information age are being built in great profusion here. The anthropologist Joseba Zulaika sums up this curious double identity of his countrymen in the twenty-first century: "We want to be the Red Indians of Europe, and the most post-modern culture on the continent. The tension between these two poles is very productive, and we have to learn from it. It is a way of reinventing our identity…"

The small mirror of the Rioja Alavesa reflects both these aspects of the Basque Country. In the midst of all its antiquity, within sight of El Sotillo, a post-modern building discreetly dominates the landscape. A warm red-brick road leads between immaculate ranks of vines to this cedar and aluminium palace, coolly floating on its own reflection in artificial pools paved with artfully broken white tiles.

This is the Ysios bodega, an elegant tribute to twenty-first-century oenology by Santiago Calatrava, one of Spain's hottest architects. The aluminium roof ripples in the sunlight, undulating across a dozen sinuous arches. Calatrava says it recalls the form of a row of wine barrels.

A medieval town in a post-modern frame: Laguardia seen from the Ysios bodega, "like a fabulous accessory bequeathed by history".

But from certain angles, like the dolmens, it echoes the line of the sierra. The centre of the building leans out like the prow of a grand ship, very high windows stripped between massive cedar beams. From the wine-tasting salon behind the glass the medieval town of Laguardia, with its towers and spires, is framed on its hill like a fabulous accessory bequeathed by history.

The atmosphere within the building is one of tastefully understated affluence and power. Tens of thousands of barrels are stacked in store rooms, but the design leaves room for tens of thousands more. The barrelling process, visitors are told, gives the wine "just a *hint* of wood". Gleaming machines like enormous tumble-dryers automatically remove the stalks and pips from the grapes. Steel vats reflecting brilliant sunlight make some rooms more like a Californian laboratory than a Basque bodega. Visitors are invited to join a club to "learn about the thrilling world hidden behind a glass of wine," and have cases of Ysios delivered to their homes via internet shopping.

The daring of the Ysios bodega is by no means unique. Just a little closer to the Ebro, the medieval monuments of the town of El Ciego must now be seen in juxtaposition to the new bodega of Marques de Riscal. Designed by Frank Gehry after his triumph with the Guggenheim in Bilbao, it sits like an untidy millionaire's Meccano set above the ancient walls. (See cover image on this book).

Ancient and Modern

So what kind of country is this? The Basque Country has embraced trophy architecture famously in recent years. Not only Gehry's Guggenheim, but Calatrava's airport and Norman Foster's metro have totally re-branded Bilbao. A grimy and decaying industrial city has become a must-see destination for connoisseurs of cutting-edge high culture. Squeaky-clean IT industries boom in every Basque town and city. Many are powered by the dozens of great white windmills which stride along the ridges of the Basque Pyrenees like demented, gesticulating giants.

And yet, and yet… if dawn finds you in one of the green valleys underneath those ridges, you may see men dressed as sheep, with four giant sheep-bells attached to their backs. These *joaldunak* move eerily through the mist-sodden fields to wake their neighbours for *jaiak* (fiestas). At the fiestas they may be joined by *momotxorroak* (cattle men), *jentillak* (giants) or *basajaunak* (lords of the wood). And at the *jaiak* you will certainly see other men hoisting rocks (stone again, you see) on shoulders a sumo wrestler would envy. And you may see young men in elaborate white and red costumes, small bells chiming on their trousers, performing a sword dance along the stone banks of a river. And perhaps trophy architecture is not so novel in the Basque Country after all; an opulent *casa torre* (tower house) which could sleep a battalion—and did, in several local and international wars—stands above them. Moreover, every farmhouse in the valley may have its own coat of arms blazoned in stone (again) above the door. And perhaps a dozen of the houses call themselves, with some justification, *jauregis* (palaces).

And in case you think this is all merely folkloric, the strikingly ugly-beautiful woman behind the bar may be wearing a T-shirt straight out of last month's *Vogue*. But the slogan emblazoned on it markets revolution, not high fashion: *Jaiak Bai, Borroka ere Bai*—"yes to fiestas, yes to the struggle too." The photographs of local young men and women stuck up behind her, prisoners in Spanish jails, are reminders that the local wars are not over yet. An ETA ceasefire raised hopes for peace as this book was being written, but was violated by a bombing, causing two deaths, at the end of 2006, and was formally ended by ETA on the day we went to press, 5 June 2007.

Among the revellers, if you observe very closely, you may also find men and women who never let slip a certain strained alertness, and who are always shadowed at a discreet distance by someone else. The Basque nationalist social world, intimate as it is in many ways, finds them almost invisible. This world has become an open prison for such people, because they cannot go anywhere without a bodyguard. Academics, local politicians, journalists, judges, union leaders, entrepreneurs—anyone who has criticized ETA's terrorism in public discourse can find themselves on the group's list of "legitimate" targets.

Some of them have been shot down in pretty little towns like this one, as they bought their morning papers, or had a coffee with a friend, or returned home from an ETA-imposed exile because they could not bear to miss the *jaiak* in their home place.

You do not see openly embattled communities protected by "peace walls" in the Basque Country, as you do in Northern Ireland. But the intimate cement of Basque society is gravely weakened by a bloody fracture barely visible to the casual visitor. And that fissiparous line is not ethnically based: it snakes through families and through the *cuadrilla*, that second Basque family made up of a tight-knit group of friends from childhood. Some of ETA's victims have been native Basque-speakers who support conservative Spanish nationalism. Some were former *etarras* who have renounced violence. Others were brave politicians who preached reconciliation between the country's two great traditions, and found that building bridges could be a lethal activity.

Where a Basque stands in relation to that invisible dividing line will tend to determine many things. For some, the dolmens of the Rioja Alavesa are a reminder of the ancestral Basque past, a unique heritage which can, the most radical will say, only be authentically conserved in an independent Basque state. For others, the dolmens suggest a common Iberian ancestor for all the Spanish peoples, one strand in the conviction that the "Basque Country is not just part of Spain, it is the heart of Spain," as a conservative Spanish nationalist politician, who is also a

Basque, once told me. And these conservatives can point out that a Basque government, with more powers than any regional equivalent in Europe, has been in the hands of Basque nationalists since the Basque Autonomous Community (CAV) was established in 1980.

This is a land, then, of many contradictions. You can, of course, find ancient fiesta traditions in many other communities in Iberia. What is remarkable about the Basque case is their juxtaposition with modernity, and their polyvalent political significance. Trying to find a rational mid-point between extremes, the perceptive Basque anthropologist Julio Caro Baroja once put it like this:

> Questions about the Basque Country cannot be clearly answered *unless you see it as it is*, and see the people as having very distinct characteristics, that's true, but without that sense of being anomalous, strange and outlandish which some enthusiastic and somewhat self-obsessed Basques give themselves.

But neither, he warns, can we accept the prejudices of "anti-Basques, who are offended by the existence of a language and customs which they do not share... The Basque is not some kind of platypus or isolated creature in the concert of the peoples [of Europe]," he continues. "But neither is [the Basque] a humble, factory-farmed animal," produced to fit some standard norm.

"To see the Basque Country as it is" sets the bar very high, impossibly high in fact, because every observer, including this writer, sees the country through their own inevitably limited and partial experience. But in the pages that follow we will try to avoid the extremes indicated by Baroja, the twin stereotypes of folkloric freak show and of homogenous uniformity. We will, indeed, encounter much that is strange and archaic to the eyes of the outsider, but will find that it all occurs in a shared context common to our new century. First, however, we have to find out where the Basque Country is. And even that is a contentious question.

Bay of Biscay

F R A N C E

LES LANDES

Biarritz
(Miarritze)

Bayonne
(Baiona)

BÉARN

BASSE
NAVARRE
(NAFARROA
BEHEREA)

Mauléon
(Maule)

LABOURD
(LAPURDI)

San Sebastián
/Donostia

Irún

Gernika

Getaria

VIZCAYA
(BIZKAIA)

Asteasu

St Jean Pied-de-Port
(Donibane Garazi)

SOULE
(ZUBEROA)

Bilbao (Bilbo)

Nervión

GUIPÚZCOA
(GIPUZKOA)

Bidasoa

Urumea

P   y   r   e   n   e   e   s

CANTABRIA

C a n t a b r i a n   C o r d i l l e r a

Vitoria
(Gasteiz)

ÁLAVA
(ARABA)

Pamplona (Iruñea)

Arga

Ebro

Estella
(Lizarra)

NAVARRE
(NAFARROA)

Laguardia

Olite
(Erriberri)

CASTILE

Aragón

ARAGON

S P A I N

Bardenas
badlands

Tudela
(Tutera)

Ebro

FRANCE

Basque
Country

PORTUGAL

Madrid

SPAIN

AFRICA

N

0   30
km

BASQUE COUNTRY

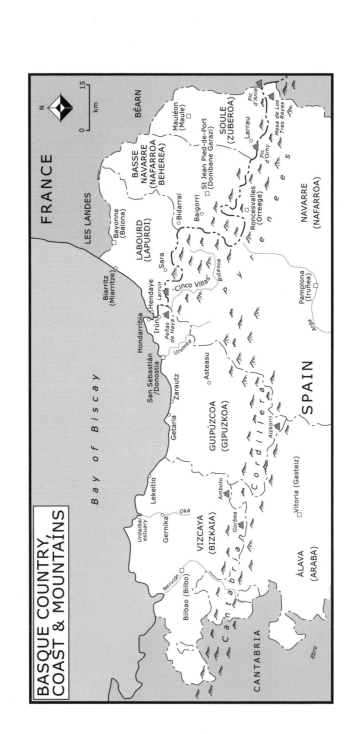

BASQUE COUNTRY,
COAST & MOUNTAINS

FRANCE

LES LANDES

BÉARN

Bay of Biscay

CANTABRIA

SPAIN

Bilbao (Bilbo)

Nervión

Gernika

Lekeitio

Urdaibai
estuary

Oka

VIZCAYA
(BIZKAIA)

ÁLAVA
(ARABA)

Vitoria (Gasteiz)

Amboto

Gorbea

C a n t a b r i a n

C o r d i l l e r a

Ebro

Getaria

Zarautz

San Sebastián
/Donostia

Hondarribia

Biarritz
(Miarritze)

Bayonne
(Baiona)

LABOURD
(LAPURDI)

Sara

Irún

Hendaye

Larrun

Peñas
de Haya

Urumea

Asteasu

GUIPÚZCOA
(GIPUZKOA)

Aizkorri

Bidasoa

Cinco Villas

Aya

Pamplona
(Iruñea)

P y r e n e e s

NAVARRE
(NAFARROA)

BASSE
NAVARRE
(NAFARROA
BEHEREA)

Bidarrai

Bigorri

St Jean Pied-de-Port
(Donibane Garazi)

Roncesvalles
(Orreaga)

SOULE
(ZUBEROA)

Larrau

Mauléon
(Maule)

Pic
d'Anie

Pic
d'Orhy

Mesa de Los
Tres Reyes

0   15
km

N

Chapter One

Where Are We, Exactly? And What Will We Call This Place?

Izena duen guztiak izatea ere badauke: Everything with a name exists
Izenak ez du egiten izana: A name does not make something true
Basque proverbs

The Basques occupy a very small corner of the world, but they have been there for a very long time.

The Basque Country, even in the broadest interpretation of that problematic phrase—no term is neutral here—looks compact on a map. What appears to be bounded by a nutshell, however, quickly expands on closer inspection. This is a space which is "labyrinthine, heterogeneous, vast and complex to the observant traveller," as the novelist Bernardo Atxaga puts it.

This book is based on the premise that there are seven provinces which can be properly called "Basque". Four are under Spanish jurisdiction. Vizcaya, Guipúzcoa, and Álava have a considerable measure of self-rule as the Comunidad Autónoma Vasca (CAV), while Navarre has a stand-alone autonomous government. Three are administered by Paris: Labourd, Basse Navarre and Soule, and have no administrative identity, being subsumed within the *département* of the Pyrenées Atlantiques. These apparently innocuous statements will irritate, even infuriate, many of the contemporary inhabitants of these territories. But there are good historical and cultural reasons for this definition, and on that basis we will sketch out the Basque Country's geographical limits.

On the Spanish side of the border, the Basque coast extends little more than sixty miles, flying like Julio Medem's bird-camera in *Euskal Pilota*. Looking from the east, it starts at the bay of Txingudi, where the Pyrenees drop down to the elbow of the Bay of Biscay. At its western limit it meets the province of Santander, just beyond Bilbao. On the

Heavy lifting and hard labour: *harri-jasotze*, or rock-lifting, like several other traditional Basque sports, is rooted in the physical strength required to farm the steep Basque hills.

French side at Bayonne, the Adour river, which marks the Basque border with Les Landes, is even closer to Txingudi, nine hours' walk on a coast sloping north-east of the Spanish frontier.

Follow the rising line of the Pyrenees' spinal column south-east, and again you can hardly travel 75 straight miles and stay in Basque territory. You will reach the limit on the flat peak of the Table of the Three Kings, just short of the dramatic summit of the Pic d'Anie. But if you swing south-west out across Pyrenean foothills and the plains of Navarre, you can add another ninety miles before meeting the deepest southern boundary with Aragon, crossing first the spectacular badlands of the Bardenas Reales, and then the flatlands of the Ribera.

The Basque Country's second big mountain system is a mixture of Pyrenean offshoots and the eastward limits of the Cantabrian Cordillera. This system runs westwards from the Pyrenees, more or less parallel to the coast. It reaches its dramatic climax in the Picos de Europa in Asturias, well to the west of the Basque borders with La Rioja and Burgos (Castile). The highest Basque peaks in this range are between 3,000 and 5,000 feet, but their proximity to sea-level lends them an imposing grandeur. Characteristically, their northern faces are abrupt and rocky, and they are more easily approached from the gentler and grassier southern slopes. This mountain system divides most of the Basque region into an Atlantic climate zone to the north, and a smaller Mediterranean climate zone to the south, which merges with the Castilian *meseta*.

In this Mediterranean zone, taking in the Rioja Alavesa and Navarre south of Pamplona, all rivers flow into the Ebro, which continues southeast through Aragon to Catalonia. The Basque Mediterranean climate area is relatively arid, as you would expect. It has a wealth of Romanesque monuments, and produces excellent red—and a few fine white—wines.

In the Atlantic zone most of the rivers flow more or less south-north, into the Bay of Biscay. Green is the dominant colour here, in many subtle and lovely shades—when the sun is shining. Let that sun go in, and gloom can fall with menacing abruptness, all the greens fading into dull greys. But if there is mist, or *sirimiri*—the drenching Basque drizzle which imperceptibly penetrates even the most rainproof clothes—the atmosphere can shift quickly again to a kind of melancholy enchantment. This mountain landscape is so sharply and unpredictably carved with valleys, running at all angles, that one can easily, and enjoyably, get lost half a dozen times during an afternoon's drive.

The temperate rainfall here has stimulated intensive farming on land which is not particularly fertile. Intensive, but generally not mechanized, so that much of the countryside looks curiously archaic. The characteristic steepness of the Basque hills, small though they often are, makes tractors impractical. The typical arable landscape here resembles a crazy patchwork of market gardens more than modern farmlands.

Individual physical strength is the key to the hard labour this land demands. Many of the popular "primitive" Basque folk-sports, like rock-lifting, log-cutting and hay-mowing, derive from the qualities prized in Basque farming. It is possible, even today, to see a man throw his shoulder to the yoke alongside his oxen to keep a plough moving uphill, or stoically scythe a meadow on a near-vertical slope.

Between these smallholdings and the bald karstic peaks that tower above them, forestry is dominant. Some magnificent ancient beech woods survive, but conifer plantations are now also widespread. Higher again, but before the clay thins down to scree, are calm expanses of pastoral alpine meadows, filled with the sound of sheep bells and cow bells.

Still in the Atlantic zone, on the southern side of the Spanish-French border, the hills often extend right down to the sea, making the coastal roads feel at times like a switchback inside a corkscrew. This produces abruptly contrasting vistas, often of breathtaking beauty, following in kaleidoscopic succession. Softly curving sandy Atlantic beaches alternate with tortuously twisted strata of sandstone and sometimes slate, punctuated by occasional estuaries.

These estuaries have very few remaining wetlands or dune systems, due to intense human exploitation. And for many centuries the Basques have exploited every natural harbour, so that this coast is studded with some twenty ports. They range from the post-industrial super-port at Bilbao, to villages whose intimate scale belies historic links to world maritime history. The smaller ports, like Getaria and Lekeitio, are still making a painful transition from a collapsing fishing industry to tourism.

To the north, the French Basque Country shares this green and pleasant Atlantic ecosystem. The hills are mostly gentler here (apart, of course, from the Pyrenees), and stand back further from the coast. And there are much starker contrasts. Even the most remote inland valleys of Guipúzcoa and Vizcaya are generally prosperous with busy towns and villages. But the hinterland in Basse Navarre and Soule is depopulated and poor, though rich in indigenous Basque traditions. The French Basque coast is also gentler than its southern equivalent, more typical of the great west-facing Atlantic beaches further north, in France, and much further south in Portugal and Morocco. The conversion of the fishing ports to tourism generally happened earlier here than on the southern side. This has made a big impact on the architecture of Biarritz and St.-Jean-de-Luz, which reflects the faded grandeur of nineteenth-century promenades, spas and casinos. The French Basque villages are often very beautiful, but there is a downside: their pristine perfection, especially near the coast, has more than a slight hint of the heritage park about it.

Given the close links that have always existed across the political frontier that divides the Basque Country, the contrast when you cross it, even today, is striking. The northern side looks cleaner, its parks more manicured, its houses seem more recently painted. "Well," a Spanish Basque may say, shrugging a weary shoulder: "What do you expect? Those French people [who suddenly cease to be Basques in such conversations] bring all their rubbish south and dump it here." French Basques, for their part, tend to regard their southern neighbours as a little uncouth, and more than a little emotional and unstable in their politics. Anyone who has moved between the Italian *Mezzogiorno* and Milan, or between Belfast and Dublin, will find these north/south borderland stereotypes oddly familiar. Here, however, the northern self-assurance is not based on early industrialization. Indeed, in this respect the Basques invert the Irish and Italian models, because the great industrial take-off here occurred on the southern side of the border. So any airs affected by the northerners can be attributed more to French attitudes towards Iberia in general—the doubly racist assertion that "Africa begins at the Pyrenees"—rather than to any innately Basque experience.

Writing eighty years ago, Rodney Gallop expressed these distinctions from a haughty but affectionate English perspective in his charming, idiosyncratic and wittily illustrated classic, *A Book of the Basques* (1930): "The slothful spell of the South is upon them [the French Basques]. Yet one has only to cross the Bidassoa [sic] to find that the [Spanish] Basques are in every sense the Northerners of Spain... the French Basques seem to lack all ambition."

There have been many changes since Gallop spent happy years studying Basque folk customs, including the orientation of the typical tourist: "The foreign visitor has always shown a disposition to concentrate on the French Basque Country at the expense of the Spanish provinces." The opposite has been the case in recent years, especially since the advent of the Guggenheim, though there are signs that the *Côte Basque* is regaining ground. And the increasing tendency to market tourism in cross-border packages, and set up cross-border institutions, will probably bring about a kind of north-south equity.

The Urban-Rural Divide

The deepest divide in the Basque Country is not across the border, but between city and countryside within each territory. The rural world is the repository of the essence of Basqueness—as it is dreamed of by Basque nationalists. It is where the Basque language is strongest, where the dances, orally composed verses and *force Basque* sports which embody traditional culture can be found in their purest forms.

The growth of the Basque cities, especially Bilbao, is often portrayed from this perspective as having severely diluted indigenous culture, even poisoning it, according to the most traditional voices. But Bilbao was also the motor of a dynamic industrial economy that has made the Basque Country, or at least its southern provinces, what they are today. The iron ore in the hills above the city has been exploited for many centuries. The steel industry, coupled with shipbuilding, brought great wealth to the city's merchants, which was exhibited ostentatiously in palatial new districts like Neguri. While this new bourgeoisie was predominantly Basque in ethnic origins, the pull of profit drew it into the orbit of Madrid, and its attachment to Basque particularity tended to fall away.

The Bilbao industrial revolution also attracted tens of thousands of workers from less fortunate parts of Spain. According to the first nationalist ideologues, who found their voices at precisely this moment in history, the immigrants contaminated the city with their licentious morals and Marxist ideologies.

It one of history's ironies that the most radical and committed nationalists in the Basque Country today, grouped around the terrorist

Beasts of burden: oxen are still used where Basque hills are too steep to take a tractor, but their colourful yokes are prized by collectors as relics of the past. They are mostly seen today in rock-dragging competitions, an archaic sport which gives Basques yet another opportunity to place a bet.

group ETA (Euskadi ta Askatasuna, Basque Homeland and Liberty) pay verbose lip service to far-left Marxist doctrines. One of ETA's ideological difficulties has been to find where the "oppression" of Euskal Herria fits into the mould of international revolution. If the Basques are some kind of colony of an imperialist Madrid in an economic sense, this is a strange empire, because the periphery has long been wealthier than the metropolitan capital.

Outside Bilbao, and especially in Guipúzcoa, small and even medium-sized industries are spread out through all the towns and most of the villages. This creates a curiously unsettling sense of temporal as well as physical dislocation. One sharp bend in the road can bring you from the verdant countryside, with oxen ploughing, into a *plaza* of stone-faced medieval houses, their great oak doors patterned with iron studs. This impression of an ancient culture will be abruptly contradicted as you exit the village. Another twist in the road will bring you face to face with a shiny—or filthy—factory, where huge articulated trucks queue up to take engine parts to the auto industries of Germany or Italy, or pâté to the post-modern restaurants of Barcelona or Cannes.

The final element that must be mentioned in our brief territorial overview is the sea itself, *itsaso*, the medium which defines the Basque relationship with the world more than any other.

> My people
> has always had a harbour,
> but nothing to hold on to firmly,
> our harbour is the sea,
> the furious sea,
> which stretches from Bayonne to Bilbao...
> The sea is our language,
> from Bayonne to Bilbao.

So sings Imanol Larzabal, one of the legendary Basque singer-songwriters who emerged in the 1960s, in the song written by Koldo Izagirre, *Baionatik Bilbora*.

The Basques are often accused of insularity, especially by other Basques who have become weary of the murderous parochialism of radical nationalism. "The Basque problem could be solved if every Basque had a satellite dish and an air ticket," said the late Mario Onaindia, a prolific ideologue, historian (and Basque-language novelist) of the 1980s and 1990s. Onaindia was one of the senior ETA leaders from the Franco period who, like a number of his comrades, abandoned violence with the advent of democracy, and ultimately rejected Basque nationalism altogether, becoming a scourge to the ideology he had once so militantly espoused.

Onaindia's prescription seems unlikely to be effective; indeed it misses a key point. The Basques may have stayed in one place for a very long time, but they have never been strangers to the wider world beyond their shores. Few peoples have been so at home for so long on the world's oceans. Basque fishermen will follow their quarry wherever it leads them. This is not just the case today, when over-fishing drives the few remaining captains to the Indian Ocean, or forces unemployed mariners to sell their legendary skills in Latin America's Pacific ports. It was also true long ago when they followed the cod much further, in terms of time and isolation, to the coast of Labrador, probably just after Columbus reached the Caribbean. One of Columbus' own captains was a Basque. And after Ferdinand Magellan was killed in the Philippines, it was Juan Sebastián de Elcano from Getaria who brought home the first fleet to circumnavigate the globe. Tens of thousands of Basques migrated to the Americas, and hundreds returned as wealthy *Indianos*. They built the mansions flaunting magnolia trees you can find in every Basque village, and endowed the construction and artwork of many fine churches. But this vast experience was not enough to entirely dilute atavistic attitudes, best expressed in the proverb "land of foreigners, land of wolves". A similarly inward-looking perspective is indicated by the fact that, traditionally, the Basques have had just one name, *Erdera*, for all the languages in the world except, of course, their own language, Euskera. Likewise, the Basques' word for their green-white-and-red national flag is simply *ikurriña*, "the flag".

The integrity of the Basque quarrel, to paraphrase Churchill on Northern Ireland, remains most unfortunately intact. The cultures which both imagine and shape the Basque landscape are at once refreshingly diverse, and deeply problematic. The total population is a little less than 3,000,000, with more than two-thirds in the CAV, 500,000 in Navarre, and barely 250,000 in the French Basque Country. About 25 per cent of Basques use Eukera as a daily means of communication, with a peak of 44 per cent in Guipúzcoa and a mere eight per cent in Álava.

I referred earlier to the irritation my simple outline of Basque geography could engender. There is hardly a sentence I have written about the seven provinces which would not provoke the wrath of one group, or another. Many Navarrans, for example, see their province as a totally separate entity from the Basque Country, and would regard Navarre's presence in this book as a kind of annexation. Most citizens of the three French provinces, while recognizing their cultural Basqueness—it does help attract the tourists—are suspicious of any definition which lumps them with their turbulent neighbours south of the border.

Conversely, a rather slim majority of citizens of the CAV would be equally offended by any definition of the Basque Country which did *not* include Navarre and the French provinces. Their position is summed up in the old Basque nationalist slogan, *Zazpiak Bat*, "the Seven are One". Many of them, indeed, would contest the use of adjectives like "French" or "Spanish" in this context. They speak of Iparralde, the "northern region", not the French Basque Country. They call the Spanish side Hegoalde, the "southern region". And many of them regard Navarre as the Basque province *par excellence*, the heartland, though only about 20 per cent of Navarrans share these sentiments.

We will have to negotiate such politico-linguistic minefields many times in the course of this book. The very names of the provinces, indeed the names of almost every town and district, are contentious. Should we speak of the province of Guipúzcoa (Spanish), or of Gipuzkoa (Basque), and is its capital San Sebastián (Spanish) or Donostia (Basque)? On the French side there may be three variations for a single town: St.-Jean-de-Luz (French), San Juan de Luz (Spanish), and Donibane Lohitzune (Basque).

While respecting the multiple and overlapping identities which both enrich and trouble the Basque landscape, I propose a pragmatic approach. Because they are most familiar to English-speaking readers, we will generally use the Spanish and French names respectively for the provinces and better-known cities and towns. Their Basque names can be found on the maps (pp.xxv-vi) or in parenthesis where they first occur. We will use Basque names for lesser-known towns and villages in Basque-speaking areas. But where the Basque name for a better-known town has passed into general usage, usually because it is very similar to the Spanish, as in Zarautz and Gernika, we will use that version.

Then there is the vexed question of what to call the whole region. There is something attractive about Euskal Herria, literally "the land of Basque-speakers". It has the virtue of automatically including the whole cultural area, including Navarre and the French Basque Country. But we must also bear in mind that this phrase has been, to a degree, appropriated by radicals close to the thinking of ETA in recent years. This despite the fact that ETA itself stands for Euskadi Ta Askatasuna, the Basque Country and Liberty. Euskadi (originally Euzkadi) was the neologism coined to describe the seven provinces as a national unit by the father of Basque nationalism, Sabino Arana, in the late nineteenth century. But Euskadi is now the official designation of the CAV, so the radicals have shifted back to the older Euskal Herria to insist on a claim to the whole territory. If you investigate further, you will find varied spellings, like Euskalerria and Eskual Herria (a French Basque form). Then there is Vasconia, briefly popularized by the radical nationalist Federico Krutwig in the 1960s, and Las Provincias Vascongadas, an old-fashioned formula for Guipúzkoa, Álava and Vizcaya, often regarded as pejorative by Basque nationalists. In English, Mark Kurlansky, author of the entertaining and beautifully written—if unreliable—*Basque History of the World* (1999), used Basqueland, which has a nice ring to it. But, for the sake of familiarity, we will generally stick to the most widely used and politically neutral phrase, the Basque Country, a translation of the Spanish País Vasco, and perhaps as close as English can get to Euskal Herria.

Why are these issues of naming and identity so contentious here and so often linked to charges (from several opposing directions) of racism, ethnic cleansing, terrorism, even genocide? To answer that question comprehensively is well beyond the scope of this book, but the issues will recur in almost every chapter. What follows is a short historical sketch, which will not reach any definitive conclusions, but may at least provide a context in which the questions raised here may be better understood.

Capstone conundrum: did ancestral Basques build the *Sorginetxe* dolmen in Álava? As the historian Roger Collins puts it, the scholarly study of Basque origins is "linked at not many removes to political debate and even terrorism."

Chapter Two

A Short Version of a Long History: From the Stone Age to the Civil War

> Ultimately, what is striking is not the enigma of the [Basque] past in itself, but the existence of a people bewitched by the ethnographic spell which has been cast over that enigma.
>
> Joseba Zulaika, *Del Cromañon al Carnaval*, 1996

The origins of the Basques, and of their language, Euskera, are at once enticingly mysterious and politically contested. This has been a complex combination, and at times a lethal one. A vacuum of hard evidence has sucked in a deal of lunacy. Larry Trask, a linguist who has looked coolly and hard at the language side of this question, carries a warning on his website that gives a witty indication of the wildness of some of the speculation. "Write to me," Trask invited his readers, "but:

> Please note: I do not want to hear about the following:
> Your discovery that Basque is the secret key to understanding the Ogam inscriptions/the Phaistos disc/the Easter Island carvings/the Egyptian Book of the Dead/the Qabbala/the prophecies of Nostradamus/your PC manual/the movements of the New York Stock Exchange.

Was he exaggerating? Not much. As late as 1825, a learned cleric was still claiming that Euskera was the language spoken in the Garden of Eden, and theories which are just as wacky still proliferate today in only slightly less learned circles. The website of Edo Nyland confidently proclaims that "until Orthodox Christianity arrived in Europe everyone spoke Basque, including the early Irish Gnostic Christian missionaries."

To make things more complicated, new facts sometimes suggest a degree of convergence with these old fantasies. There is no relationship between Euskera and the Irish language, but recent DNA research at Trinity College, Dublin and elsewhere has established significant genetic affinities between Basques and people from the west of Ireland, distinguishing both from more easterly European populations.

The Basques share other biological indicators with each other which confirm that they are a distinctive ethnic type. Fifty-five per cent of Basques have blood of group O, as against 40 and 43 per cent respectively for the Spanish and French. The Basques are much less likely than their neighbours to have blood of groups A and AB. Other blood studies show that Basques are Rhesus negative in proportions which are exceptionally high by global standards.

You may be wondering why any of this rather arcane information matters very much. For much of the last 120 years, many Basques (and many politically aware Spaniards) would have told you that it matters a great deal. As Roger Collins puts it in *The Basques* (1990):

> For few other peoples of the world, and surely no other in Europe, can the scholarly study of their origins and earliest history be a matter of such direct and contemporary importance, linked at not many removes to political debate and even terrorism, as is the case with the Basques... the present state of Basque nationalist arguments *and the counter-thrusts of its centralizing opponents* are such that few statements relating to the people, their history and their language can be regarded as neutral. [italics mine]

The significance of the past in this context, therefore, depends to a great extent on the cultural and political interpretation you put on it. From the late nineteenth century, there was a dynamic and polemical relationship between research, which suggested that the Basques had evolved biologically *in situ*, and the emergence of Basque nationalism which, like most nineteenth-century nationalisms, had a strong racial component. If the Basques really were a unique people, then their case for carving out an independent state was that much stronger. Blood groups duly became a topic of passionate debate in Basque nationalist circles. So, in the 1930s, did skulls.

Anthropology and the Skull of the Basque Ancestor
As Joseba Zulaika points out, the Basques did not invent this passion for anthropology, racial biology, ethnology and linguistics. Senior European figures in these mainly new disciplines saw the Basque Country as a marvellous opportunity to do serious field work among primitives, without the bother of travelling to far-off and dangerous jungles. They brought to the western Pyrenees an obsession for cranial measurement in the service of "racial classification". Paul Broca, the founder of the Société d'Anthropologie de Paris in 1859, personally examined seventy skulls secretly removed from a cemetery in Zarautz. All this was done in the name of science, but in many cases these anthropologists had a distinctly unscientific faith in the superiority of northern European "races".

The research of these eminent men offered Basque nationalists "the foundational narrative with which to cement their identity," in Zulaika's words. The resulting ethical burden for today's anthropologists is a heavy one. Zulaika, a leading contemporary Basque figure in this field, is not entirely joking when he describes himself as "a recovering anthropologist".

The outstanding Basque anthropologists of the last century were Telesforo de Aranzadi, a cousin of Miguel de Unamuno, and a priest, José Miguel Barandiarán. They inherited cranial preoccupations from their northern European predecessors, but they rejected the idea of racial hierarchies. As *vasquistas* ("Basqueists"), though not political nationalists, they were obsessed with the idea that their Basque ancestors might, alone among Europeans, have evolved into *homo sapiens* in their native place. A cave at Urtiaga, near Itziar in Guipúzcoa, offered them up a skull that seemed dramatic proof of this thesis in 1935. The skull had similar measurements and proportions to its typical modern Basque counterpart. But its position in the strata deposited in the cave told the anthropologists that it was at least 10,000 years old. A Basque Cro-Magnon man had been verified by hard science. Or so it seemed at the time.

The outbreak of civil war found Barandarián still digging away at Urtiaga. The conflict brought him to the brink of tragedy, but farce saved the day. Barandiarán packed the precious skull in a suitcase, and took it on the train to Bilbao. There, at Atxurri station, he was confronted by Republican militia, who were understandably suspicious about his macabre luggage. They thought he might be hiding evidence of a war crime. He thought he was the guardian of the Basque Ancestor. Understandably confused, they finally let this self-effacing priest go about his strange business.

It is important to be fair to these scholars. They reported on their discovery in tentative and carefully scientific terms. Barandiarán himself developed new doubts about the skull's antiquity while the scientific evidence still seemed to support his original findings. Decades later, more modern dating methods showed that the skull was much more recent than he had estimated, dating from no earlier than 1500 BC and possibly as recent as 200 BC. The strata in the cave had, apparently, been frequently disturbed and displaced. It remains an indication of a long Basque lineage in one place, but lacks the magic Cro-Magnon label, by a long shot.

Urtiaga's real significance lies not in the anthropologists' discovery and analysis, but in the way in which Basque nationalism interiorized its apparent results. Even if the skull had been Cro-Magnon, as a sample of one it was very flimsy scientific evidence of such very ancient Basque roots. This did not bother the ideologues of the Partido Nacionalista Vasco (PNV). They found it lent a patina of intellectual respectability to a deep emotional yearning for proof for some very special status for their people. This yearning was, very understandably, intensified by the historical moment in which the skull had been found. The aggressively racist Franco regime would soon set out to eradicate most aspects of Basqueness in the name of Spanish nationalism. The skull was a symbol of Basque resilience, a prehistoric response to the horrors of contemporary history. We may be a small people, the Basques could say, but we are Europe's true originals; compared with our longevity, the Spanish Golden Age pales into insignificance. We may have little literature in our own language, but Basques were painting masterpieces on the walls of our caves long before the Spanish nation had been invented, or the Prado had been dreamed of.

Zulaika captures this extraordinary aspect of the Basque nationalist relationship to the past—and of how we foreigners love it—in a classic study of his own small community in the village of Itziar, *Basque Violence: Metaphor and Sacrament* (1988).

In connection with their linguistic insularity, Basque identity is founded on an acute sense of their enigmatic past. Their being a "mystery people" is also what seems to be of most interest about Basques to outsiders.

Identity runs in an unbroken line from the ancestors who came from nowhere else but [the caves of] Urtiaga and Ekain, who achieved their human condition right there in those nearby underground dwellings. These caves provide for Basques the tangible context in which their imagination of the past finds its home… in conversations with Basques it is not unusual to hear expressions such as "that happened *only* 5,000 B.C."

Many Basques today reject the traditional nationalist account of prehistory, but many others still cling to it. This clinging creates a dangerous contempt for the "spurious period" of historical time, when the Basque Country as we know it today was really forged. Contemporary Basque nationalism is well aware of the negative resonance of terms like "race" since the Nazi Holocaust, and usually substitutes cultural, linguistic and even purely political definitions of Basqueness for racial criteria. But the racist rhetoric of the PNV's first ideologue, Sabino Arana, still finds an echo in some Basque conversations, and also provides an easy target for Spanish nationalists and modernizing Basque "anti-nationalists".

Bandiarián's work had other dimensions which were ripe for political harvesting by Basque nationalism. His extensive ethnographical studies would also be seized upon for contemporary political and cultural purposes. His meticulous and copious tabulation of everything from farm implements to funeral customs, from folk dances to pre-Christian myths, were a massive underpinning of the legacy of his people. An unconscious marriage of science, sorcery and politics was taking place. It produced some fantastical offspring, but they had deep repercussions in the real world. Basque nationalism would sit out the long winter of Francoism comforted by the contents of ethnographic museums and obscure anthropological essays. Basque artists, even such pioneers of the cosmopolitan avant-garde as Eduardo Chillida, would seek inspiration in the forms of primitive hay forks and ploughshares. Amateurs eagerly pursued further discoveries, a form of cultural activism which evaded Madrid's repressive censorship. In 1969, as ETA was cutting its teeth as a different form of opposition, a spectacular world-class set of cave paintings, with some especially fine representations of horses, was found only five miles from Urtiaga, at Ekain. The Stone-Age artists were, of course, assumed to be *Euskaldunak*, in both senses of the word—ethnic Basques, and speakers of Euskera.

Qui dit Basque dit Catholique, says the French proverb, but while the Basques continued to fill their churches, ancestor worship was the real religion of the region's nationalists.

A Stone-Age Language?

In daily life there was no more tangible, or more threatened, evidence of the ancestors than Euskera, which has proved a more reliable indicator of Basque originality than the shape of Basque brain pans. The identity of people and language is manifest in the word *Euskaldun*, which as we have seen designates both "Basque person" and "Basque-speaker" in Euskera.

Euskal Herria similarly merges the concepts of region, people and language. Euskera's origins continue to baffle scholars, starting with learned contributions from such heavyweights as Wilhelm von Humboldt (1767-1835) and Louis-Lucien Bonaparte (1813-91). We can easily dismiss the contention, made by the seventeenth-century Basque historian, Esteban de Garibay, that the grandson of Noah, Tubal, brought the language to the Basque Country. But it is much harder to make convincing positive assertions about connections with any living language. Tentative links have been traced to certain Caucasian languages and to Berber. The idea that a mountain people migrated in a north-south sweep several millennia ago, and found familiar homes in the caves of the Pyrenees and in the Atlas Mountains, has a certain attraction. Alas, the consensus today is that such links as do exist between these languages are insufficient to establish any definite common parentage.

The venerable age of Euskera may be indicated by the presence of a root-word *haitz* (or *aitz*)—stone—in the names of many common implements, such as knife and axe. Rodney Gallop records *Aitz-tturr* as a "small stone for tearing: i.e. scissors". And one need go no further than the numerals to appreciate the distinctive nature of much Basque vocabulary. The number three, for example, has a similar form in languages ranging from French to Sanskrit. But when the Basques put two and one together, they get *hiru*. In the first ten numerals in Euskera, only *bi* (two) and *sei* (six) look familiar to Indo-Europeans. When you get as far as nine, *bederatzi*, you begin to get the point of the title of the first attempt to codify the language, Manuel de Larramendi's *El Imposible Vencido* (1729)—"The Impossible Overcome". As for the grammar, its difficulty is neatly summarized by Jeremy MacClancy in his fine essay, *Biological Basques, Sociologically Speaking* (1993):

> The definite article is not a separate word but a suffix; nouns used with numerals remain in the singular; auxiliary verbs vary according to the number of objects as well as to the number of subjects; instead of prepositions, Euskera employs a host of suffixes and prefixes which vary depending on whether the word to which they are attached refers to something animate or inanimate.

The suffix for the definite article is –a, and for the plural –k. So *baserri* is "farmhouse", *baserria* is "the farmhouse", and *baserriak* is "the farmhouses".

Several recurrent combinations of consonants immediately look unfamiliar in a European context: "tx" sounds similar to "ch" in English. "Tt", "tz" and "ts", and "x" as an initial consonant, are a little harder to convey in non-technical terms.

The syntax is enough to bend the brain of a foreigner. Making a simple sentence negative is daunting. *Ni Bilbon bizi naiz* means "I live in Bilbao", literally "I Bilbao-in to live am." If you want to say the opposite, it becomes *Ni ez naiz Bilbon bizi*—"I not am Bilbao-in to live." One genitive case (there are two—let's not go there) is formed by adding *-ren* to the definite article: "the beauty of the sea" becomes *itsasoaren edertasuna*, "sea-the-of beauty-the". Many neologisms, especially in personal names, have been invented since Sabino Arana's generation pioneered the craze. It is often sufficient to substitute a "k" for a "c" in a Spanish name or noun to make it defiantly *basko*. So the Spanish Conchita becomes Kontxita. With the radicalization of Basque nationalism, substitute "k"s have passed into international Spanish as an indication that your *radicalismo* is truly *radikal*. Squatters in Madrid and Mexico City now call themselves *okupas*.

How about simpler things, like affirmations, negations and greetings? If you want to say yes, say *bai*. If you want to say no, just say *ez*. Goodbye is *agur* (but *agur* can sometimes also mean hello), *egun on* is "good morning", and both *kaixo* and *aizu* roughly translate as "hi". Oh, and *eta* means "and", a coincidence which makes many outsiders (especially Spanish policemen) see references to terrorism in every second Basque sentence.

All that said, many foreigners (though not, I must confess, this writer) who make the effort do become fluent in Euskera. Nor should you imagine that the language has lived in splendid isolation from French and Spanish. Many lexical elements have been exchanged with both languages. The great Euskera scholar, Koldo Mitxelena (Luis Michelena), who performed the Herculean task of uniting the disparate Basque dialects in a single language, found evidence that its syntax has also had a structural impact on the development of its neighbours.

While it has so far proved impossible to find a confirmed relative for Euskera among living languages, vanished forms of communication offer some clues which again suggest a long Basque sojourn in the Pyrenees. Larry Trask's theory is that Basque is the surviving descendant of Aquitanian, a language spoken in southern Gaul and the Pyrenees which the Romans found incomprehensible. But the Aquitanians, he says, left enough written records of names (of gods and people) in Latin texts to establish a pretty solid link to contemporary Basque. And new discoveries, still to be fully analyzed, will fuel further debate. In the summer of 2006 a group of archaeologists in Álava found stone inscriptions with Basque phrases from daily life dating from the third or fourth century AD. They mentioned activities like eating and drinking and, intriguingly, an apparent reference to a "blue star", all in words close to current usage. This was a major leap back in time—the earliest previously known Basque transcriptions were in manuscripts from the tenth century. Euskera did not appear in complete texts until the French Basque Bernart Dechepare (or Bernat Etxepare) published a seminal collection of poems, *Linguae Vasconum Primitiae*, in 1545.

Trask wrote that Basque extended as far north as the Garonne in Roman times, and as far south-east along the Pyrenees as the Val d'Aran, an area which is now Catalan-speaking, and in eastern Navarre. He made two crucial claims: first, he found no link between Basque and

Celtiberian and Iberian, two of the other main languages spoken on the peninsula in the Roman period. Secondly, he found no evidence that Basque was spoken in Roman times in much of the heartland of today's Basque Country: not in Vizcaya, not in Álava or western Navarre, and only possibly in Guipúzcoa.

Trask was an academic linguist, but his two arguments manage to run counter to the mainstreams of *both* the ideologically constructed pasts which are cherished by opposing groups in the Basque Country today. Basque nationalists may be happy to hear that there is no link between Basque and other Iberian languages. But they will be distressed with the implication that sacred sites like the Stone-Age cave-paintings in Ekain in Guipúzcoa, or in Santimamiñe in Vizcaya, may not have been the creations of Basque-speaking ancestors, after all.

Not One Nationalism, but Three

Basque nationalism, as is hopefully clear by now, is not the only political actor guilty of playing highly charged political games in the Basque Country. It is important to remember that there is not one but *three* nationalist ideologies competing for the soul of this small people— Basque, Spanish and French. While it is not expressed so overtly, the Spanish nationalist perspective has another myth which Trask's findings puncture. This is the idea that the Basques are actually the original *Spaniards*, proto-Iberians, the pure origin of a race subsequently "contaminated" by Jews and Arabs. That idea, too, according to Trask, has to be set aside.

To see the Basque Country whole, you need a kind of triple vision, which can simultaneously focus on the Basque, Spanish and French nationalist versions of events. These are often contradictory but they are not necessarily mutually exclusive. They contain essential insights into Basque reality, but no single narrative tells the full story. It may seem odd to lay such emphasis on seeing the world here through political filters. But this is one of the most highly politicized places on earth, where almost any of the normal ingredients of daily life—language, gastronomy, sport—can be and is co-opted to reinforce one or the other point of view.

For example, Trask's thesis does endorse, to an extent, the nationalist view that Basques have been in the Pyrenees for a very long time.

Indeed, it is ironic that the French Basque Country, and eastern Navarre, two areas where nationalism barely gets a look-in at the polling booths today, may be the very places where the Basque ancestors were longest established.

And while Spanish nationalists may have to forget about the Basques being proto-Iberians, there is some basis, later in history, to their argument that the Basque Country is "the heart of Spain". Basques were prominent in the Christian *reconquista* of Islamic Iberia, and many Basque fighters—often mercenaries like many on both sides of that complex conflict—settled in Castile, the heartland of what was to become the Spanish nation-state. So here is another irony: the very Pérezs and Sánchezs who brandish Spanish flags in conservative marches against Basque nationalism in Madrid today may be of Basque origin themselves.

It is easy to extend this argument that the Basques are an essential part of Spanish life. The Basques gave Spain navigators like Juan Sebastián de Elcano and *conquistadores* like Lope de Aguirre, subject of Werner Herzog's movie *Aguirre Wrath of God*. The Basque contribution to Spanish—and world—culture, in the broadest sense, has been enormous. St. Ignatius Loyola, founder of the Jesuits, and St. Francis Xavier, that order's pioneering missionary, were both Basques. The Basque novelist Pío Baroja and the Basque philosopher Miguel de Unamuno were key figures in the "Generation of '98". This was the group of intellectuals who attempted to make sense of Spain as a once-great imperial nation which lost most of its last remnants of empire—Cuba, the Philippines, and Puerto Rico—in 1898, just as its European neighbours were expanding their overseas dominions. Both wrote in Spanish, but both had intimate and complex relationships with their Basque identities.

The best-known contemporary Basque novelist, Bernardo Atxaga, writes in Euskera, and has described himself as standing, somewhat uncomfortably, in the middle of a river between the banks of Basque and Spanish nationalism. His novels are translated into Spanish (and more than twenty other languages, including English), and his *Obabakoak* won the *Spanish* National Narrative Award in 1989, as well as a fistful of Basque prizes and a nomination for the European Literary Award. A *New York Times* critic mixed things up nicely by describing this quintessentially Basque book as being "as Spanish as *paella*", a dish which is in any case Valencian, not Basque, in origin.

Go to a website dedicated to the Basque painter Ignacio Zuloaga, and you will see he has two museums dedicated to his work. One is on the Basque coast at Orio. The other is in Pedraza, a quintessentially Castilian town in Segovia, because Zuloaga spent many years in the south, and captured the atmosphere of *la España profunda* to a unique degree. Eduardo Chillida is widely recognized as one of the key figures of international sculpture in the twentieth century, and yet his work is intimately linked to the Basque landscape. That is where much of his best work can still be found, like the "Comb of the Winds", embedded in the rocks above the beach at Ondarreta in San Sebastián, or the many pieces in the marvellous Chillida Leku park near Hernani. The work of Jorge Oteiza, Chillida's aggressive rival for the title of best Basque sculptor, is also ubiquitous. He too now has a museum solely dedicated to his work, in Alzuza near Pamplona, and he too is undoubtedly a figure of international significance.

French and Spanish rugby and Spanish soccer would be terribly impoverished without Basque participation, or so friends who know about these things tell me. Try to imagine their national teams, they say, without ex-Real Sociedad players Xabi Alonso (now a Liverpool FC hero) and Mikel Arteta (currently playing for Everton), and rugby giants like Imanol Harinordoki (Biarritz RFC) and Daniel Larretxea (formerly of Bayonne RFC and now playing for English league champions, Sale Sharks). You may have to imagine this sooner than you think, because Basque nationalists are demanding the right to field their own team in international competitions. When you remember that Wales has its own rugby team, and even Northern Ireland has its own soccer team, this seems pretty reasonable. But for obvious reasons it is not an argument that is digested with any pleasure in Madrid or Paris.

As for gastronomy, Basque cuisine dominates Spain's rich range of regional cooking to an extraordinary extent. It is not just that two of the top restaurants in the whole peninsula, Arzak and Martin Berastegui, can be found in a single Basque city, San Sebastián. The most popular culinary programme, indeed one of the most popular programmes of any kind, on Spanish TV is presented by Karlos Arguiñano, a Basque chef.

The Basque film industry went through a phase of acute introspection when it took off in the 1980s, while benefiting from multiple subsidies from the Madrid, CAV and provincial administrations. But today Basque directors like Julio Medem are as likely to deal with sexual ecstasy and existential angst in Madrid or Majorca as they are to focus on specifically Basque questions.

Turn to economics, and again you find the Basque Country as an engine house of the peninsula, consistently punching well above its weight in both industry and finance.

And yet, despite all this, the Basques are different, so different that many of them do not feel Spanish or French at all. Medem's own afore-mentioned documentary, *La Pelota Vasca/The Basque Ball*, makes this uncomfortably clear. The depth of that cleavage was evident in the out-rageous anathemas issued against this director by Spanish cultural mandarins of left and right. It was easier to call Medem a useful fool for terrorist propagandists, or accuse him of being as "naïve as a Swiss NGO", than to face the straightforward testimony of his interviewees. If Basque nationalism is sometimes visceral, irrational and intolerant, so is its much more powerful Spanish counterpart.

The Basque Sense of Difference

The Basque sense of difference is rooted in a history which—and this is the difficult part—is at once distinctive from the normative Spanish or French experience, yet interpenetrates constantly with the histories of its larger neighbours.

Spain has been moulded by its exposure to two great colonizing powers, the Romans and the Arabs (as well as enjoying the cultural contribution of a significant Jewish population). Everything from the Spanish language to Spanish architecture and Spanish music bears the mark of these formidable presences. The Basques, on the other hand, remained *relatively* untouched, in their mountains and forests, by these waves of invasion, occupation and assimilation. There is no reason to believe that the Romans could not have occupied the whole Basque Country, had they wanted to. Pamplona [Iruñea], now the capital of Navarre, is of Roman origin, and there are also extensive Roman remains in Álava. There were significant trading settlements, at least, on the coasts of Vizcaya, Guipúzcoa, and Labourd. But there seems to have been no formal Roman administration north of the Cantabrian Cordillera, and certainly there was none in the Basque Pyrenees.

The general absence of Roman fortifications around their coastal trading posts has been taken to indicate some kind of military failure on the part of the empire. It may indicate just the opposite: that the Basques put up no significant resistance to the presence of traders, and entered into mutually beneficial relations with them without much conflict, but also with little cultural interaction.

Basque nationalists, as we have seen, date the distinctiveness of the Basques from much further back in time. The historian Roger Collins, after very cautious deliberation, thinks the linguistic evidence manifest in topography and archaeology does tilt the balance in favour of explaining the Basque presence in the Pyrenees from the Neolithic period onwards. But, as MacClancy points out, there is an equally well constructed argument that they arrived more recently, so that "the origin of the Basques remains an open question."

Collins himself remains tentative even when he reaches the Roman period, and for long centuries thereafter, writing in *The Basques*:

> The scant, fragmentary and frequently contradictory evidence for the earliest recorded periods of Basque history is almost too frail to bear any substantial construction, and can reduce the aspiring chronicler to the rank of novelist.

For all that, he continues, the period from the Romans to the late twelfth century, "is a crucial one in which, solely amongst all of the former pre-Indo-European peoples of Europe, the Basques were able to survive, to resist cultural assimilation and to retain a language divorced... from all other living speeches of the continent." Then he adds an equally important counterpoint: "At the same time these centuries saw the failure of the Basques to develop political unity or even find the impulse to do so. Their cultural tenacity was thus totally separate from any form of political cohesion based under independent self-government or the growth of nationhood." Basque nationalists, attempting to construct a credible historical ante-chamber for the emergence of their ideology, have made strenuous efforts to wrestle their way around this fact, but their energies have so far generated more heat than light.

As the Roman Empire declined, the Basques do not appear to have proved an obstacle to the Vandal and then Visigothic forces who advanced through the western Pyrenees during the fifth century. But their apparent passivity evaporated as the Visigoths became established in the Navarran lowlands centred on Pamplona, which the Basques raided repeatedly. The Visigoths quickly established their authority over almost all of old Roman Spain, but the Basque Pyrenees were again an exception.

As the emerging Frankish kingdom to the north began attacking the Visigoths across the Pyrenees, the Basques seem to have become progressively more belligerent, probably due to the increasingly frequent passage of troops through their territory. This phase, where the Basques became regarded as notorious "brigands" by more conventional armed forces, finds its most famous instance at the battle of Roncesvalles [Orreaga] in 778.

By this time, the Visigothic kingdom in Iberia had been largely replaced by the rapid expansion of the Berber and Arab forces who had invaded from Morocco. The Frankish emperor Charlemagne entered Spain to exact tribute from the Moorish emirates, and returned home through the Basque Pyrenees. At the pass of Roncesvalles his rearguard was massacred and his baggage train plundered by Basque warriors. Curiously, by the time the *Chanson de Roland*, which would immortalize this episode, was written down three centuries later, the identity of the villains of the piece have changed. They are no longer Basques, and have become the infidel "Moors".

Sancho: the Greatest Basque Political Figure?

It was only much later, in the eleventh century, that the entire Basque Country came under a single jurisdiction, for the first and only time in its history. This occurred under the leadership of the Navarran king Sancho Garcés III (1004-35). He expanded his kingdom as far north as Bordeaux, as far west as León, and almost as far south as Huesca. The composite kingdom of Sancho, known as "the Great", is often seen by Basque nationalists as a prototype for a modern Basque political entity. In 2004 Sancho's reign, including a rather stereotyped portrayal of Muslims, was the subject of the Soule *Pastorale*, an enormously popular pageant-play tradition in Iparralde. On the millennial anniversary of his accession to the throne, he was described in a preface to the text of the pageant as "the greatest political figure so far produced by the Basque Country."

Was Sancho's kingdom Basque in any meaningful sense? He may have spoken Euskera, and most of his subjects certainly did. But it is worth noting that when Sancho acquired sovereignty over Vizcaya and Guipúzcoa, it was not so much because of strong organic connections between Navarre and these provinces, but indirectly, because he had gained control of León, which at that time dominated the Basque coast. And the title he gave himself was not "King of the Basques" but *Rex Hispaniorum*, "King of the Spains". So is Navarre, as Basque nationalists claim, the mother province of their nation, or is it, as the Spanish historian Claudio Sánchez-Albornoz has it, "the grandmother of today's Spain"?

The answer is surely "both/and" rather than "either/or", though that kind of ambiguity offends political dogmatists of all stripes. We will see evidence of Navarre's deep Basque roots in the chapters to come. But it is important to point out that an Islamic dynasty allied to the caliphate of al-Andalus ruled Pamplona for most of the eighth century. And that the Christian Basque who then supplanted this dynasty, Iñigo Aritza, founded a principality in Navarre which became "the dominant power in Christian Spain… at the spearhead of the Reconquest," according to Marianne Heiberg in *The Making of the Basque Nation* (1989), a book full of refreshingly open-minded insights.

In any case, Sáncho III's kingdom quickly broke up when he bequeathed it, in fragments, to his four sons. As Collins says: "no sense of racial, linguistic or cultural unity seems to have existed that proved itself greater than [the Basques'] internal divisions." Sancho's brief empire "was not to have any impact on their [the Basques'] self-awareness or aspirations." Indeed, we could say that this monarch has more influence on the Basques today than at any time since his own reign.

The medieval Basque Country, then, was a deeply divided territory, parts of which would repeatedly make alliances with, or fall subject to, foreign powers on its borders. Matters were made more confused by the tendency of each small valley to fight with its neighbour, in inconclusive and bloody quarrels known as the "war of the bands". These were feuds between noble warlords loosely grouped in two rival factions, led by the Oñaz and Gamboa families respectively. They were not so much territorial wars as contests to measure the strength of the combatants at any given moment. The family banners—red and blue respectively—persist today as the distinctive colours of contestants in pelota games. Collins again: "Overall the Basques remained, in the late Middle Ages as in the early, politically divided, subjects of different kingdoms, and with no sense of nationhood of their own. Indeed, such a concept is anachronistic if applied to them."

Some sense of unity must have been fostered by the common use of a most uncommon language throughout the region. But Euskera's own divisions into dialects which could barely communicate with each other undermined any unifying tendency. And Spanish, and not Euskera, replaced Latin as the local language of administration and high culture, which suggests that the old language made little impact in the political sphere.

Special Rights and the Ancestral Oak

If one thing characterized the Basque Country right up to the last decades of the nineteenth century, it was its extraordinary diversity of its administrations. Vizcaya, Álava and Guipúzcoa had all been coerced or co-opted, depending on your political point of view, into association with the new and ascendant power of Castile and León by the year 1200, with only Navarre retaining a separate kingship (until 1512). But each province, and often districts *within* the provinces, had their own special *fuero*, or charter of rights, practices and customs. Vizcaya retained the status of a separate territory until 1876, and Navarre retains the title "kingdom" to this day.

Local charters were commonplace throughout Spain, and indeed in much of medieval Europe. Basque *fueros*, however, seem to have devolved exceptional powers to the local authorities. They certainly remained in operation longer in the Basque Country than anywhere else on the Iberian Peninsula. But because they were specific to each province, and sometimes even to each village, they actually worked against the establishment of unified Basque institutions, whereas a more general *fuero* conferred an early sense of national unity on Catalonia. Yet Basque nationalists see the *fueros* as recognition that the region's association with the emerging Spanish nation-state was voluntary, and conditional on the Spanish king conceding sweeping autonomous powers. This concession is symbolized by the traditional obligation of each king of Castile, and later each king of Spain, to swear to uphold the *fueros* of Vizcaya at a ceremony under the ancestral oak in Gernika (see p.58-9).

Heiberg describes the powers granted to the Basques as "possibly unique in Spain". They included general exemption from torture, from arbitrary arrest, and from military conscription for service outside their own territory by the king. These privileges, which were generally only granted to nobles in other regions, created a powerful sense that the Basques enjoyed a kind of "universal nobility". In fact, many of these privileges may have been granted for pragmatic reasons. They may have been granted in order to undermine the power of the local nobles, since their feuds were creating such mayhem. What has often been described as the "egalitarianism" of Basque society, and traced back to Neolithic times, is therefore probably of quite recent origin. As the anthropologist Juan Aranzadi comments acidly, in the Basque case the Neolithic period "did not arrive until the twelfth and thirteenth centuries."

In addition, the Spanish crown accepted that it had no right to levy taxes in the region. The most striking privilege of all, however, was that the line of Spanish customs posts remained on the Ebro until the nineteenth century, making the Spanish Basque Country a duty-free zone. Heiberg suggests that these concessions may have been intended in part as incentives to migrants to populate and defend a border region where Castile had no standing army.

Proposals to abolish these economic privileges were central issues in the Carlist wars, which plunged Spain into bloody conflict twice in the nineteenth century. The Basques were deeply involved in these wars—on both sides.

The Carlist Wars: the Basque Rift Deepens

In the Basque Country the Carlist wars were an expression of the deepening of a long rift between the countryside and the towns. The fault lines run back to the twelfth century, when urbanization began in earnest. Seven hundred years later, the rural/urban rift had become a chasm. The rapidly industrializing cities found that the *fueros* left them in the worst of all worlds. Their products were subject to customs duties in the Spanish market, while they had no protection from British or Dutch competition in the internal Basque market. The urban merchants wanted to shake off ancient privileges which were turning into chronic

Armed struggle: some of the best moments in Julio Medem's film *Vacas* are set in the Carlist wars, like this scene in which Carmelo Gómez (left) and Kandido Uranga, rival neighbours, are thrown together in the horror and absurdity of battle. Courtesy Sogecine.

handicaps in the emerging world order. The *fueros* were inhibiting their ability to exploit their pivotal geographical position between Madrid, Paris, London and Amsterdam.

In the countryside, however, the peasantry feared ruin if they were exposed to the duty-free import of Castilian livestock and cereals, or lost their rights to graze common lands or exploit natural resources held in common. The *fueros* also decreed that wood and iron were municipal property. Modest but productive smelters and smithies could be found along every Basque river, directly serving local communities on a small scale. Urban liberals wanted the commons privatized so that industrial-scale manufacture, oriented towards exports, could flourish.

The first Carlist war was sparked by a dynastic struggle, but its deeper causes were economic and cultural. In 1833, after the death of Ferdinand VII, his brother, the pretender Don Carlos, claimed the throne, which was then occupied by the queen regent, María Cristina, representing her infant daughter Isabella. What was really at issue in this war, and in its successor in 1872-76, was the political future of Spain.

Urban liberals supported the queen, and rural conservatives favoured Don Carlos. The Carlists generally represented the obscurantist Catholicism of *La España Negra*; the liberals leaned towards Enlightenment values. In a foretaste of Spain's twentieth-century Civil War, British, French and German volunteers and mercenaries fought on both sides. In the Basque Country, these wars became a kind of struggle for the soul of a nation which had not yet been born. Much of the worst fighting, in both wars, took place in the Basque region.

The traditionalists in the Basque countryside, especially in Navarre, were Carlist diehards because they believed that Don Carlos would respect their ancient liberties, encapsulated in the *fueros*. The Basque cities, and especially Bilbao, were predictably Liberal. Julio Medem's sur-realistic film *Vacas* uses a vendetta between two families as a metaphor for the Basque conflict, then and now. Some of its best moments are set in the bloody chaos of the Carlist wars.

The first war ended in 1841 with a negotiated defeat for the Carlists, in which some *fueros* were retained. The definitive triumph of the liber-als in 1876 spelt their final abolition. In the view of the Carlists, and of Basque nationalism as it subsequently emerged, this was an unprece-dented tragedy. To this day, Basque nationalists routinely assume it had a catastrophic yet ultimately regenerative impact on national conscious-ness—a curiously parallel sentiment to Spanish perceptions of the "Disaster" of 1898.

The Basque liberals, however, were naturally happy to see customs tariffs shift to the coast, administration centralized and the commons privatized. But their belief in the free market had its limits. In a neat double whammy, they promptly negotiated a fresh raft of fiscal privileges for the region, tailored to their specific needs, known as the *Concierto Económico*.

The rest of the century saw the population of Bilbao triple, and Vizcaya become the most densely populated province in Spain, as indus-trialization accelerated. The increased population was largely made up of impoverished immigrants from Andalusia, Extremadura and Galicia. This new industrial working class became one of the seed beds of Spanish socialism, and both the PSOE and its associated union, the UGT, put down deep and permanent roots in the hard and dirty steel towns springing up on the left bank of Bilbao's Nervión river.

Not only the Carlist countryside, but also the urban lower-middle class, looked on in growing resentment as two new actors appeared to be squeezing them off the political, social and cultural stages "in their own country".

One actor was the industrial and financial oligarchy. It had Basque surnames but was now economically married to big capital in Madrid and Barcelona. This new elite inherited two things from the old Basque aristocracy, with which it was well connected: vigorous relationships with the capital city, and a barely concealed belief that they were "more Spanish than the Spanish" because of their "purity of blood". The oligarchy energetically jettisoned traditional Basque values like *berdin-berdin*—egalitarianism.

The other actor was the rising proletariat, mostly non-Basque in origin, often militantly atheistic and revolutionary. And, Basque traditionalists liked to add, shamelessly promiscuous in its morals.

Sabino Arana: Inventor of Basque Nationalism

That was the view of the most influential ideologue to emerge in the Basque Country in the nineteenth century: Sabino Arana. He and his brother Luis constructed a nationalist project for the Basque Country which, though it drew heavily (and often capriciously) on tradition, was also distinctively modern. So modern that it is the inheritors of Arana who have dominated every Basque government since the CAV was established in 1980, and who can claim the Guggenheim Museum and a booming IT sector as their initiatives.

Arana (1865-1903) came from a Carlist family, but his people were shipbuilders with three yards in booming Bilbao, not peasants from the green Goiherri valleys, nor sailors from Lekeitio. He did not even speak Euskera, though he managed to learn it, with difficulty. His virtual invention of Basque nationalism was as much a search for an identity as an expression of it. To say this is not to deny his ideology political legitimacy. All nationalisms are inventions to some degree, replacing the diversity of reality with a comforting homogeneity. As the French historian Ernest Renan put it, "getting its history wrong is part of being a nation."

Arana grafted significant elements of his Carlist legacy onto his new plant, though his followers would be regarded as traitors to Spain by traditional Carlists. His loathing for immigrants was pathological. His ideology was nourished by xenophobia. (In fairness, we must remember that a degree of racism was mother's milk to most nascent nationalisms in nineteenth-century Europe.) He was a terrifyingly zealous Catholic.

This religious inheritance from Carlism was enshrined in the very title of the party he founded, though not in the Spanish version of its name, the one which rather oddly, is mostly used today. In Euskera, however, the Partido Nacionalista Vasco (PNV) becomes Eusko Alderdi Jeltzalea (EAJ). *Jeltzalea* is not only one of the many new Basque words coined by Arana, but is minted, somewhat awkwardly, out of an acronym he also invented, JEL. This stands for his favourite slogan, *Jaungoikoa Eta Lege Zarra*, "for God and the Ancient Laws". The phrase is still prominent on the PNV's website today, though the party omits to translate it directly. Instead, the site renders it in fuzzy fashion as "an expression of a transcendental concept of existence, linked to an affirmation of the Basque nation." The party goes on to describe its ideology as "humanist" and "non-confessional", words which must have Arana fuming from the gates of heaven.

Arana claimed that the basic principles of Basque nationalism were revealed to him on Whitsun Day. But he had no Christian love to spare for his Spanish brothers and sisters in the tenements of Bilbao and the mining villages round about them. He admonished his Church for wasting its charity on such degenerates. "They do not pray with us," he commented sniffily. The fact that they danced cheek to cheek in public places was sufficient to indict them of chronic depravity. His belief that the Basque "race" was superior to the Spanish was quite explicit, ironically sharing an ideology of purity of blood with the Castilians he spurned. He called them *maketos*, an offensive term for immigrants. As recently as the 1950s, a PNV ideologue would dismiss a new wave of migrant workers as "Koreans", and the name stuck.

Arana's distaste for the deracinated Basque oligarchy was equally visceral on the surface. But it masked a sneaking regard for the robust energy with which these businessmen were endowing his homeland with unprecedented economic power. Like Éamon de Valera in Ireland, he harked back to an Arcadian past ("if we were poor, and only had fields and livestock, we would be happy"). But it was the countryside's symbols that he wanted to harvest, not its agricultural produce. The *baserri*, the

Basque family farmhouse, was the new nationalism's desirable residence par excellence, but few nationalists actually lived in one, at least in the early days of the movement. Peasant dances and peasant costumes were core elements in the movement's liturgy, but that does not mean that PNV leaders actually worked in the fields, or wanted their daughters to marry anyone who did.

Arana founded the PNV in 1894, and by the time he died nine years later, at the age of 38, it had become a significant force. He left behind not only an ideology but a flag (the *ikurriña*, which looks like a red, white and green union jack) an anthem (*Gora ta Gora*—his words to a traditional air) and a name for this new-and-ancient nation: Euskadi. In fact, he spelt it Euzkadi, though all other Basque words related to the Basque language begin with Euskera's root syllable, "Eus". Arana was trying to suggest a link with the Basque word for the sun, *eguzki*, harking back to the solar symbols so dominant in Basque mythology. This was an interesting nod in the direction of pagan roots for such a Christian ideologue to make. Pagan roots would also fascinate many ETA supporters from the 1960s onwards, but the "z" has disappeared from "Euskadi" for good. It is a measure of Arana's influence that these key symbols—flag, anthem (albeit without his words) and name—have all been in official use by the Basque Autonomous Community (CAV) since the early 1980s.

Arana's greatest gift to the PNV was his ambiguity. He had started out proclaiming the party's goal to be total independence from Spain (and, even less realistically, from France). Quite suddenly, he apparently accepted that "maximum autonomy" within the Spanish state was more desirable. He was ill and in prison at the time he expressed this view, which casts doubts on his motive for shifting his ground, and the documentary evidence is inconclusive.

From that day to this, the PNV has succeeded in appealing simultaneously to two sets of Basques: to those who are happy to settle for the cultural (and financial) benefits of a strong regional government within the Spanish state, and to a more radical but still substantial minority who want to sever all links with Madrid. Quite often, indeed, the same individual party members appear to hold both positions at the same time, one with their heads, and the other with their hearts.

Despite the dependence on rural symbols, the PNV's first successes were in the cities, where they gained support from the Basque middle class, squeezed between monopolizing capital and radicalizing labour. In the countryside the Carlists, who had after all been shedding their blood for a *Spanish* monarch, were deeply suspicious of a movement that was appropriating their language and traditional customs for an entirely novel political project. Gradually, however, many of the small towns and villages were won over, especially in Vizcaya and Guipúzcoa, but less so in Álava and less again, with critical consequences, in Navarre.

As for the French Basque Country, it figured in the PNV's adoption of the ideal of *Zazpiak Bat*, "the Seven are One", but the party failed to make its presence felt north of the border. The centralizing force of the 1789 French Revolution had stripped that part of the Basque Country of local privileges almost a century before the Spanish Basques lost theirs. Much more recently, the impact of the First World War, in which Spain was neutral but many French Basques died at the front, consolidated the sway of French patriotism over the Basques north of the Pyrenees. However, Euskera and folk traditions remained (and remain) strong there.

The Civil War: the PNV Stands—Reluctantly—with the Republic

South of the border, neutrality in the First World War was excellent for business, but the subsequent depression also intensified a class war. Bilbao became the second most violent city in Spain, after Barcelona. Some of the street fighting was inter-union, as militants of the UGT engaged in dockside shoot-outs with members of ELA, the union the PNV set up to give native Basque proletarians a Catholic option in the workplace.

However, the hostility between the PNV and the PSOE was not universal. The philosopher Miguel de Unamuno, then a socialist sympathizer, moved from caustic opposition to Basque nationalism at the turn of the century to a more comprehending position as early as 1906. He wrote in the magazine *La Lucha de Clases*:

> Cannot socialism be translated into the Basque spirit? That most of [socialism's] first apostles and propagandists neither were from here nor know of this spirit has damaged the cause of socialism in Vasconia. A doctrine, regardless of its universality, can be made fruitful only by injecting local sentiments into it.

As Spanish politics polarized with the advent of the second Spanish Republic and the international rise of fascism, an uncomfortable but real rapprochement developed between the PNV and the Basque left. General Franco and his fellow generals launched their "Christian Crusade against Communism" on 18 July 1936. But most of the very Catholic PNV stood firmly, if reluctantly, with Spanish republican democracy, although they loathed the anti-clerical excesses and revolutionary passion of some republicans. For Franco and his allies, the PNV's decision to challenge his uprising in the name of the Basque nation and of democracy was an unforgivable betrayal.

The beleaguered republic rather grudgingly rewarded the PNV's loyalty by belatedly granting autonomy to Vizcaya, Álava and Guipúzcoa. The first Basque government was formed by a pluralist coalition led by the PNV, but including the PSOE, Republicans, and even the PCE. This historic administration would only last a few months. In Álava, the PNV failed to mobilize effectively against the uprising. As for Navarre, the Carlists and other conservatives made sure that it was the only province in the whole of Spain which produced a popular uprising *in favour* of the generals. Significantly, Navarre was not even mentioned in the autonomy statute. The rest is well known: the burning of Irún, the rapid advance of the insurgents across Guipúzcoa, the unprecedented Nazi bombings of Durango and Gernika, and the siege and betrayal of Bilbao.

A Nightwatchman in Navarre, a *Conquistador* in Bilbao

Lesaka is a Basque-speaking village in the north of Navarre, right up against the border with Guipúzcoa. It still preserves the tradition of *bertsolarismo*—of folk poets who spontaneously compose verses in Euskera in public competitions. In the 1980s a friend invited me to the town's San Fermín fiestas. We had a meal with her elderly father, a most accomplished *bertsolari* who had some difficulty conversing in Spanish. The topic of the Civil War came up, and this man casually mentioned that he had fought "with Franco's lot". A young communist at the table, not used to eating in such politically mixed company, rather rudely demanded an explanation. "Well," said my friend's father patiently, "the *requetés* (Carlist militias) came into Lesaka on the morning of 19 July. They ordered all the young men to come out of their houses, and said:

'Christians to this side of the plaza, Reds to the other.' I was a Christian, and I wasn't a Red, and I did not want to get shot. I went with the *requetés*.'

He was not exactly a Francoist by conviction, however, and contrived to shoot himself in the toe at an early stage of operations. Honourably invalided home, his war pension was attached to the job of *sereno*, or town crier and nightwatchman. He fulfilled this position for the entire period of the Franco dictatorship, and the Franco administration paid him weekly for a job he carried out by calling out the hours, and the news that all was well, which it usually was, in the Basque language.

On the other side of the Peñas de Haya, the series of sharply crested granite peaks which separate Lesaka from the coast, the dictatorship was a very different story. Unlike Navarre (and Álava), Vizcaya and Guipúzcoa were treated as "traitor" provinces throughout the Franco period. The speaking of Euskera in public was prohibited, even in church sermons where most of the villagers could not understand Spanish. The Basque Church, which had generally supported the republic, was regarded with the deepest suspicion. Some priests were shot. All symbols of Basque nationalism were banned. "This horrible, evil nightmare called Euzkadi... has been defeated for ever. Vizcaya is again a piece of Spain through poor and simple military conquest," boasted the first Francoist mayor of Bilbao, José María de Areilza. He sounded like a *conquistador* on an exotic continent, though he was in fact a native of Bilbao, coming home.

It is prudent to take a longer view of history, Basque nationalists might have told him, had they been able to speak at all at the time. In fact, to paraphrase the historian Antonio Elorza, the dictatorship made a grim reality out of Sabino Arana's fantasy that the Basque Country was an occupied and subjugated nation. And those circumstances would give birth to Euskadi ta Askatasuna, ETA, and forge an entirely new, and bloody, impetus to full Basque independence. But we will leave that story to another chapter, and instead explore the estuary of Urdaibai, a mini-region rich in symbols of Basque identity, and of Basque diversity.

Flag, tree, parliament, nation: traditional dancers and musicians salute the ancestral oak at Gernika's parliament house, symbol of Basque nationhood. Ironically, a plaque on the convent in the background proclaims that "Christ will reign in Spain."

Chapter Three

Bai, Bai, Urdaibai: Cave Paintings, Painted Trees, Tree of Gernika

If you look northwards from Gernika's Casa de Juntas, beside the ancestral Basque oak trees, or from within Chillida's nearby and appropriate sculpture, *The House of my Father*, a conical hill may catch your eye. Its neatly triangular peak is broken by the faint outline of a building, a sanctuary church.

The hermitage of San Mikel de Ereñozar (1,500 feet) dates from the sixteenth century, though it was built on the site of a small fortress at least four hundred years older. The summit's natural defences include not only the hill's steep sides, but also an almost impenetrable thicket of holm oak. This hardy evergreen bears no obvious resemblance to the more familiar broadleaf "English" oak, which is the symbol of Gernika, and of Basque democracy. According to the official literature of the Casa de Juntas, it is also the symbol of "the Basque soul".

In terms of natural history, though, the holm oak has at least as good a claim to be the emblem of the region. Hilltop stands of this tree are among the only remaining patches of native Atlantic Cantabrian forest along the Basque coastal hills. Just a little further down the slope of Ereñozar, alien but profitable lines of eucalyptus and massed ranks of Monterey pine can be seen marching upwards, displacing the ancient woodlands. These clashing forests exemplify the perennial Basque struggle between reverence for heritage and energetic pursuit of wealth. The advance of invasive mono-cultural vegetation and the surge in urban sprawl raise questions about who is winning the battle for the Basque soul in Urdaibai, the most emblematic Basque valley.

Look back carefully at the Casa de Juntas from the town below and you will see that this venerable parliament building is not dominated by oaks, as you might have expected. The current "tree of Gernika" is a modest oak sapling, planted here in 2005. Its predecessor dated from

1860, surviving the 1937 bombing but still died relatively young in 2004. A section of the trunk of the grandparent, perhaps three centuries old, is preserved nearby, reverently encircled by stone columns. Patriotic Basque visitors still search for acorns from the current tree, to plant them as far away as Idaho and Venezuela. An especially passionate nationalist told me he has planted one on the farm he has bought in Navarre, to grow as a silent witness to a heartfelt territorial claim.

But, as I was saying, the dominant tree as you approach the building is not an oak. It is a giant eucalyptus. This Australian exotic has been incongruously planted on the margins of the Park of the Peoples of Europe, which backs onto the Casa de Juntas. That such a tree can stand tall in such a place is a small indicator that the Basque authorities are not always quite as sensitive to tradition as they like to claim. The exhibitions about the origins and nature of Basque democracy in the Casa de Juntas present a cosy and homogenous version of Gernika and its hinterland, Urdaibai. The reality is much more complex and much more interesting. This valley represents rich and varied sediments of significance. It encompasses many different senses of what it is to be Basque, and of where the Basque Country has been, and where it may be going. These strata, some deriving from the distant past, coexist uneasily in the present, and extend into the future.

It is doubly ironic that this eucalyptus, an alien plant which often displaces native vegetation and guzzles scarce water, also stands only a few hundred yards from the headquarters of Urdaibai Biosphere Reserve. Urdaibai (possibly deriving from *urde*—pig or wild boar—and *ibai*, river) is the name the River Oka takes as it becomes an estuary, between Gernika and the coast ten miles to the north. Biosphere reserves are designated by UNESCO as regions demonstrating innovative approaches to conservation and sustainable development, as "living laboratories for people and nature".

These reserves recognize human economic and cultural activities as part of the ecosystem, rather than excluding them beyond high fences. One of the goals of Urdaibai is the conservation of indigenous biodiversity, but the prevalence of eucalyptus and other invasive alien plants in this landscape suggests that the outcome of this experiment remains in doubt.

Though its outskirts are plagued by invasive acacias, there are still some fine holm oaks in the harbour at Mundaka, the small fishing port (and surfer's Mecca) tucked into the western lip of the estuary. Here the oaks' roots are lapped by saltwater, a reminder that the native Cantabrian forest once carpeted all of Urdaibai right down to the shore. But that is a rare sight now. A workshop organized by UNESCO and Urdaibai Reserve in 2005 heard that native woodlands had been reduced to 6.5 per cent of the area, while commercial plantations had surged to 55 per cent. The participants issued a stinging indictment of the Basque administration's failure to conserve the traditional landscape, here in the valley where Basque democratic traditions are said to have been born.

The holm oaks have survived down in Mundaka, and up at the summit of Ereñozar, because they can thrive on scant accumulations of soil in the crevices of karstic limestone. This is the rock which gives most of the Urdaibai river basin its characteristic horizon. Each watershed is formed by a line of little hills whose sharp gradients give them curiously pointed peaks, making them seem higher than they are. Ereñozar's summit is the most acute of them all.

Karstic limestone is very permeable, allowing rainwater to gradually ease apart and penetrate its crevices over the millennia, until the whole hill system is half-hollow, a honeycomb of caves and hidden passages. The novelist Bernardo Atxaga talks about the "instability of the Basque ground" in symbolic terms, but you can frequently apply the phrase to the far-from-solid Basque earth. The result of karstic instability in Urdaibai has been remarkable. Under Ereñozar, it has created a place whose meaning is itself unstable, shifting, and uncertain.

Santimamiñe and Forua: Palaeolithic Paintings, Roman Smelters

Far below the church on the peak is a second and more natural sanctuary, which was evidently much appreciated by the first human inhabitants of the region, but was unknown at the time the chapel was built.

The entrance to the caves of Santimamiñe was discovered by a group of schoolchildren in 1916, though some reports say it had been known to locals for many generations. The caves inevitably attracted the assiduous anthropologists José Miguel de Barandarián and Telesforo de Aranzadi, who began an eight-year initial excavation in 1918. They found themselves face to face with one of the wonders of the European Stone-Age world: galleries adorned with finely wrought paintings of bison, horses, deer, goats and bear. They are comparable to the images at Lascaux in the Dordogne and at Altamira in Santander. Archaeological evidence suggests the caves were occupied by humans for long periods, from Upper Palaeolithic times (35,000 BC) down to just two millennia ago. Whether any of the earlier occupants can meaningfully be described as Basques is, as we saw in Chapter Two, highly problematic, but Basque nationalist culture appropriated them in any case.

The caves would again become a shelter for local people for a very brief period in the twentieth century, or so I was told when I first visited them in 1975. Gernika was bombed from the air by the Condor Legion on 26 April 1937. Picasso's response to this event, titled after the Spanish name of the town, *Guernica*, has become one of the key images of modern warfare, indeed of modernity itself. His images of bulls and horses hideously distorted by the bombardment contrast grimly with the elegant animals portrayed in Santimamiñe. Some of the survivors of that horror, fearful of further attacks and of Franco's advancing soldiers, followed an atavistic instinct and took refuge in the caves which may have been home to their distant ancestors. Some of these refugees were probably just glad to have found one of nature's air-raid shelters. Others believed they had come home. I have only oral evidence for this story, but it reflects events elsewhere. Some of the many caves around Itziar were certainly used as refuges during the Civil War, and ETA has since used caves as arms dumps and possibly to hold kidnap victims. Legends have an uncanny way of becoming history in this country.

The core Basque nationalist creed is not content with ancestral cave-dwellers. It also insists that the Basques managed to stand above the more recent tide-lines of invasion that swept across the Iberian Peninsula. These isolated hill-dwellers and adventurous sailors were never conquered by the Romans, Visigoths or Arabs who set the foundation stones of Spanish history, nor was their blood intermingled with that of the Jewish craftsmen and traders who moulded part of the Spanish soul. The Basque mansion, said the old-style nationalists, was constructed in Basque stone alone.

At Forua, across the valley from Santimamiñe, and within sight of the small rise on which Gernika is situated, is hard evidence that things were not as simple as that. Sturdy brick foundations and a wealth of domestic and cultural artefacts show that there was an extensive Roman settlement in this valley for hundreds of years. It was, however, a trading post rather than an administrative or military centre.

The local Basques cultivated cereals on the flood plain here, and there was a rich stock of game and fish to supplement the Roman settlers' diet. But it was iron, not food, which attracted the Romans to Forua. The estuary gave them easy access to the sea, enabling them to export the mineral that would be the single greatest source of Basque wealth in the centuries to come. The Romans set up smelters and forges along the river, using ore traded from the hills nearby. For all its cultural roots in rural life, the Basque Country has had industry in its veins for a very long time.

Txatxaramendi: the Fishing Industry Learns to Fly

As we have seen, even Sabino Arana favoured industry in practice while eulogizing rural simplicity in principle. Contemporary Basque nationalist commitment to industrial innovation is demonstrated in Urdaibai, in an imposing but discreetly located building a few miles downriver from Forua. The headquarters of the Institute for Fisheries and Food Products Technology (AZTI-Tecnalia) is close to the mouth of the estuary, on the seaward side of the island of Txatxaramendi. This ambitious project was set up in 1981, shortly after the first post-Franco Basque autonomous government took office.

Before we look a little more closely at AZTI, it is worth stressing how much authority Basque governments have under Spain's very decentralized democracy. The Comunidad Autónoma Vasca is ruled by what is arguably the most powerful regional administration in Europe. Based in Vitoria [Gasteiz], the capital of Álava, the Basque Government [*Eusko Jaurlaritza*] raises and spends its own taxes, and controls its own education system, health service and housing, among many other services. It also has its own police force, the Ertzaintza, though the Spanish Guardia Civil is still responsible for airports, borders and some counter-terrorist functions.

AZTI, which was restructured in 1991 as a private non-profit foundation, was a rather visionary initiative of the first such government and the provincial administration of Vizcaya. Initially, the institute was focused on one of the quintessential Basque occupations—and preoccupations: fishing. The Basque fleet, already under severe pressure from international competition, was gearing up for Spanish entry into the EEC (now European Union) at that time.

AZTI's principal objective was to assist the industry to meet these challenges. It offered scientific data on the state of fish stocks, and guidance on re-equipping ships to compete with more advanced countries. The institute rapidly rose to international prominence in this field. But that did not prevent the equally rapid decline of the industry from factors outside the institute's control, especially over-fishing and increasingly aggressive competition. So AZTI has broadened its brief to follow the fish from the dockside to the dining table. It has gone on to look at the question of "the food of the future" and cutting-edge developments in other fields as well.

AZTI has collaborated in the production of fish-substitutes, including a passable and popular imitation of a great delicacy. *Angulas* are the elvers, or baby eels, for which Bilbao's Nervión river was once, and is again, justly famous. A combination of over-fishing and pollution caused the eel population's collapse in the 1980s. (The stock has since made a healthy recovery.) The Japanese are willing to pay outrageously high prices for these tasty morsels, so Basque business sense has won out over Basque gastronomic passions, and almost all of today's catch goes for export. At home, Basques are learning to make do with a product known as La Gula, an ersatz food made up of pulverized Alaskan ling crafted to take the "shape, colour, taste and texture" of the elvers. AZTI is also working on substitutes for caviar, and for anchovies. Such developments seem a little depressing, especially in a region renowned for its superb primary produce for the table.

Yet the man who led AZTI in the early years of this century, Xabier Goirigolzarri, has seen the future, and is convinced that it will work: "We consult young chefs about the direction cooking will take. I know my daughter will not buy the same fish my wife buys. Young people do not have time to go the market to look at the day's catch. Our surveys show that they want three things: they want to be sure that the fish is fresh; they want it to be quick and easy to prepare; and they do not want there to be any smell produced while cooking, that irritates the neighbours in apartment blocks. We are working to meet these criteria. We want to put the products of the future into the market now."

This is progress of a sort, but for those who remember the scent of garlic and grilled hake, spilling into the street from dozens of kitchens, as one of the signatures of any evening stroll in a Basque town, it also represents a great loss.

Today, AZTI's investigations range as far as the development of very small pilot-less planes. Bristling with sensors and satellite communications, these little gadgets are economic and convenient substitutes for the helicopters currently used by factory ships to find the ever-decreasing stocks of fish in the oceans. They can also assist in weather forecasting. But they may, of course, also have many military uses, of which AZTI cannot be unaware.

AZTI's impressive headquarters is situated on the flight path which saw the Condor Legion's Junkers, Heinkels and Messerschmitts rumble up and down, testing new technologies as they rained death on Gernika on 26 April 1937. Could the same valley be witnessing today the quiet development of delivery systems appropriate to, though not intended for, chemical or biological weapons of mass destruction? Could a future Basque government, with a long tradition of campaigning for peace, be tempted to export weapons of war? In a globalized world dominated by post-modern irony, that appears not to be impossible.

Moving swiftly on to happier and healthier topics, AZTI's investigations also focus on other areas of undoubted benefit to humanity. Our corneas tend to reject contact lenses made of non-organic substances. The sea offers us a solution, says AZTI. Extracts from the shells of crustaceans can be blended with the lenses, and the rejection rate drops dramatically.

All this is magic beyond the dreams of the ur-democrats who gathered beneath Gernika's oak tree to settle local matters in medieval times, and millennia beyond the brilliant visions of the cave-painters of Santimamiñe. Whether we see things any more clearly now is a different matter.

The Basque passion for research and development raises interesting questions about the Basques' relationship with Spain. The CAV is investing 1.4 per cent of its GDP in R&D, as against 1.1 per cent in the Spanish state. Imagine if Belfast and Derry had been making a similarly significant contribution to British commercial science in the 1990s. Could John Major ever have made the statement in the Downing Street

Declaration, so crucial to the Irish peace process, that Britain has "no selfish, strategic, or economic interest" in Northern Ireland?

Mundaka: Surfers, Ecologists, a Left-handed Wave

Another pioneering development lies across the estuary from Txatxarramendi, but this one seeks to go back in time rather than to anticipate the future. Until the 1950s an imposing line of sand dunes rose above and behind Laida beach, which still dominates the eastern side of the river mouth. But the post-war bathing boom set the conditions for their destruction. Thousands of tramping feet loosened the roots of the plants which stabilized the dune system. A freak storm in 1956 then swept the weakened dunes away overnight. The natural tendency of the tide and wind patterns should have rebuilt them spontaneously. However, the flattened expanse of sand only enhanced Laida's attraction for sunbathers. The relentlessly increasing human footfall denied vegetation any chance to take root. Without plants to build up and bind sand ridges, no new dunes were formed. The beach itself continued to erode, losing more than 50 per cent of its area by the mid-1990s.

In 1999 the University of the Basque Country (UPV) decided that Laida was an ideal place for a major practical experiment in ecological restoration. This is the optimistic scientific practice dedicated to healing damaged ecosystems. Working with Urdaibai Biosphere Reserve staff, university ecologists cordoned off central sections of the beach from human access. The next step was to set dense rows of willow rods in the sand, to accelerate the dune-building process.

Seen from the road above today, these stark lines of dark wood look quite unnatural, rather as though some strange crop had been planted in error. They have, however, had the required effect: the wind has piled up sand against them. Then the eco-workers planted hundreds of thousands of appropriate plants including sea spurge, sea holly and tamarisk. This vegetation has re-engaged the natural binding process which keeps dune systems relatively stable. The dunes are climbing back towards their original height, and should recover their original territory over the next twenty years.

As a poster on the beach points out, the growing dunes will in turn extend the beach area, so that bathers will benefit from their restoration.

So, of course, will wildlife. Scarce species like the little ringed plover, an endearing shorebird with a smart suit of black, white and coffee-coloured plumage and a bright yellow eye-ring, will find some refuge in their shelter. When the dunes are fully stabilized, they will be re-opened to the public, offering further space for leisure pursuits such as discreet sunbathing, picnicking and birding.

Furthermore, according to the restorers, the dunes are capturing sand which would otherwise have blown upstream, and built up steadily on the riverbed. They will thus reduce the amount of dredging required to enable boats with deep draughts to be launched from a shipyard upriver at Murueta. Adding all these benefits together, the case for restoration seems incontrovertible. It satisfies the demands of human leisure and business activities, and the best interests of the animal and plant communities, thus meeting the key criteria of a biosphere reserve.

Nevertheless, the restoration of the dunes at Laida has been intimately linked to an angry controversy about the disappearance of the Wave of Mundaka, a development which sent the global surfing fraternity into apoplexy. This is a wave with a capital "W" because, like a Second Set of Eyes in an Atxaga novel, it points to an experience outside the range of ordinary life.

"The disappearance of the Wave is due to a conspiracy between the Basque government, the Urdaibai Reserve, the ecologists at the University of the Basque Country and the shipyard at Murueta," a hotel receptionist in Mundaka told me angrily in 2005. She spoke with the kind of enviable certainty characteristic of politically-committed Basques, but this question transcends mere politics. The rows of unused keys behind her head attest to the damage that Wavelessness has done to her business. Tiny Mundaka has four hotels, while nearby Bermeo, with ten times the population, only has one. Before the Wave disappeared, it was almost impossible to get a room here. But the Wave also transcends business. It represents a way of life and an international community with a sense of its own identity almost as strong as that enjoyed by the Basques themselves—though its history is a great deal shorter.

The first surfer to be recorded off the Basque coast was Peter Viertel, film writer, and husband of the actress Deborah Kerr. He was spotted riding the waves at Biarritz in 1957, where he was working on the screen version of Ernest Hemingway's *The Old Man and the Sea*. Surfing folk-

Now you see it, now you don't: there are few waves in the world to compare to Mundaka's, and none in Europe, which made its controversial disappearance all the more shocking to surfers.

lore has it that some native Basques had already experimented with home-made boards, but they were not famous so we do not know their names.

Viertel had happened on one of the best surfing spots in Europe. Today it is impossible to walk down the elegant promenades of Biarritz, Zarautz or San Sebastián without bumping into a surf board, but it took the international surfing community a long time to follow Viertel's lead. This is hardly surprising—a sport associated with Hawaii, Brazil, California and Australia does not fit easily into the rain-drenched image of the Bay of Biscay. By the late 1980s, however, the world's best surfers were coming to the Basque coast, and Basque names began to figure among the world's, or at least Europe's, finest exponents of the art.

Very quickly, scruffy little Mundaka began to be favoured by surfers over the exquisite watering holes of the Basque *corniche*. The village rapidly gained the extraordinary distinction of being selected as one of eleven sites for the Billabong Pro World Championship Tour (WCT), an elite annual competition between the top 44 international surfers. Brazil and Hawaii were the next, and final, venues, so excitement was already at fever-pitch when the WCT and its entourage of some 10,000 spectators and hangers-on reached the Basque coast. The lure of Mundaka was, of course, the Wave.

The Wave started about 100 yards beyond the harbour mouth, which faces east across the estuary. It formed in the channel where the Atlantic rushes, north-south, to merge with the out-flowing river at high tide. It gained its extraordinary energy from a little-understood formation of sand bars on the ocean floor. At its best, the Wave was a marvel. It was unusual in that it was "left-handed"—breaking to the left from the point of view of the surfer, to the right from the stance of the beach-bound spectator. It could form a "tube" or "tunnel" up to twice the height of an average adult, and extending for 1,000 feet—straight towards the dunes across the estuary at Laida. There was nothing like it in Europe, and few waves like it in the world.

Mundaka has survived its years of fame remarkably intact. Its restaurants and bars remain traditional, and it has not sprouted pizzerias and hamburger joints. In fact, its restaurants are strangely old-fashioned for the coast; some feel as if they have not been refurbished since the 1950s, though the food is as fresh as this morning's catch. The small port is hardly a jewel of the coast in any architectural sense, but it has an attractive sense of intimacy. Almost inevitably, though, about a quarter of Mundaka has been ruined by barbarous speculative building, dating from the Franco period and continuing today. Nevertheless, there are very handsome *miradores*—those glass-encased balconies which add grace to so many Basque streets—in the Santa Katalina Plazatxoa.

Such scenes attract few tourists, however, while the Wave made small fortunes in the town, and kept a lot of small businesses afloat. And then, in 2003, the Wave began to falter, breaking lower and shorter. By 2005 it had ceased to break at all, and the Billabong WCT pulled out. Craig Sage, an Australian now living in Mundaka, is a former director of the WCT and pioneered European, and especially Basque, participation in the event. But in these conditions, he told the press, to continue with the Billabong "would [have been] like holding a world cup final on a dirt pitch."

But why should the dune restoration project at Laida be blamed for abducting the Wave? Of course, restoring a sand formation on one side of an estuary is bound to impact on sea bottom configurations on the other side. But old fishermen in the village say that the Wave was there when Laida was intact, before the 1956 storm. Indeed, some of them say the Wave has always been subject to dynamic cycles, appearing and disappearing over several years as the sand shifted around the bay due to natural causes.

The surfers and their friends, however, had observed something untoward in 2003, just before the Wave melted away. The Laida dunes had not been reconstructed solely due to sand naturally accumulated by the willow cuttings set by the ecologists. A huge quantity of sand had been dumped there by a dredger working for the Murueta shipyards. The presence of this large industrial concern, halfway up the estuary towards Gernika, is a major challenge to the biosphere reserve concept. It employs many people, and creates more wealth than the tourism generated by the WCT, according to the Basque government's director of biodiversity, Josu Erkiaga. While it should arguably be shifted to Bilbao, which is only half an hour to the west, he contended that that would represent a defeat for sustainable development, the idea that industry and nature can flourish side by side. In any case, as Murueta has prospered it has begun building bigger ships with deeper draughts. So it periodically needs to dredge the estuary down to Mundaka in order to sail them out to sea. Whether such dredging is compatible with the ecological integrity required of a biosphere reserve is certainly open to question.

The director of the reserve, Xabier Arana, called for calm, reminding the surfers that waves which depend on sandbars are, by definition, "unstable and impermanent". Once again, we are faced with the instability of the Basque ground, and the complexity of Basque arguments.

Finally, in mid-2006, a Basque government investigation, in which AZTI participated, conceded that the 2003 dredging, which removed six times more sand than any previous operation, was the "primary cause" of the loss of the Wave. Yet it optimistically insisted that the Wave would be restored by natural forces, possibly in time for that year's Billabong WCT. Just as this book goes to press, that optimism was justified: the Wave has returned in all its glory, and Mundaka has again taken its rightful place among the surfing hotspots of the world—until something else shifts in the Basque ground.

Paranoid as it sounded, the hotel receptionist's conspiracy theory had hit some sensitive home bases. University ecologists had indeed accepted a sand boost for their project from a dredging operation which was environmentally very suspect. The biosphere reserve managers did not appear to have kept a close eye on the shipyard. AZTI should perhaps also have raised more questions about what was happening right under its office windows. And the Basque government does invest in all three institutions. Nevertheless, this was not any kind of conspiracy. The Basques are simply learning the hard way that, even when you manage your own affairs—no Spanish institution was involved here—thorny conflicts of interest remain to be resolved.

Oma's Enchanted Forest: a Threat to the Basque Nation?

There has been another conflict of interest in Urdaibai, which has been much less manageable than the Wave controversy, and reveals the ugliest face of contemporary Basque political culture.

In the secluded valley of Oma, between Ereñozar and Gernika, a magical work of art has become the target of brutal vandalism. The elderly artist who created it has become the victim of intimidation and death threats. The Painted (or Enchanted) Forest is a piece of land art which dares to rival Santimamiñe's nearby cave paintings for the wonder and delight it evokes in spectators. Its maker, Agustín Ibarrola, lives in a classic Basque farmhouse on the valley floor, just below his creation. His isolation makes him easy prey for his persecutors. Oma's natural tranquillity has been shattered on several occasions by radicals who have painted slogans like "ETA, kill him" on his white walls, and pelted his red roof with stones late at night. They have cut down some of the painted trees and have repeatedly defaced many more of them.

For a high-profile artwork covering several acres, the Painted Forest is rather hard to find. You can approach it from the valley floor, about two miles east of Santimamiñe. This is a steep climb and it is easy to take a wrong turn. Or you can take a dirt road, wracked with potholes and gullies, along the southern ridge of the valley. There you come to a sign, broken and lying on the ground when I last visited. You can only read *Baso Margotua*, "painted forest" in Euskera. The Spanish version has been blacked out by an aerosol spray. The local municipal administration at Kortezubi, controlled by the PNV, has been less than diligent about maintaining and encouraging access to this key work by a Basque artist.

Take the path downhill, between expanding eucalyptus groves and the occasional sweet chestnut. Gradually, Monterey pines begin to dominate. Suddenly a yellow diamond blazes out of the wood. Half the outline is painted on one pine, half on another, so that its upper and lower points have to be imagined, somewhere between them. From here on, what you see is more or less up to you.

I confess to something of a prejudice against land art, perhaps even against art in natural settings. Art is one thing, nature another, and they should not mix, a little voice in my head recites primly. This is nonsense, of course. The Egyptian pyramids, at least as we see them now, add dimensions to the desert, and vice versa. But painting trees? Even Lenin balked when a group of radical artists approached him after the revolution and proposed painting every tree in Moscow red.

Ibarrola won me over in sixty seconds. Looking up to the right, a group of figures, purple with white outlines, seem to be running through the trees on which they are painted. You could easily miss them, and perhaps, by focusing on them, I missed something else. That is how it goes as you wander on into this labyrinth of images. There are little stone arrows set in the ground to show you where to stand for key views. But it is easy to miss them, too, and I suspect the artist may have placed some of them a little mischievously, and may have placed others where there is little to see.

The first figures seem like males, wearing *txapelas* (Basque berets). Then women and children start to melt out of the wood, indicated by a hint of breastly curvature, a sense of scale. Close-up, the paint itself is thick and rubbery, the cracks and wrinkles in the bark lending a texture Jackson Pollock might have envied. There are deep and viscous reds now, and mauves superimposed on purple. On some paths the painting is almost pure abstraction, multiple blue horizontal lines, yellow diagonals, then suddenly a white heart. Further on, hints of continuity between trees shade imperceptibly into another group of unmistakeably human figures. They are vivid with movement, brilliantly choreographed. They seem to be involved in a chase, though whether they are pursued or pursuing, fugitives or stalkers, will depend on your mood. And perhaps on how much you have learned about the artist's circumstances. Some of the children, if that is what they are, appear

The trees have a thousand eyes: Agustín Ibarrola's Enchanted Forest at Oma, which became the target of a hate campaign by ETA.

increasingly infantile, almost foetal, their faceless appearances an open canvas for our projections.

A white circle, pure geometry, seems wittily incongruous in this irregular setting. But there is really no circle at all, just the connections our perceptions make between separate white marks on wood. Another yellow diamond, smaller this time, seems to float among Red Indian war-paint daubs of green and blue. There are some oak trees now, with some kind of mildew on the leaves, another living pattern. The roots of the pines make their own sinuous art on the forest floor.

Broaching a ridge, the eyes have it. The whole forest is watching you, oval pupils unblinking on every tree, a startling rendering of psychedelic paranoia. By the top they have become totem poles, pillars of celebratory colour, yellows, purples, reds, greens, mauves, whites, blues, oranges. You smile involuntarily at every turn, as though Miró had been daubing from the sky. A shift in mood can turn the eyes into targets, an impression heightened by a host of figures slipping into vision from the left, stark, white outline only, everywhere, all around you. Hostile now, no doubt about it, menacing. A jagged white line zigzags from tree to tree, like the tape the police erect around a crime scene. Happier, then, to turn back just a little, to where the trees are wrapped in warm colours half-way up their height, and the bark itself is taking on the soft pinks of the declining sun, or where a distant image is morphing into an erotic sylph.

Why should such an exhilarating artwork have attracted such violent antipathy from ETA supporters? In repeated assaults they have hacked down some trees altogether, and mutilated the paintwork on others. Many more have been painted entirely grey. This seems an interesting reflection on the mindset of the vandals, who in other contexts like to flaunt the rainbow colours of eco-radicalism and libertarianism. Their graffiti denounce Ibarrola as "a Spaniard" and "an honorary fascist". Demands for an amnesty for ETA prisoners are coupled, with no apparent sense of incongruence, with the aforementioned appeals to that organization to "kill Ibarrola."

Since these slogans refer to the artist's perceived politics, rather than to his work, you might think that Ibarrola represents some vestige of the old regime, or rejects any expression of Basque identity. On the contrary, Ibarrola is an ethnic Basque, was born in an iconic *baserri* in 1930, and always wears a *txapela* (Basque beret). He was a militant anti-fascist in his youth, joined the Communist Party (PCE) and spent many years in jail and exile under the dictatorship. His early and middle periods are dominated by images of striking Basque workers, clenched fists raised, and by more playful representations of Basque nationalist movements like the "March for Liberty". The latter series recalls relatively idyllic days of peaceful democratic struggle and celebration during the transition from Francoism.

Ibarrola's political trajectory since then is typical of a grim and sterile dialectic which has driven many Basque leftists almost full circle. They have shifted from militant left nationalism into political positions close to the Spanish nationalist right, impelled by their view that ETA has itself become a "fascist" movement, and that the PNV's version of Basque nationalism is sectarian or even racist.

The persistence of violence in a democratic society poisoned all relationships. Ibarrola was outraged by ETA's killings of local councillors, academics and journalists in the 1990s. He was furious at the impunity which the perpetrators and their supporters appeared to enjoy from the Basque police, under PNV control. He came to believe that the PNV was unwilling to pursue ETA effectively because it shared its dream of independence. He joined anti-terrorist platforms like Basta Ya! and the Foro de Ermua, where his condemnations of ETA segued increasingly seamlessly into condemnations of Basque nationalism in general.

His comments outraged the PNV, which deeply resents being tarred with the broad brush brandished by the anti-terrorist lobby. But that kind of offence can hardly be compared to the offence caused by stones raining down on an isolated farmhouse, inhabited only by Ibarrola and his wife, in the middle of the night. His political stance cannot excuse for a moment the PNV's failure, over a long period, adequately to protect Ibarrola's artistic reputation, his art, and his personal security.

He is widely regarded, at home and abroad, as one of the three great Basque visual artists of his generation, along with Jorge Oteiza and Eduardo Chillida. The Painted Forest is one of the cultural treasures most publicized by the Basque government's Department of Tourism. Yet the PNV mayor of Kortezubi, Marco Bastegieta, refused to condemn the stoning of his house, "because of Ibarrola's attitude to Basque nationalism". And the PNV cultural councillor for Vizcaya, Belén Greaves, refused to protect the Painted Forest from further attacks, and asked for the matter not to be debated again. She used the extraordinary excuse that such a debate would "only remind the attackers of its existence."

It must be said that the PNV eventually came to its senses; the Vizcayan authorities have now invested €78,000 in restoring the forest after attacks. The Basque government has also recently shown much more active solidarity with the artist and his forest, including a high-profile visit in 2005 by the *lehendakari* (Basque first minister), Juan José Ibarretxe. But one still sometimes hears Basque nationalists discuss the affair as if Ibarrola was somehow to blame for own persecution.

Gernika: Democracy, Bombs and Paradoxes

Ibarretxe was sworn into office as *lehendakari* under the sacred oak at Gernika. He used the same form of words as the first *lehendakari*, José Antonio Aguirre, when he took office under the shadow of the advancing Francoist troops in 1936.

> Humbled before God
> on foot on Basque soil
> in memory of our ancestors
> under the tree of Gernika
> before you
> representatives of the people
> I swear to faithfully carry out my duties.

Aguirre's brave little government, cobbled together between rival Basque nationalists, socialists, communists and anarchists to cope with the emergency of civil war, lasted less than a year. The bombing of Gernika would be one of the nails in its coffin. It would also become the century's icon of the horror of total war.

The *Times* journalist W. G. Steer, whose extraordinary career has been so engagingly reconstructed in Nicholas Rankin's *Telegram from Gernika* (2003), broke that ominous story to the world. As a meticulous eye-witness to the aftermath of the bombing, he collected three unexploded German incendiary devices, stamped by their factory of origin, and used them as hard evidence that the Nazis' intention was to burn the town. That is confirmed in a diary note by the Luftwaffe commander, Wolfram von Richthofen, that the explosives and incendiaries used in combination had been a "complete technical success".

Indeed they had been. The Germans chose a market-day Monday afternoon, when the town was packed with civilians. The Condor Legion "bombed it and bombed and bombed it, and *bueno*, why not?" in the words of an "honest" [Francoist] staff officer cited by Rankin. Yet the ludicrous Francoist propaganda version that the town was burned by retreating Basque nationalist forces is still peddled by some Spanish rightists today. "Revisionist" historians do not go that far, but claim that the casualties were greatly exaggerated. Rankin's re-examination of Steer's account strongly suggests that they were not. Hundreds were killed, thousands maimed.

Today, Gernika is the home of a fine Peace Museum, which sponsors uncensored debate on conflict resolution. The museum's centre-piece is a multi-media exhibit, which places the visitor in a nearby house on the day of the bombing, listening to the verbatim account of a survivor. The experience is not for the faint-hearted, as special effects put you at the centre of a firestorm of destruction.

Steer, reporting on the real thing, found that the tree of Gernika was untouched, and that the stone seats of the tribunal behind it were scattered with pink blossoms, blown in by the blasts. The symbolic city had been saved, presumably by accident; the real one was in agony:

> We tried to enter, but the streets were a royal carpet of live coals; blocks of wreckage slithered and crashed from the houses, and from their sides that were still erect the polished heat struck at our cheeks and eyes. There were people, they said, to be saved there… But nothing could be done, and we put our hands in our pockets and wondered why the world was so mad and warfare become so easy.

Ignacia Ozamiz told oral historian Ronald Fraser of a conversation in the midst of all this madness, recorded in his *Blood of Spain* (1994). Her husband had just emerged from their burning house with some papers and money.

> "Oh, if only you had managed to save my sewing machine," I said. He went back in. As he came down with the machine, he found the staircase alight. He threw the machine out of the window, only just managing to jump out himself. "Woman, I got your machine but it nearly cost me my life." "Why did you go up?" "To do you a pleasure."… I've got it still.

Fraser also notes that a cow was driven into one smoke-choked shelter, and started "to shriek." Incidents like this must lie behind some of the distorted images of animals in Picasso's painting. This now hangs in the Reina Sofía museum in Madrid. Requests to bring it to the Guggenheim in Bilbao, even temporarily, have been turned down. Concerns about its conservation are the public justification for this decision; the real reason is probably a fear that the Basque nationalists would never give it back.

"They got the art, we got the bombs," was the typically acerbic response of the then PNV president, Xabier Arzalluz. Whatever the rights and wrongs of keeping *Guernica* in the Spanish capital, this remark caused legitimate offence to Spanish Republicans who remember the civilian death toll inflicted daily on other cities by Francoist bombers as the war went on. Moreover, Arzalluz's predecessors had, according to an account by several contemporary Basque artists, blown their chances to own *Guernica*. Picasso himself had offered it to the Basque government in exile in Paris after the war, and José Antonio Aguirre rejected it as a painting unworthy of the subject. It seems that the conservative Basques were outraged by a typically frivolous remark allegedly by the bohemian painter. He had boasted to one of the men present, in a stage whisper, that the curious representations of fingers in the image were not fingers at all, "but the organ you and I have between our legs."

Gernika had been recognized as an international symbol of democracy and liberty by artists and philosophers long before Picasso. During the Napoleonic wars William Wordsworth wrote that it would be better for the sacred oak to be struck by lightning and die than to live under Bonaparte's tyranny. "How canst thou flourish at this blighting hour?" he reproved the tree,

> If never more…
> Those lofty-minded Lawgivers shall meet,
> Peasant and lord, in their appointed seat,
> Guardians of Biscay's ancient liberty.

In these lines he encapsulates the view that Gernika is the seat of a very old democracy. Jean-Jacques Rousseau also endorsed the town's traditions: "Gernika is the happiest town in the world. Its affairs are governed by an assembly of countrymen who meet under an oak tree and always reach the fairest decisions."

Basque nationalists have good cause to cherish the practices associated with Gernika and its oak tree. History is vague about the origins of the link between oaks and democracy, but it seems that local assemblies, in which all male householders were represented, took place under several oaks in Vizcaya from early in the Christian period. Fires were lit, and horns were blown, on mountain tops throughout the province to summon the worthies together. Gradually Gernika became the assembly that represented all the others, and the Casa de Juntas became the home of a powerful provincial parliament. The small church which used to house this assembly was replaced by the current parliament building in 1826.

Parallel to this practice, from early medieval times each Lord of Vizcaya had to swear to uphold the *fueros* of the province before their authority was accepted. As we saw in the previous chapter, when Vizcaya came under Castilian overlordship in the thirteenth century, the King of Castile was required to travel to Gernika for the same purpose. Kings of Spain would honour this custom for seven centuries. Rights enshrined in the *fueros* included habeas corpus, exemption from torture, and from compulsory military service outside the province.

As we have seen, the abolition of the *fueros* following the Carlist wars in the nineteenth century brought the dual role of the Casa de Juntas—as local parliament, and as nexus between the Spanish monarchy and Vizcaya—to a close. The building and the tree were maintained, however, and now play a central if rather confused symbolic role in the life of the Basque Autonomous Community. Vizcaya once again elects *Junteros*, whose executive, the *Diputación*, forms a powerful layer in the local administration. General assemblies of the *Junteros*, which are largely ceremonial occasions, take place once again in the Casa de Juntas.

Yet it is notable that it is now the Basque first minister, representing three Basque provinces, who is sworn in at the tree, and not the King of Spain, since the *fueros* no longer exist. The current monarch, Juan Carlos II, made a courtesy visit in 1981, but the occasion was not a happy one. The eleven parliamentary deputies of Herri Batasuna, the political wing of ETA, greeted him with clenched fists. Before they were ejected, they managed to sing an a cappella version of the nationalist civil war anthem which ETA has made its own, *Eusko Gudariak*, the Song of the Basque Soldiers. The position of the oak tree in modern Spanish-Basque history is still not fixed.

The Casa de Juntas now functions on a daily basis mainly as a visitors' centre. The interpretation given of its significance is largely according to the canon of Basque nationalism. For example, the audiovisual panels here, and at the much more extensive, and often impressive, Museo de Euskal Herria next door, give the impression that "the Basques" were the losers in the Carlist wars. This ignores the fact that many Basques fought on the winning Liberal side in these conflicts. This attempt to homogenize history, ignoring its awkward and lumpy elements, may be a characteristic of nation-building, but it leaves many Basques feeling excluded from their own institutions today.

The Casa de Juntas video shows a young boy going to sleep with an acorn from the oak under his pillow. In scenes occasionally reminiscent of the surrealism of a Medem movie, but more often like an advertising feature, he dreams of the forest which gave birth to the oak. He imagines a Basque history which stretches from the cave paintings of Santimamiñe to the Guggenheim Museum. It is a film which, quite legitimately, leaves open the dream of Basque independence. But it fails to acknowledge the fears of those Basques for whom such a development might be a nightmare.

The exhibition also quotes Tirso de Molina in praise of the ancient oak, perhaps to show that great Spanish writers, as well as French philosophers and English poets have recognized the qualities of early Basque democracy. De Molina was the most prolific playwright of Spain's sixteenth-century Golden Age. He wrote that

> The Tree of Gernika has conserved
> the antiquity that makes its lords famous,
> tyrants have not stripped its leaves,
> nor does it give shade to converts or to traitors.

The reference to "converts" is interesting here. Tirso de Molina was referring to Jews and Muslims who attempted to retain their rights after the Christian *reconquista* by becoming Catholics. They were often expropriated, and sometimes massacred, despite their conversions. The playwright is echoing the old belief in "purity of blood", which was revived in early Basque nationalism, and which, ironically, coincides neatly in its racism to Spanish chauvinist prescriptions.

Straight across the street from the oak tree stands the enclosed convent of the Sisters of St. Clare. At a discreet height, a little bronze relief of the Sacred Heart, set against the Spanish royal coat of arms, proclaims that "Christ will reign in Spain." The woman who screened the video for me was young, bright and very fashionably dressed, the epitome of modern European Basqueness. I could not resist asking her how this public proclamation of Spanish identity had survived, right beside the sanctum sanctorum of Basque nationalism. She laughed and dismissed the nuns' plaque rather airily as "a vestige of the past, with no significance for us now." Since the convent belonged to the church, she continued, the Basque government had no say in what was expressed on its walls. She added, as an afterthought, that there were no Spanish sisters left in the convent now, much less any Basques. "They are all Latin Americans these days," she said, adding, with apparent satisfaction, "there are hardly any vocations in the Basque Country any more."

What, one wonders, would Sabino Arana make of this secularized nationalism, expressed in the very place where the "Ancient Laws" which he had always linked to religion, are still celebrated?

The ideological paradoxes of Basque and Spanish nationalism may seem abstruse to readers from countries where nationalism has ceased to be an article of political faith. But questions regarding the nature of the nation and "vestiges of the past" are still extraordinarily alive throughout the Spanish state.

It so happened that the last time I drove into the Urdaibai valley I was listening to the COPE radio station. This channel is controlled by Spain's Catholic bishops and is shrilly critical of the country's "regional nationalisms", while asserting the "unity of the Spanish fatherland" as a supreme civic value, almost as an article of the Christian faith. It is the licensed voice of the Spanish nationalist right. "Forget all that nonsense about the Basques and Catalans being Europe's first democrats," the presenter was saying, in the hectoring style of an American shock-jock. "Forget about British claims that the Magna Carta was the first charter of citizens' rights, controlling the fiscal powers of the monarch. History now shows that the parliament of León was the first to meet, fifty years before the Magna Carta, and it limited the king's ability to levy taxes. We Spaniards should stop flagellating ourselves about the Franco dictatorship. We were the first democrats in Europe!" Ironically, the presenter seemed to be accepting the Basque and Catalan nationalist cases by implicitly excluding them from this definition of Spain.

Gernika disappoints visitors who are seeking some essence of Basqueness. Or maybe it just disappoints. Like many heavily bombed towns, its destruction and reconstruction have evacuated much of its sense of the past, a curious sensation in a most historic place. The bombing can be blamed for the lack of the kind of lively and atmospheric old quarter which is the heart of most Basque towns. Yet this does not entirely explain the air of neglect which hangs over much of the place. Some of the squares and public spaces are scruffy, even tawdry.

The streets have an unfortunately provincial air, in sharp contrast to the new metropolitan confidence of the big Basque cities, and the warm charm of many of the smaller towns. More disappointingly still, the Casa de Juntas and its oak trees do not quite live up to their legendary reputation. Perhaps they are being crushed under the weight of contradictory symbolism. On the one hand they represent a universal tradition of democracy and human rights, reinforced by the anti-fascist imagery sent around the world by Picasso. On the other they represents the *fueros*, a specific political regime which is sentimentally precious to Basque nationalists, but which has little real meaning today, and had been dumped by many other Basques more than a century ago.

If there is an essence of Basqueness here, maybe it lies in the broader valley beyond the town limits, where history, nature, art, politics, science, sport, gastronomy and industry bump up against each other in everyday life. And maybe it lies in much less celebrated places, some of which we will now set out for.

Chapter Four

The *Frontón* at the Heart of Life: the Power and Beauty of Pelota

The *frontón*, like Proust's madeleine, contains within itself the collective memory of the Basques, a memory which, like all memories, is constructed on the basis of what is happening in the present.

Olatz González Abrisketa, *Pelota Vasca, Un ritual, una estética*, 2005

You are spoiled for choice if you want to play pelota in the little village of Zizurkil, where there are three options within 200 yards of each other. A so-called "industrial" *frontón*, roofed in and with seating capacity for hundreds of spectators, is quiet on an average weekday afternoon. Fitted out immaculately for professional championships, it is open to the street on one side and would seem an ideal place to practise, but attracts only one youth. Kitted out in sports gear, he doggedly bats a ball with a *pala*, or solid wooden racket, against the *frontis* or fore-wall which gives the pelota court its name.

Just around the corner, a big gable wall and paved courtyard is being used by two adolescent girls and a boy. Their casual game is more a rhythmic background to their conversation than a competition.

The real action is taking place close by, but it would be hard to find the game were it not for the alternate staccato slaps of skin against leather, then of leather against old stone. In the shadowy space under the church porch, four teenage boys are playing a deadly serious game of *mano*, bare hands hammering the ball at a wall pockmarked by centuries of similar treatment. They know every cranny, every nook, and they use that knowledge with great skill to send the ball in unexpected directions at great speed. They are watched intently by a dozen villagers. A two-year-old repeatedly totters perilously close to the players, mesmerized by the *tuc, toc, tuc, toc, tuc, toc* rhythm.

Zizurkil's plenitude of *frontones* is not exceptional. It would be hard

Multi-functional *frontón*: the pelota court in the lovely French Basque village of Sara doubles as the *plaza mayor*.

to exaggerate the omnipresence of pelota in Basque life, especially in the smaller towns and villages. "Pelota is the quintessential Basque sport," wrote Pío Baroja (*El País Vasco*, 1940). The great German Basque scholar, Wilhelm von Humboldt, said 150 years earlier that the game is "the principal fiesta of the Basque Country" (*Los Vascos*, 1998). An inscription on the *frontón* in the village of Banka tells us that pelota is simply "the most beautiful among all games". Most Basques would probably agree, though football attracts far more paying fans. Julio Medem's documentary *The Basque Ball: the Skin against the Stone* uses heart-stopping images of pelota as his central metaphor for the Basque conflict. Orson Welles was there before him: he made pelota the primary focus of his BBC documentary on the Basques, which is prominently quoted in Medem's film.

Serafín Baroja, the novelist's father, gave the sport a new name when he christened a *frontón* in San Sebastián *Jai Alai* (the joyful fiesta). Pelota goes by this name in the US (especially Florida) and Latin America, where Basque emigrants made it a very popular and lucrative sport in the nineteenth and twentieth centuries. With the possible exceptions of ETA and Euskera, pelota is the best-known sign of Basqueness in the world today.

Inevitably, pelota figures large in Basque mythology. The *jentilak*, legendary giants who rejected Christianity, are said to have played it with the great boulders scattered by glaciers on upland meadows in the Pyrenees and Cantabrian mountains. Contemporary myth-makers may transform the giants into Neolithic shepherds, but the first documentary evidence of pelota in the Basque Country is a 1509 prohibition against the sport in the "cemetery" of the Cathedral of Santiago in Bilbao. This was probably the porch, where burials often took place at the time. So the boys in Zizurkil today are indeed following a long tradition, though not necessarily a Stone-Age one. In the late Middle Ages, the church porch could still accommodate all the public functions which would later separate out into the key sites of the Basque town: worship, burial, public assembly and ball court. Pelota was often simply played in the street, against any convenient wall.

Handball had in fact been played in various forms throughout Europe since Roman times or earlier, so that at first sight there is nothing specifically Basque about *la pelota vasca*. Yet it is true that the Basques, on both sides of the Pyrenees, continued playing handball when most other places either refined it into games like tennis or badminton, or gave it up altogether. It is also true that many of the modern refinements of the game were developed in the Basque Country. However, pelota in various forms also remained popular into the modern period in other parts of Iberia; an indigenous version (handball) exists today in Ireland; and it is still played very widely and very well in the neighbouring region of La Rioja.

"Pelota is as *riojana* as it is Basque," says Olatz González, rather surprisingly, since she titled her recent magisterial study of the sport *Pelota vasca* (2005). She argues that it is not a unique association with the sport which gives the Basques the right to claim pelota as their own, but the way in which it permeates and reflects so many aspects of Basque society. Many Basque males start spending time at the *frontón* as soon as they can walk, and many would like to take their last breath watching (and betting) on a good match.

González's book is fascinating in that she repeatedly illuminates the power of tradition, but shows just as often how tricky a concept tradition can be. She writes that traditional beliefs about, for example, the prevalence of matriarchy and egalitarianism in Basque society are "inventions". But she adds that, like all such inventions, "they have a grain of truth in them," if only because "the traditional Basque culture which makes up our image-system has become part of modernity within ourselves." She shows that it was the Basque cities, and not, as most people think, the villages, which forged the intimate relationship with pelota the Basques know today. However, as city life was transformed by industrialization, the countryside indeed became the "reserve" which protected the sport, and which now supplies many of its best players.

More Than a Game

The Basque Country is home to a bewildering variety of pelota games. It can be played with leather gloves of various sizes, or with several kinds of curved wickerwork scoops, of which the banana-shaped *cesta-punta* is the best-known. Other versions require racquets or rigid wooden bats (*palas*). And then there is *mano*, played with the naked hand, the most popular version today for professionals, and in some ways the most dramatic to watch. The form of the *frontón* varies greatly. Sometimes there is only a *frontis* (fore-wall), often there is a left-hand wall as well, and occasionally a rear wall comes into play. The configuration of players changes radically according to the game played. Opposing teams and individuals can either play side by side, squash-style, as in *mano*, or facing each other, tennis-style, as in the "long" games like *rebote* and *laxoa*, which today are mostly restricted to Iparralde.

Mano, played singles and doubles against a *frontis* and left-hand wall, is now so dominant on the Spanish side of the border that many Basques think it has always been that way. But González demonstrates that this style only became popular 150 years ago, when the introduction of elasticized rubber gave a much faster bounce to the leather-covered ball. Traditionalists were outraged, and it was commonplace to see *frontones* with signs prohibiting this innovation. The traditionalists won north of the Pyrenees, where "long" games still dominate and a single wall forms the characteristic French Basque *frontón*. But the innovators won across the border. By the 1870s, most southern *frontones* there had acquired a left-hand wall.

It was not only the style of play which was shifting in this period, as social attitudes to the game were also changing. Pelota, like most sports, had initially been fiercely local and tribal. "Unamuno said that even in his time 'the people went to pelota matches as if it were a continuation of the wars of the bands,'" says González. She points out that the colours of those wars, red and blue, remain the standard Spanish Basque contestants' colours today, but that they no longer signify factional loyalties. She argues that the introduction of a complex and lively betting system led to a much more sophisticated appreciation of the game.

The system works like this: if you start a match with a bet on the favourite, but the underdog begins to make the running, you are allowed to make a second bet, to cover at least some of the losses you are now likely to incur on your original punt. But the bookie will only accept this bet if he can find another punter in the crowd to take you on. If the tide turns again, you can seek out another wager, and yet another, right up to match point. Half or more of the fun of attending a pelota match can come from watching the hectic flow of the betting. You could try listening as well, but the calls are a baffling cacophony to the outsider. Imagine a score of auctioneers competing at a dog track, during the race. Unamuno described the voices of the bookies as "the barometer of the match". Antonio Peña y Goñi, writing at the same period (the 1890s), thought they were the "one of [the game's] most important and substantial ingredients", and commented on their "cries, howls and bellows", "a cacophony using every register of the vocal chords." It is much the same today.

Up to 22 bookies (*artekariak*, or "intermediaries", in Euskera) stand facing the spectators. Eyes in the back of their heads, ears tuned to every voice among hundreds, they chivvy betters to take on new odds as every point is scored. The mental agility and physical stamina required is remarkable. Because of the noise level, there is a signalling system: a punter touching his head means a bet for the red team, touching their arm a bet for the blue. The bookies stuff betting slips into a slit tennis ball and hurl them up the stands with staggering accuracy. Meanwhile, they are taking other bets on mobile phones from punters watching the match on TV. They know all their clients' voices, and their characters. Nothing is signed, and debts are paid (most of the time) on an honour basis.

The impact of this system has been to foster a critical eye for good performance rather than blind support for an individual player, creating a most discriminating audience. "Betting has a downside," says González, "because of the large amounts of money lost. But it does enhance an objective appreciation, an understanding of the game which goes far beyond loyalty to local heroes."

For most of the last century, Basque pelota had a reputation for honouring fair play and good play, on the courts and in the stands, which British cricket or Wimbledon Centre Court might have envied. In the last few years, however, a new kind of younger fan has emerged, who has no interest in betting and chants support for favourites and abuse at opponents as eagerly as any soccer fan. Perhaps due to the boosting of individual images through massive TV coverage, the pendulum seems to be swinging back towards partisanship.

The *frontón* in the Basque Country is much more than a sports venue. It is a public space as significant as the *plaza mayor*, to which it is often adjacent. Like the bull-ring in old towns in Castile, it sometimes *is* the *plaza mayor*, or an extension of it, as in the French Basque village of Sara. It is a core venue for fiestas, when it may be used successively for exhibition matches, dances, markets and displays of agricultural prod-

Playing hardball with handball: in *mano*, the players literally leave their skin on the court, and sometimes dislocate their arms.

ucts, and of course for the huge meals in which a whole community eats together. It may also be used by exponents of other traditional skills, like *bertsolaris,* log-choppers and rock-lifters.

More contentiously, it is also a stage for political rallies. González points out that this creates a clash of values, because the *frontón* is a public space par excellence, where the whole community should feel represented. Indeed, where other indigenous traditions have tended to be appropriated as Basque nationalist icons, pelota has been inclusive, integrating immigrants in a fundamental indigenous pursuit. But political events are by definition divisive, representing only one fraction of the people.

Radical groups have further undermined this unifying function, using the *frontón* as a kind of permanent political megaphone by painting slogans and murals on its walls. Entire generations have grown up playing under such edifying messages as *Iraulza ala Hil,* "revolution or death". In Zizurkil a giant mural covers the whole of one informal *frontis,* showing a proposed high-speed train as a monstrous snake devouring the landscape. Sometimes murals come from the less overtly political world of the fantasy comic, featuring lurid creatures smoking outsize joints.

Lions, Foxes and Magic Moments

All this is a far cry from the noble and immaculate simplicity of the *pelotari* and *frontón* portrayed in classic twentieth-century art and posters. Curiously, both Basque and Spanish nationalists endorsed this image; pelota was one of the few aspects of Basque life enthusiastically endorsed by Franco. But while most fans would prefer the clean and elegant lines of the *frontón* to be universally restored, commercial interests have also launched an assault on this aesthetic. The huge increase in TV coverage over the last 15 years, coupled with a concentration of most of the business of professional pelota in the hands of a single confederation, has created a rash of temporary advertising on the left-hand walls of *frontones* for big matches. It may only be a matter of time until some advertising becomes permanent.

Qualities like nobility and honesty are often seen as central to the character of a great *pelotari*, and to the game itself. In fact, they are often only half the story because cunning, and even deceit, are also essential to pelota. A solo player has to embody these opposing qualities in one person, but the double value system can most clearly be seen where *mano* is played by teams of two. One player in each team is positioned towards the back of the court, where great strength is required. This player is the "lion", with a strong, noble and straightforward style. The forward player is the "fox", required to be extremely agile mentally and physically, constantly attempting to fool his opponents as to where he will place the ball. To say that a person is *muy pelotari* ("a very pelota type of person") is not to say they are strong or straightforward, but to say they are brilliantly astute, to the point of deviousness.

Speculation on national characteristics is always risky, but it is tempting to say that these diverse qualities do reflect central aspects of Basque behaviour. The phrase *Palabra de Vasco* (the word of a Basque) has been widely used for centuries in the entire Spanish-speaking world to indicate that one's word is one's bond. And it is very generally true that Basques, when they do give their word, stick by it with exceptional integrity. But it is also true that it is important to listen to what a Basque does *not* say. They do not waste words or suffer fools gladly. Basque card-playing is noted for its deadpan bluffs, its unpredictable use of the *hordago* or ultimatum. Basques tend to be extremely astute negotiators, and may well place the bouncing ball of a conversation where you least expect to find it.

All these points are debatable, of course, but there is no argument about which two characteristics above all others are required of the *pelotari*. He must show courage and endurance in the face of severe pain and exhausting stress. Hands are bandaged for protection before a *mano* match, but there is no painless way of slapping a stinging ball with great force. This is hardball, no doubt about it: players literally leave their skin in the *frontón*, and sometimes dislocate their arms. One champion, writes González, lost two kilos in every match; another used to urinate blood after playing.

You may have noticed by now that, with the exception of the informal game in Zizurkil, all the references we have made so far have made to pelota have been masculine. Yet women play pelota a lot, informally or at amateur level. One woman even defeated a champion, *Beloki*, in a private challenge match—an extraordinary achievement given general male/female disparities in physical strength. Women used to compete professionally in racquet pelota, and did very well at it. But though Basque women dominated the sport, it was largely played in Madrid and Barcelona. There was an air of the *demi-monde* about the sport, and González found former players so reluctant to talk about their youth that she did not include them in her book. Why don't Basque women play Basque pelota where it counts, as professionals today? "A woman's league could be created, but it hasn't been and it won't be," says González. "This represents Basque reality very well," she continues. "Equality issues seem to have been resolved for women in modern Basque society, but this situation suggests something different":

> The plaza, the *frontón*, as a public political space is masculine. The archetypal Basque games—pelota, log-chopping, rock-lifting—are masculine. When the *frontón* is used for these rituals, women cannot enter. It is very subtle. You can participate at various levels, but you can't play where and when it really matters. In the most representative moments in our society, women don't exist.

González nevertheless clearly takes enormous pleasure in participation as a spectator, writing of "communion", a sense of an "eternal moment" which can be generated by a game well played, from which, paradoxically, she does not feel excluded at all: "At any moment, between those *pelotaris*, that *pelota* and this *frontón*, the magic may happen, that moment of uncontainable beauty, of definitive harmony, in which you feel you are participating completely."

Chapter Five

Cinco Villas: Pío Baroja, Flying Mari, Sword Dances and Sorcery

I would like to make little nocturnal sacrifices now and then.
                                    Julio Caro Baroja, *Los Baroja*, 1972

"Don't you even raise your eyes to the house called *Itzea*," the nuns used to tell schoolgirls on trips to Vera de Bidasoa in the 1920s. "That's the home of the devil Baroja."

Taking the nuns' anathema as a compliment, we will begin to look for modern Basque literature here, in the sleepy Navarran village of Vera [Bera]. This is the capital of the Cinco Villas, five of the most delightful hamlets to be found anywhere in the Basque Country. They nestle below the north-western Pyrenean foothills, on either side of the middle reaches of the Bidasoa river.

Itzea was the home chosen by Pío Baroja, always referred to—by those who respect and love him—simply as "Don Pío". The English critic C. A. Longhurst considers him the "most important Spanish novelist after [Benito Pérez] Galdós". He places him among the "big four" Spanish writers of the last century, with the poet Antonio Machado, the philosopher and novelist Miguel de Unamuno (also a Basque, though, like Baroja, not always recognized as such) and the playwright and novelist Ramón María del Valle-Inclán. Baroja's deceptively direct and simple style won him an international readership, and he was a major influence on Ernest Hemingway, among many others.

Immediately, of course, that S-word gives us a problem. If Baroja is Spanish, can he also be Basque? Most nationalities would be delighted to claim such an illustrious figure as their own. But Baroja, like almost all Basque writers of his period, wrote in Spanish, and for some Basques this rules him out of the national canon. Yet his imagination was saturated in Basque folklore, not a little of which he had invented or embellished

River dancers in Lesaka: young men perform the *Makil Gurutzea* over the Odin as part of the town's San Fermín fiesta, a festival which can outshine its better-known namesake in Pamplona.

himself. He was familiar enough with Euskera to draw extensively on local folk songs and proverbs in their original versions. His descriptions of the landscape of his beloved Bidasoa valley, at their best, capture its misty, intimate qualities superbly well. So his preference for the Spanish language might be forgiven were there not a worse stroke against him, in terms of mainstream contemporary Basque cultural politics: he was acidly, mercilessly sceptical about Basque nationalism. This scepticism has been shared by other members of his intellectually distinguished family, which includes his brother, the accomplished painter Ricardo Baroja, and his nephews, the eminent anthropologist Julio Caro Baroja, and the filmmaker and writer Pío Caro Baroja. Julio Caro, in a brief introduction to one of Don Pío's key Basque novels, *Jaun de Alzate*, describes the novelist as a *vasquista* (Basqueist) "who thinks that is possible to be a Basque, pure and simple, without being a nationalist, a Carlist, or even a Christian."

Baroja's mocking scepticism made him enemies everywhere, as well as friends in odd places. Julio Caro describes his uncle's politics in the 1930s like this:

> He held a poor idea of the Spanish monarchists, and of the king himself. But he had no better impression, at a personal level, of the republican leaders, the majority of whom he considered hollow figures. To say this in public was to get the reputation of a bitter man, a man possessed by demons, irascible and mad.

In the first days of the Civil War he was almost shot by the Carlists who swarmed north from Pamplona in support of the military uprising against the Republic. His well-known anti-clerical views were an abomination to these traditionalist Catholics, and he quickly slipped across the French border. But he did not join the chorus of intellectuals and artists campaigning for Spain's embattled democracy. He had no love for Franco's dictatorship but, as an old-fashioned liberal, he also loathed and feared the radicalism of the Republic. He returned to Spain after the dictator's victory. He suffered some censorship but no persecution, despite periodic outbursts against him by the Catholic Church. One Jesuit publication, which classified writers according to what we might call their religious correctness, defined him as "impious, phobic about the clergy, and dishonest". The Falange, the most independent-minded faction in Franco's ideological family, nominated him for the Nobel Prize for Literature. They apparently published, without his permission, a collection of his work under the title *Judías y demás ralea* ("Jews and Other Riffraff"). Their campaign was unsuccessful.

Baroja died in 1956 as a grand, if cantankerous and awkward, old man of Spanish letters. Fifty years later, the Basque autonomous institutions let his anniversary pass almost unrecognized. Navarre's autonomous government, implacably opposed to Basque nationalism, was happy to claim him, as a Spanish writer, and did rather better by him. But the reality is that he shares both identities, Basque and Spanish. This should be one of his glories, but makes him suspect in the sectarian cultural climate which so often darkens Basque skies.

It may be illuminating to compare his status with that of James Joyce in Ireland. Joyce wrote in English, and punctured the pretensions of Irish nationalist ideologues with fiercely comic precision. He was banned in the de Valera period, and his lascivious Molly Bloom was initially no competitor for the chaste Caitlín Ni Houlihán, endorsed by W. B. Yeats as an icon of Irishness. But for many years now that has all been forgotten. Molly Bloom's erotic monologue is heard on mainstream Irish radio. Images of Joyce—and of other heterodox Irish writers in the English language, like Yeats himself, and Samuel Beckett and Brendan Behan—proudly decorate the walls of Irish bars all over the globe.

There are, as always, instructive differences between the Basque and Irish cases. Ireland (most of it) has at last acquired the confidence of a country with many decades of independence behind it. And the Irish language, despite (or because of) the efforts of the nationalist ideologues Joyce despised, is no longer a primary sign of Irish identity. In a nicely paradoxical twist, the Irish ability to repeatedly outperform the English in their own language has become a quietly celebrated source of national pride.

There is another contrast: the kind of creative interplay between two languages that enriches Hiberno-English is almost entirely absent from Spanish work written by Basques. The linguistic chasm between Euskera and *Castellano* is simply too vast for that kind of cross-fertilization.

Whether an independent Basque Country would eventually hold Baroja in higher regard is a moot point. In any case, you do not see Pío

Baroja's frail and bookish face staring from the walls of many Basque taverns today.

Nevertheless, there is something very Basque about his scepticism and calmly lucid pessimism, though his canvas extends far more widely than the Basque Country, with some of his best-known novels, like the Dickensian *La Busca*, largely set in Madrid. The sadness which pervades his work has a curious dignity. Yet he never takes himself entirely seriously either; his very scepticism does not permit it. "What I don't understand, I don't understand. As far as I am concerned, no one knows, or will ever know, why we are born into this world, or for what end, if indeed we have any purpose in being here, which I doubt," says Jaun de Alzate, arguing with Christian proselytizers, in Baroja's eponymous novel.

You find echoes of Baroja, conscious or otherwise, in countless Basque conversations today. Perhaps I might take the example of a friend of mine, José Ignacio. He is a man of fiercely independent opinions, and fits very few Basque stereotypes. But there are two entirely predictable and very Basque things about him. One is that the sardines he cooks in his gastronomic society in Zarautz are always mouth-watering. The other is that he will conclude almost every dinner there, as he drains the last glass of the early morning, with words along these lines, no matter what we have been discussing: "Well, what do you expect? Life is shitty, in general. That is not surprising. We are not up to much, any of us. Humanity is a rather small thing, after all." "*Que barojiano eres tú*," his wife María Pilar will respond. To be *barojiano* is, for many Basques, simply a reflection of the human condition. There can be few higher plaudits for a writer.

An Enemy in His Own Country?

But do the Basques read Baroja? "Less than a hundred of them, today, this country regards him as an enemy." This is the highly partisan view of his surviving nephew, Pío Caro Baroja, who has replaced his elder brother Julio as the gatekeeper of the family reputation, and of its voluminous archives, at *Itzea*.

This imposing mansion, which Don Pío bought with his mother in 1912, remains on the very outskirts of Vera. Only a couple of houses have been built beyond it, where an old road, once part of the spider's web of smugglers' trails between the Bidasoa river and the French border, disappears into up into the woods on the mountain slopes.

Pío Baroja was born in San Sebastián in 1872, and spent his childhood between that city, Pamplona and Madrid, where he studied medicine without distinction. His doctoral thesis, appropriately for the theme of so much of his later writing, was simply entitled "Pain". His first and only medical practice was in the Guipuzcoan village of Cestona, home to one of a dozen fashionable spas in the region, and the only one which survives today. His patients, however, were mostly the rural poor, and gave him a brief but intimate and intense contact with the Basque countryside. He soon abandoned medicine, but maintained that contact during the many summers he spent in Vera de Bidasoa.

Baroja's output was vast, and perhaps as a result, often infuriatingly slapdash. In his early career he was closely associated with the "Generation of '98", which sought to reinvent Spain in the early twentieth century after the *Desastre* of that year, the loss of Madrid's last imperial possessions. Several other key figures in this movement were also Basques, including Unamuno and Ramiro de Maeztu. Baroja contributed to Ortega y Gasset's seminal *Revista de Ocidente*, but he did not share that stylist's obsession with "great formal perfection". According to Julio Caro Baroja, Don Pío preferred a "direct, rapid manner of writing". This can result in clear, crisp and accessible prose. It can also make for self-indulgence and sloppy writing.

Plagiarizing his Native Place

Jaun de Alzate is one of the key Basque novels in the Baroja canon. The name is taken from a family of warlords who lived in Vera in medieval times. But Don Pío pushes the action back to the moment when Christianity triumphed over paganism in the region. He makes Jaun de Alzate the last spokesman for a vibrant and fantastical culture, undermined by a bloodless and killjoy religion. In so doing, the novelist freely admits that he is "plagiarizing the myths of my native place, and dressing them up to my own taste." So Jaun sometimes sounds like Lucretius, and sometimes rather like—in fact very like—the anti-Semitic Pío Baroja. He laments coming of "histrionic priests with their Jewish gods and church bells to wake us in the morning."

In *Jaun de Alzate*, Baroja blames early non-Basque immigrants for the imposition of Christianity on the region. One suspects he took a mischievous pleasure in this, since Basque nationalists blamed atheistic Spanish immigrants for undermining Basque Christianity and traditions in the nineteenth and early twentieth centuries.

This book's scenario lays bare a curious aspect of the novelist's relationship to Basqueness, a relationship shared by his nephew, Julio Caro. Their passion for Basque traditions, invented or otherwise, could hardly be equalled by any Basque nationalist. But Don Pío liked to celebrate these traditions as if they occurred spontaneously, without any manipulation from political movements or religious authorities. Unsurprisingly, these traditions often only existed within the pages of his novels. If Sabino Arana, the PNV, and latterly ETA and its political wing Batasuna, have attempted to create the Basque Country in their own image, so too did Baroja. And he liked to dress his anti-Semitism in Basque peasant dress, a nasty tendency which has its parallels in Basque nationalism's periodic espousal of "purity of the race".

As ever, his dry wit saves him from taking it all too seriously. "The Basques are so traditionalist," he writes at one point, "that they sometimes know what their fathers did, but never what their grandfathers got up to." *Jaun de Alzate* also echoes a perennial Barojian theme: self-deception ("the vital lie") is indispensable for human survival. The novel also expresses Baroja's precise and passionate observation of the landscape of the Bidasoa Valley. This passion and several other *barojiano* Basque motifs are also present in marvellously distilled form in an essay, simply entitled *País Vasco* in the collection *Fantasías Vascas*. In a few brief paragraphs, he sketches the topography of the whole Basque Country, digresses for a lyrical account of a specific landscape, and finishes with a highly idiosyncratic account of the "warrior instinct" of the Basque character. As he rode out to visit his patients:

> The village was sleeping, the houses were looming out of the night, black and damp; on the river a blue mist was rising which dissolved into fragments. I went up the hill paths on horseback in the mist, thinking about nothing. Often, on the summit I saw the whole valley full of white fog, and up there the sun shone brilliantly and the sky was as blue as sapphire. Sometimes the clouds surged, running through the

naked trees, whose black branches seemed themselves to be thick smoke, and the fog enveloped me.

Those mountain mists are an indelible memory for me... they over-whelmed my soul forever; they do not leave it now, they never will.

Baroja then suddenly confesses to "an honest and heroic dream, infantile and brutal". He sees himself as a chieftain at the time of the warlords, or perhaps during the Carlist wars, burning the enemy's farmhouses, robbing the village coffers, and seducing the priest's niece. He imagines the pleasure of escape on horseback, to sleep beneath the stars on a bed of dry grass.

This is a curious fantasy for a man who shrank from sexual encoun-ters and violent adventures, prizing his quiet life above all else. What is more remarkable is that he extrapolates from it a "warrior instinct" which he applies to all aspects of Basque life, from business (the ambi-tious and grasping Bilbao oligarchy) to religion (the militant Jesuit philosophy of St. Ignatius, representing "the will of the race".) Never afraid to generalize, he sees the Basque character as anarchic yet with-drawn: "Silent and antisocial, when Basques want to communicate, they sing." This is a strange statement from a Basque who suffered from some-thing approaching logorrhoea, but Baroja was ever the exception to his own rules, and perhaps all the more Basque for that.

His nephew Julio Caro has also left a remarkable testimony to his own love for the Bidasoa Valley in *Los Baroja*, his fascinating family memoir. Here he draws conclusions every bit as bold and sweeping as his uncle's about the relationship between the Basque Country and Castile:

I felt anguish every year on returning from Vera to the *meseta*. Obviously I have no love for Castile...For me the ideal landscape is that of valleys, hills, woods and rivers. If you can make out the sea in the distance, better again...So, to approach Castile from Vera was to swap life for death.

While both Don Pío and Julio Caro Baroja were dismissive of Basque nationalism, it is evident that they shared, to a remarkably intense degree, some of the sentiments that underlie that ideology. But their line of thinking here runs counter to the mainstream of both main factions in the Basque quarrel. Spanish nationalists are deeply attached to the mystique of Castile, while most Basque nationalists (at least before ETA) identified their politics very closely with their Catholicism.

Today, the old seat of Jaun de Alzate's family, a stone's throw from *Itzea*, has been rebuilt as a small chic villa with stained-glass artwork on its front wall. If you look over that wall, however, you will see a poster over the front door, calling for the repatriation of ETA prisoners with the ubiquitous slogan *Euskal Presoak, Euskal Herrira*. Old quarrels take new forms. Pío Caro Baroja says, not entirely in jest, that you can meet the Cura Santa Cruz, a bloodthirsty Carlist priest, on any Basque street today.

Vera de Bidasoa is the largest and most accessible of the Cinco Villas, which makes it the least obviously attractive of these villages, even though the substantial industrial estate which keeps it prosperous is tucked away discreetly in nearby woods. The old main road from Irún (and therefore France) to Pamplona ran straight through Vera's narrow and impossibly right-angled main street. As traffic increased in the post-war period, the rude intrusion of hundreds of trucks a day knocked the heart out of the town. An ugly 1960s post office and some apartment blocks completed the job. A new bypass road has not brought the centre back to life. The volume of private cars now approaches that of commercial traffic ten years ago, and the main street's central bend still requires a one-way traffic light.

Up the hill, however, the church of Santesteban has a marvellously muscular Gothic ceiling. There are several fine and spacious mansions in its environs, scrupulously maintained. The big surprise is the town hall, quite unlike any other in the area. On a smart white plaster background, its frontage is decorated with neoclassical figures representing Courage, Prudence, Justice and Temperance. The latter features a maiden deliberately spilling a pitcher of wine onto to the ground—not something that would be regarded as a virtue in any Basque community I have ever encountered. A sign tells us that the figures were redrawn from eighteenth-century originals by Julio Caro Baroja, another small instance of the multi-disciplined contributions of this extraordinary, if difficult, family towards their community.

That contribution receives some recognition in a local school, which is named after Pío's painter brother, Ricardo. The school sign, however, crudely attempts to render his name retrospectively more Basque by

Guardian of the family archives: Pío Caro Baroja in the library in *Itzea*, the mansion where his uncle, the novelist Pío Baroja, and Pío Caro's older brother, the anthropologist Julio Caro Baroja, used to work.

spelling it "Rikardo". The letter "k" hardly exists in Spanish, so modern Basque orthography often inserts it simply to be different, not because it existed in traditional Euskera. It is hard to imagine the Barojas being flattered by this kind of linguistic tinkering. Another recent example, which happily has not prospered, was the attempt to change the name of Arturo Campion (1854-1937), a Basque scholar and novelist of Italian origins, into "Kampion", a spelling he never used himself.

Etxalar: Witches, Pigeon Shoots and Carmen

Etxalar, well off the main road and deep in a flat-bottomed valley, is the only other town in the Cinco Villas to lie to the east of the Bidasoa, towards the French border. Its position means that contraband was, until EU entry, the mainstay of the local economy. Right up to the 1980s, you might have been struck by the unusually cordial relationship between *guardias civiles* and local people in these towns. The booming illicit import/export business meant deep pockets, greased palms, guards snug in the bars and smugglers secure on mountain trails.

Etxalar has been also closely associated with witchcraft. One of the two obvious roads towards the border—there are several others which are not clearly marked—goes through Zugarramurdi and Urdax. These villages were the site of a particularly notorious witch-hunt by the Holy Inquisition in the early seventeenth century. Its findings were so outrageous that they ultimately undermined the authority of this institution. Thirty-one men and women, a substantial proportion of the adult population of these tiny hamlets, were tried prior to an *auto de fe* in Logroño. Thirteen died in prison and six at the stake. Things were even worse in Iparralde in the same period, where the notorious witch-finder Pierre de Lancre burned dozens of witches; estimates range from a credible 80 to an unlikely 600. These events created the sensational impression that the entire Basque Country was infested with witchcraft sects.

Were the Basque witches simply the unfortunate peasant victims of foolish or demented clerics? Were they induced by torture, or simple intimidation, to confess to crimes conforming to the credulous fantasies of their persecutors? Or were there elements of a pagan and polytheistic "Old Religion" persisting in isolated rural areas where conversion to Christianity had been superficial?

There is a good case for both arguments. Undoubtedly, people snatched from remote villages and imprisoned in alien cities, subjected to the threat or reality of loathsome torments and interrogated in languages they did not understand, must have suffered from hysterical fantasies. Or they may simply have made false confessions to end their suffering. Yet pre-Christian beliefs have undoubtedly persisted in cultures much less isolated than Zugaramurdi and Urdax were then. There is plenty of evidence that belief in the old Basque gods, especially the ubiquitous Mari, co-existed with the Catholic faith well into the last century. Julio Caro Baroja did much meticulous investigation in this field, and documented the survival of many pre-Christian practices. Zulaika writes that: "at the *baserria* where my father served in his youth, the master of the household frequently used to watch Mari flying. One night she would go in a given direction, the next in the opposite one, but always travelling the same route between the two highest mountains of the area. My father was himself in his early twenties the subject of frightening witchcraft tricks." He has recorded an old woman who was convinced that a witch was in the room with them during the interview.

And he has himself encountered events which defy rational explanation. There is evidence in stone as well. The coat of arms of every village in the Bidasoa Valley includes a *lamia*, a kind of succubus or fresh-water mermaid.

The whole issue is somewhat complicated by the zeal with which some radical Basque nationalists, and indeed some radical feminists, have espoused the cause of the witches as representing an instance of Basque resistance to Spanish and French domination, or to the imposition of patriarchy on an ancient matriarchal culture.

Don Pío, of course, exercised all the privileges of a fiction writer in his treatment of witchcraft. The old gods and demons are a constant presence in *Jaun de Alzate*. Jaun himself respects the old gods as social institutions, but he is sceptical about witchcraft. In a telling exchange he says to the Christians: "If we need fictions, I prefer mine to yours."

The theme of witchcraft fascinated Baroja, and his readers, and he indulged this fascination to the full in tales like *La Dama de Urtubi*, an elaboration of a legend attached to a castle in the French Basque Country between Urrugne and St.-Jean-de-Luz. Through multiple narrators, he allows himself to put forward the view that the Inquisition effectively invented witchcraft. Then he recounts a ripe old yarn about an *akelarre* (sabbat), portrayed primarily as a fusion of a licentious masked ball and a peasant orgy. But the story is larded with colourful details which can be taken with as much, or as little, salt as the reader's taste dictates: the corpses of babies are exhumed and burned as torches to light the lustful scenes; hordes of toads attend, dressed in monk's habits, and so on. And in the midst of all this, Baroja finds a pulpit to inveigle in favour of the old matriarchal religions of the earth, and against the Semitic patriarchal practices of Jews, Christians and Moors.

The other official road across the mountains out of Etxalar leads to the lovely village of Sara. But it first passes by a kind of war-zone known as Palomeras, the place of the doves. It is well worth stopping off here for a stroll along the green ridge, commanding much of the small Basque provinces north of the border. But you need to walk with care here in the shooting season. This small pass is favoured by vast numbers of migrating woodpigeons, which are slaughtered annually by a small army of hunters. All year round, you will stumble on bunker-style hides, covered in military camouflage. There are even brick towers, which provide a solid shooting platform right up in the canopy of the pines. Etxalar claims the historical patent on a device the hunters use to bring high-flying pigeons within range. This is a kind of boomerang, shaped rather like an outsize table tennis bat. They are fired high into the sky, timed to drop back over an incoming flock. The birds take the spiralling shadow to be a stooping bird of prey, and plunge down for cover—straight into a deafeningly intense field of fire. You can see these devices in the ethnographical museum in Elizondo, further up the Bidasoa watershed in the Baztan Valley, and in the Musée Basque in Bayonne, where the patent is attributed to Sara.

Men are not the only hunters here. One of the most predatory and desirable women in modern European fiction came from Etxalar, or so she claimed. In Prosper Mérimée's novella *Carmen* (1845), on which Bizet's opera was based, José's strong Basque accent betrays his origins to Carmen while he is escorting her to jail. She asks him, in Euskera, where he comes from, and finds that he is a native of Elizondo. "And I'm from Etxalar," she exclaims. "Your village is only four hours from ours. I was kidnapped by gypsies who brought me to Seville. I've been working in the cigar factory to earn enough money to return to Navarre and be with my poor mother..." Despite her "atrocious" Euskera, José falls for her threadbare story, with tragic consequences for them both. Her ruse is a minor part of the plot, but it permits Mérimée a brief digression into Basque exotica, with José expounding on the universal nobility of the Navarrans, his prowess at pelota, and his deadly skill with the *makila* (Basque sword-stick), with a few phrases in Euskera thrown in. Bizet retained some of the original dialogue, but made his Carmen too much the epitome of the sultry Andalusian to pass her off as a Navarran on stage for more than an instant. His José immediately calls her Basque bluff, while still succumbing to her charms.

Carmen's outrageous flirtatiousness would certainly have been out of place in the Navarran valleys of that period, but her fierce pride and independence would not have been. There is conflicting evidence about how far extramarital adventures were tolerated. Some of the traditions related to witchcraft hint at subterranean erotic freedoms, but social conventions were very strong. Pierre Loti's *Ramuntcho, A Tale of the Pyrenees* (1897), the novel which helped create the vogue for French Basque folklore, has a protagonist who suffers no initial stigma for being born out of wedlock.

His mother had fallen from grace with an urban Don Juan. She is fully accepted back into village life when she concludes the affair, though a shrewish neighbour eventually finds a way to punish both of them.

Rodney Gallop, a more reliable source than Loti, but given to rather sweeping judgements, wrote: "Adultery is most severely condemned. Should the slightest breath of suspicion link the names of two persons who are not free to marry one another, these may awake one morning to find a tell-tale trail of fresh grass or rushes linking the doors of their houses, as a mark of public disapproval." However, he noted that the Basques "are singularly lenient towards the misconduct of unmarried persons. Should a girl find herself in trouble, she will be held up to ridicule in improvised songs, but she will not be expected to marry her lover, nor will she have difficulty in finding a husband. The latter indeed will not merely overlook the existence of an illegitimate child, but will welcome it into his home just as primitive man must have welcomed every prospective pair of able hands." (Gallop was writing in the 1920s, and not all Basques are convinced by this rather rosy picture of rural sexual mores. Bernardo Atxaga, for example, offers anecdotal evidence of a level of repression which caused unmarried mothers to commit suicide.)

The streets of Etxalar are stretched over the valley floor, divided by little streams. Broad green fields are subdivided by neat and narrow walls, generations old, often simply slabs of sandstone or slate set vertically. The homes here, even in this large and open context, look enormous. Some date from the fifteenth century. This village gives a good introduction to the "big house" look of traditional rural architecture in the Navarran Pyrenees. We are, after all, next door to Baztan, where each house has its own coat of arms and is, theoretically at least, a dwelling for noble men and women. It is easy to see that universal nobility, and cavernous dwellings, did not mean universal wealth. Many of these families were very humble in economic terms, and some still are.

All of them must, in any case, come to dust, as Etxalar's important collection of traditional headstones, equalled outdoors only in Sara, reminds us. These are small stone monuments, about three feet high. They are capped with discs, possibly solar or lunar symbols in origin, sitting on short pillars which slope sharply inwards. The effect is of a circle imposed on the apex of a slender triangle. This could clearly also represent the head and shoulders of the deceased. Their various names in Euskera indicate varying interpretations: *harri gizona* (stone man), *ilargi* (moon-light of death) and simply *hilarri* (death stone). Most of Etxalar's headstones are from the seventeenth to nineteenth centuries, but some are much older. The Christian cross and the Star of David are often carved within the disc, which may also contain the name of the deceased's family or, more likely, of their family home. The *lauburu* ("four heads"), a curvy Basque cross or swastika rather like the fan symbol on a car dashboard, and other solar symbols possibly of Neolithic origin, also occur. Like many emblems of rural life, this type of head-stone went out of fashion during the nineteenth century, but has enjoyed a strong revival in recent decades, with the *lauburu* a very frequent element.

"The cross was Basque before it was Christian," Pío Baroja's Jaun de Alzate tells a group of missionaries. In the increasingly secular Euskal Herria of the twenty-first century, where nationalism is perhaps the strongest religion, we may soon be able to say that the cross is Basque after it was Christian, too.

Lesaka: River Dancers in Little Venice

The remaining three of the Cinco Villas lie west across the Bidasoa towards Guipúzcoa, each more remote than the previous one.

Lesaka is a good place to be when the sky falls in Euskal Herria, as it often does. Mist tumbles silently down the precipitous hillsides that wall in the town, making a moist and cosy womb of the bed of the valley. It is a very good place to be when the bells announcing the fiesta of San Fermín roll through the dampness—the church as usual stands high above the village, well above cloud level in these conditions. The sound is at once muffled and amplified, rolling in stately fashion from great stone house to great stone house, echoing in your bones as palpably as in your ear-drums. BAAH-BOING-G-G, BAAH-BOING-G-G, BAAH-BOING-G-G, BAAH-BOING-G-G, repeating endlessly. Then they do stop and after a moment's pause the sound of drums and the shrill *txistu* flute echoes along a distant street, fading. And then more drums, and braying *dulzainas*, on a nearby street, approaching. There is a sense that the whole small town is gathering, closing in on its oddly triangular *plaza mayor*.

I will stick my neck out here, and say that there is no fiesta in the Basque Country to match *los sanfermines* in Lesaka. The fame of its namesake in Pamplona has run around the world, propelled by Hemingway's prose and countless photographs and video clips. But Lesaka has something very special and very rare, a series of elaborate formal rituals in an intimate, human-scale setting. They are performed with grace and elegance but without pretence, within a general atmosphere of well-mannered bacchanalia.

The fiesta starts, as many do, with rockets from the town hall balcony the day before the saint's day. As each one fizzles briefly over the *plaza zaharra* (old plaza) and then vanishes immediately into the mist, now at rooftop level, a woman sings a single heart-stopping stanza in a rasping tone. This is an unofficial contribution from the *izquierda abertzale*, the radical Basque nationalist left, which tends to support ETA. A banner is dropped from the town hall balcony, carrying the same message as the singer's verses. "The fiestas are for everyone. We are not all here. Bring the prisoners home." No-one applauds, nor is there any move by the authorities to remove it, a reflection perhaps of the weary stalemate before the ceasefire almost everyone wants in the summer of 2005, but which will not come for another nine months.

The mist turns into *sirimiri*, but the fiesta continues regardless. It is time for the *tamborrada infantil*, a drumfest involving dozens of little children. They brave the drizzle without complaint, filling the plaza with insistent rhythms. The fiesta uniform of white shirts, white pants and red berets are *de rigueur*. Well-prepared parents have draped transparent plastic capes over the lucky ones. Finally, there is homage to the local accordion teacher, from all his pupils over many years. The *alegría* remains irrepressible, even though the squeeze boxes are sodden.

Next morning, the finest and fittest young men in the town are kitted out for the fiesta's main event, Lesaka's unique *ezpata danza* or sword dance, on the stone margins of the Onin. This is the largest of the three streams which repeatedly transect the town and give it a distinctive character. There are twenty old stone bridges, each only a few paces wide, and 22 fountains, giving Lesaka its sobriquet of "the Little Venice". The fact that it also has 22 bars, one for ever 100 inhabitants, has probably contributed, along with the insistent rain, to its less reverent nickname, "the Pisspot of Heaven".

The *danzaris'* basic San Fermín uniform is supplemented by green, red and blue sashes, by embroidered scapulars displayed on their chests which include an image of the saint, and by brightly coloured panels studded with tiny bells stitched onto the outside legs of their trousers. Linking their hands with slim red and white rods, they lead the municipal authorities, and most of the people of the town, to the parish church of San Martín de Tours. Outside the porch, they perform the *Makil Gurutzea*, a dance using the rods to make a kind of human snake which seamlessly eats its own tail. Then the whole congregation enters the church under their raised "swords".

From the inside, this towering Gothic building could easily be mistaken for a cathedral. The massive, golden-gleaming altarpiece was carved by a leading eighteenth-century Spanish sculptor, Luis Salvador y Carmona. How could an isolated rural town, whose population then did not reach 2,000 (and is not much bigger today) afford such grandeur? As so often in the Basque Country, the answer is down to the generosity of an *Indiano*, who had made a fortune in Guatemala.

This 11 o'clock Mass is the second of the day. The *danzaris* used to attend the 8 o'clock mass, which has the best music, and accompanied the parish priest to breakfast afterwards. Late nights and declining piety have put paid to that tradition, but the dance which follows this Mass is still taken very seriously.

In the centre of Lesaka, under the huge and blackened tower house from which the Zabaleta family once plundered the Cinco Villas, the Onin's flow is controlled by stone retaining walls, about three feet high and perhaps fifteen feet apart. They sprout a wild profusion of daisies. Limpid water flows just a few inches above a bed of shingles. Trout dart about fearlessly, protected within the town limits.

One section of the banks on each side is left clear for the dancers, but every square inch elsewhere is jam-packed, with many of the windows and balconies of the surrounding houses also crammed. The dancers enter from the *plaza mayor*, repeating the *Makil Gurutzea*. They then form up along the stone walls on either bank, and dance the *Zubigainekoa*, while their captain performs a spectacular solo on the bridge between then. Putting a foot wrong on these uneven surfaces would send a dancer into the river, and disgrace. But no-one ever falters, despite, or perhaps because of, an alcohol-enriched breakfast they have enjoyed earlier at the plaza's Casino restaurant. Finally a member of the town council "dances the flag" in a banner-waving ceremony on the bridge.

Most current written accounts of this riverside encounter will tell you that it celebrates and cements a fifteenth-century peace deal between the feuding neighbourhoods of Pikuzelaia and Legarrea which lie on either side of the Onin. But as usual, there is someone who can contradict the received historical wisdom. "This notion was cooked up for an after-dinner speech a few decades ago," says local historian Rafael Eneterreaga Irigoyen, "and it has been gaining currency ever since. They say the sword dance became a rod dance to signify an end to hostilities. But there is no evidence that there was any conflict between these two neighbourhoods at that time. I believe these dances have always been a matter of exuberant play, probably deriving from an older tradition of *cristianos y moros.*"

Nonetheless the town has seen a great deal of warfare. Lesaka was constantly loyal to the kings of Navarre, and was razed to the ground twice by its Basque neighbours, once from Guipúzcoa and once from Álava, in the fifteenth century. Both were acting on behalf of the kings of Castile. The town also suffered heavily in the more localized "wars of the bands" which ravaged the region in the late Middle Ages. Lesaka very sensibly eventually evicted its own warlords in the seventeenth century. The final straw came when the Zabeletas extended their avarice to the unconscionable degree of claiming all the burial places inside the church.

Rafael knows every stone in his home place, and he knows how to make them speak. He can point out the little stone heads set almost invisibly in the walls of many of the houses to ward off witches, a practice continued right up to the end of the nineteenth century. (How the cultural values have inverted: a chic clothes shop in the plaza is called *Sorgin-zulo*, the witch's hiding place.) But what about that singular turret, clinging to a corner of the massive palace of Bordienea, and perched oddly over one of the streams? "Partly a low-level watchtower, but mainly a well-placed latrine. It allowed the waste matter to drop straight into the water." He can show you where the Duke of Wellington was very comfortably billeted for three months. This palace was owned by a Catholic bishop, grateful for his liberation from Napoleon's troops by the Protestant Irishman.

At least one of the three crosses which grace Lesaka's road junctions had a sinister purpose, though Rafael recounts its function rather glee-fully. "This was the *Pilirique*, the pillory, a place of punishment or torture. The King of Navarre gave us the privilege of making our own laws. Some of them are beautifully written, listen: 'He who bears false witness, or blasphemes against God or the Virgin, will be nailed by his tongue to the cross.' The mayor had the power of life and death. The town council met under the church arches, and its decisions were read at Mass. If you were found not to know what these decisions were, by def-inition you had not attended Mass. Well, away to the *Pilirique* with you!"

With honest inconsistency he can also bring you to a spot which suggests that Lesaka's commitment to orthodoxy in religion was ambigu-ous. Almost hidden on the wall above a disused entrance to the church is a most unusual relief: two naked cherubs sitting back to back, tilting their arms backwards above their heads to support a winged head. "This is a representation of the Trinity which was specifically condemned by the Council of Trent," says Rafael. "It's not clear why, but it may have been that the Church fathers found the image of two of the Divine Persons sitting arse to arse a little disrespectful." Nevertheless, genera-tions of Lesaka's faithful have quietly defied the Conciliar Bull, and the relief remains in place.

Lesaka encapsulates many of the characteristics of a small Basque village, but it is also has a unique character. The nobility of its architec-ture, coupled with its happy arrangement of streets and streams and pedestrian walkways, give it the air of a tiny and exquisite city. The inter-penetration of urban and rural features is very typical, however, with fields of maize among its mansions, and donkeys grazing in fields along-side its streets. There is a substantial laminated steel plant, employing 1,400 people, behind a row of medieval buildings. Even in the sixteenth century, what we might call "greater Lesaka"—the municipal boundary extends right down to Vera along the west bank of the Bidasoa—boasted 17 ironworks, using ore from local mines.

Iganzi, Arantza: Healing Waters, *Baserriak* for BMWs
Take the road south and west from Lesaka, and urban impressions quickly fall away. The slopes become steeper, the hairpin bends that lead

you down into, and up out of, deep valleys more disorientating. The wet greens of the vegetation grow more and more intense. Near the pretty white village of Igantzi is a roadside shrine. Inside a small cave a spring rises which cures skin infections, especially if you bathe there on St. John's Eve. But the Christian patina wears thin if you pause here at full moon on your own. It becomes still thinner as you approach the end of the road, the last of the Cinco Villas, Arantza. Walk here after sunset, and the words of Julio Caro Baroja, defending Basque polytheism against Spanish monotheism, may come to mind:

> The man who wanders towards home on a starry night, through a valley surrounded by mountains, where you hear the sounds of leaves, murmurs of water, light breezes, all in almost complete darkness, may find himself overcome... [He may] easily believe in old and humble presences in trees, in the streams, in the rocks, in beings which are partly human, partly demonic, partly natural... in spite of my basic rationalism... I would like to make little nocturnal sacrifices now and then... to carry out little private rituals.

On a fine day, the high meadows of Mendaur, the mountain that soars to 3,710 feet to the south, beckon for an exhilarating but undemanding walk. On a day of *sirimiri*, Arantza sinks into itself, its huge farmhouses—none of its older buildings looks truly urban—looming to twice their usual size in the mist.

On a night after just such a sodden day, in 1989, I went out alone in search of a drink and some company. A huge toad flopped out of the inky blackness, and planted itself in front of me, baleful eyes immobile, fixed on mine. "*Zu sorgiña zara... sorgiña ona, oso ona...*" I found myself muttering in my very rudimentary Euskera, quite concerned to communicate appropriately with this night creature. "You are a witch, a good witch, a very good witch." There was no obvious response. "*Ni irlandan bizi naiz,*" I added inconsequentially, simply because I knew the phrase well, and my Basque vocabulary was running out, "I am from Ireland." The little beast held my gaze contemptuously for a short eternity, and then it was gone.

This encounter was probably a self-induced illusion, of course. For when I found a bar, I was back in a sad part of the twentieth century.

Four ageing single farmers sat in the cold, isolating glow of a French soft porn channel. They would not grasp the spoken words—even Spanish might be difficult for them—but the body language was universal. Men from these villages have died of Aids, contracted in super-brothels in Irún, less than an hour's drive away. My most cherished illusion, that I would spend the evening drinking wine with the locals and learning about their lives, was also shattered. As good a chance as communication with the changeling toad.

There was no accommodation to rent in Arantza in those days, but there was a splendid restaurant, the Aterpe, which attracted people from all corners of the Basque Country and beyond to risk these narrow twisting roads at night. I had arrived by bicycle, in the evening, and the owners would not see me go short of a bed. (They have since opened a large hostel.) Their son was a drummer in a Rastafarian band. His bedroom door was left open in the morning. Above his drum kit he had painted a mural in Bob Marley's greens, reds and golds, including an outline of Navarre. The words underneath were a parody of the Basque nationalist slogan *Nafarroa Euskadi Da*, Navarre is the Basque Country. His adaptation read: *Nafarroa Afrika Da*.

When I cycled back to Lesaka the next day, I was repeatedly thrown off balance, and almost off the narrow road itself, by giant refrigerator trucks. They were bringing duck pâté from the factory at Arantza to the tables of the best restaurants in Barcelona and Madrid.

Returning 15 years later, Arantza remains heart-achingly beautiful, an oasis of calm. But some of its streets are filled with luxury apartment blocks. Their slanted red roofs and white frontages with false black beams, their cast-iron balconies painted vivid blue and sporting red geraniums, all pay homage to the *baserri*. But on the ground floor, where the animals used to be stabled in the traditional structure, there are garages with automatic doors, BMWs parked where cows used to lie.

Like all the Basque Country, even the remotest part of the Cinco Villas lives in several worlds at once. I will still speak Basque there at night, to any toads I meet, but I will watch out for oncoming headlamps in the rain.

Take your pick of *pintxos*: you can choose anything from artichoke hearts with ham to prawns skewered on eggs (scrambled, with mushrooms) to go with your drink in a bar like the Victor Montes in Bilbao.

Chapter Six

Gastronomy: Some Answers to the Most Urgent Basque Question

Filosofia baino hobea da oilo-zopa: Chicken broth is preferable to philosophy

Basque proverb

The story goes that the Basques ask themselves three questions every day. The first two questions relate, inevitably, to angst about their national identity. Where do we come from? And who are we? These are, indeed, difficult questions, as we have seen, and the answers people give have serious consequences in their daily lives. The third question, however, is the most important, or at least the most urgent: where, ask the Basques, are we going for dinner tonight?

It is almost impossible to exaggerate the significance of gastronomy here, or the extent to which it permeates almost every social activity and every social class. That, in turn, reflects a lifestyle where time is still more valuable than money, where the texture of today takes precedence over anxieties about tomorrow. The survival of this value system in an advanced industrial society is as miraculous, in its way, as the survival of the Basque language, and it may be more precarious. "Even today," says master chef Josu Zubikarai, "when a cleaning woman or a quarryman takes a lunch break, they have a first, second and third course, and then there must be time for coffee. In the US, it would be a sandwich and that's it, back to work. But it is changing here, in a generation we will be like them."

Putting aside such gloomy speculation for the moment, let us get on with some not-too-onerous research. We can start in Bilbao's old quarter, in the Calle del Perro, which translates, rather unpromisingly, as Dog Street. You can walk right through the Calle del Perro in less than a minute, but you will have passed nine or ten restaurants in the process.

The Xukela serves what they call *tapas*, but which look more like a full main course. The table clothes are made of paper, but they are replaced with subtle style and no fuss between each group of customers. You might start with seven or eight large green asparagus spears, garnished with smoked ham flash-fried with garlic. That goes well with another large plate of dry Idiazabal cheese, served with quince. And a little Txakoli, the potent "green" Basque wine, for the stomach's sake, of course.

The Arriaga is a new *sagardotegi*, or cider house, across the street from the Xukela. Serious Basque gastronomes feel a little uneasy here because an authentic cider house should be as old as the orchards which surround it. The Arriaga looks spanking new, and there is no apple tree within three miles. But it is a fair imitation of the real thing, with massive stone walls and heavy wooden beams. Two enormous barrels of cider lie on their sides, right by the entrance.

Holding your glass down near the floor, just above a small wooden vessel which catches the splashes, you pull a plug from the barrel and the golden liquid shoots out under high pressure, producing a properly frothy brew. It is very important to replace the plug smartly at the right moment. If that process seems too intimidating, the staff will bring a foaming jug to your table. You will need it to digest a steaming bowl of red beans from Gernika, cooked with generous chunks of black pudding and chorizo. A side plate of *guindillas*, little pickled sweet green chillies, gives a nice contrasting bite to the beans. And that is just for starters. For your main course, try the ample fillets of cod, accompanied by delicious red peppers with crisped garlic. Dessert? *Cuajada*, curdled sheep's milk, if it is in season, with honey and walnuts. If your head can handle it, *Patxaran*—a sweet Pyrenean liquor, based on anis and blueberries—is a good local *digestif.*

A few doors further up, the Eguiluz serves superb squid in batter in a tiny upstairs room… but we cannot spend the whole chapter in the Calle del Perro. Eating one's way through the Basque Country is a continuous pleasure: monkfish in Hondarribia, mackerel in Hernani, horse mackerel in Mutriku, beef in Mauleon—disappointments are very few and far between. I would not go back to Vitoria for the snails which are the *pièce de résistance* of the San Prudencio celebrations (I would rather chew black rubber, despite the spicy tomato sauce). But even that let-

Catch the light: there is considerable skill in getting a frothy shot of cider in a *sagardotegi*, straight from a huge wooden barrel.

down was more than made up for by the scrambled eggs laced with baby wild mushrooms which are the second speciality of that fiesta.

Basque restaurants are all very well and good, but there is another institution here which gives a unique flavour to a meal out with friends, though their gender balance leaves much to be desired. In any Basque village or town, you may notice one or more mysterious doors. They appear to lead to restaurants, but there are no signs outside, no menu in the window. Serious-looking men of all ages can be seen going through these doors early in the evening, carrying bulky parcels. Many hours later they will emerge again, empty-handed now, and looking a lot less serious.

These are private clubs known as "gastronomic societies" or, more colloquially, as *txokos*. Until recently an almost exclusively masculine preserve, they are still male-dominated to an extraordinary extent. While women are now generally admitted as guests, they are still largely excluded from membership and cannot enter the cooking area. The men say the presence of women throws them off their culinary stride. Many of the men are first-class amateur chefs, but some of them will never cook a meal at home, where women may exercise an equally absolute control over the kitchen. A transition to gastronomic gender equality has been promised for many years, but it is very slow in coming. The only women generally allowed in the kitchen are cleaners, paid to do the washing up.

José Ignacio's society in Zarautz is beautifully located, overlooking the Bay of Biscay and the broad promenade of this *belle époque* resort. This *txoko* has a relaxed approach to women guests, and his wife, María Pilar, has brought some home-pickled tuna, so we have a salad, and then a plate of Iberian ham, before he and I move on to the serious business in the kitchen. José Ignacio stokes a huge wooden fire under a grill, selects a gridiron from dozens hanging on the wall, lays the sparkling sardines in neat rows within it, and within five minutes we have a crisp and nutritious main course, washed down with wine. Strawberries, cheese, ice cream and coffee follow. No particular excuse is required for this kind of outing, though every special occasion should, if possible, be marked with a special meal.

From Itziar to Washington and Back

Josu Zubikarai grew up in a restaurant set up by his grandfather and inherited by his father. His home village of Itziar is perched on a hill between the sea and some of Vizcaya's most recondite valleys, though conveniently close to the main road between San Sebastián and Bilbao. Food was always central to his life, though not always agreeably so. His grandfather made him drink a small glass of wine whisked with sugar and two eggs before going to school every morning. He still grimaces at the memory.

Nevertheless, he found himself working in the kitchen as a boy, then taking summer jobs in a restaurant in Bilbao as a teenager, and finally going to sea as a cook. He rose fast without any formal training, becoming a signature chef in Madrid and Marbella. Here he encountered a remarkable Basque priest. Luis de Lezama had set up the Alabardero restaurant in Madrid to provide jobs for marginalized youths, and found himself with a highly successful business. He invited Zubikarai to launch an Alarbardero in Washington DC in 1990. Within a couple of years he was regarded as one of the best chefs in the capital, with a maximum four stars from the *Washingtonian*. His regular clients including Al Gore, then vice-president, ex-president Gerald Ford, the Rolling Stones, Placido Domingo, and the then first minister of the Basque Country, José Antonio Ardanza.

Where to go to dinner was not the only Basque question Zubikai had to answer, however. The persistent issue of Basque identity also raised its head, though never enough to cause him any serious grief. The Alabardero had a subvention from the Madrid government—and an official designation as "the best Spanish restaurant outside of Spain". But Zubikarai gave a Basque foundation to the menu, including the periodic use of Euskera in the text, which irritated some Spanish diplomats. As his fame grew, he cooked at international competitions across the US, but always used an *ikurriña*, astutely crossed with Old Glory, as his national emblem, and not a Spanish flag. He took out an American passport. "Spanish citizenship is imposed on us here," he says matter-of-factly. "There at least I could choose."

Even a Spanish identity was too much for some Americans to grasp in his early days in Washington because they confused Spain with Mexico. They expected to eat tacos, chilli con carne and tortillas made with flour instead of eggs. Zubikarai swiftly brought them around by offering first-class food and wine from all parts of Iberia. He says he was greatly helped by the 1992 quincentenary celebrations of Columbus' first voyage, which made enough of an impact to clarify gastronomic geography for his less cosmopolitan clients.

Four years ago, at the peak of his international career, he decided to return home to spend more time with his children, leaving behind him another Vizcayan chef, Santi Zabaleta to continue his tradition. By this time his cooking had evolved a strong international flavour, with a marked oriental influence. "The logical next step was for me to study in Thailand," he says wryly.

Instead, he finds himself back in the kitchen of the family restaurant, cooking meals very similar to the ones he helped with as a boy. "At first I found it very frustrating," he says, "but now I love it because I can spend much more time in the kitchen, and rediscover the roots and *fundamento* of traditional cooking. As a young man I was very attracted to the *Nueva Cocina Vasca* [A nouvelle cuisine vogue which revolutionized high-end Basque restaurants, pioneered in the 1960s by cooks like Juan Mari Arzak, Pedro Subijana, Karlos Arguiñano]. Now it is time to go back to my roots."

One of the things that delights him is the spontaneous availability of first-class primary materials. "One neighbour rings me and says she has good tomatoes, or onions, or potatoes in her allotment." The *huerta,* or allotment, is an ancillary obsession to cooking in Basque life. Every square inch of available ground space is used for growing vegetables, and where it is not available it is invented. In the Vizcayan village of Igorre, one resident grows potted potatoes right in the main street.

"Another neighbour says they have a dozen good chickens ready for the table," Zubikarai continues. "The fishermen call from Ondarroa and Getaria to say what they have caught today. When the hunting season begins, a friend lets me know when they have shot a deer, or a wild boar."

He sees some positive changes on his return, especially a more open attitude to wine. "We used to think everything that did not come from La Rioja, or La Rioja Alavesa, was not worth drinking. Now we recognize good wine from all over Spain, and from the New World."

He is not tempted, for the moment, to enter the top of the market, partly for personal reasons and partly because he believes that there will always be regular clients for traditional Basque cooking. Innovative enterprises, he points out, tend to become fashion victims, losing their clients to the Next Big Thing after five or ten years. He is concerned, but not surprised, that the standard of home cooking has sharply declined since he was a boy. "This is inevitable, with women going out to work. When I was growing up, the women spent all day cooking, if not for that night for the next day or for the weekend. At least most of us still eat one family meal a day, but young people will abandon even that, no-one has any time any more."

Perhaps it is as well that some Basque traditions have fallen off, because Zubikarai remembers how a champion rock-lifter in his youth believed he could only perform well if he ate thirty eggs a day. "Yet he lived to be a healthy old man, that's the strange thing," he remarks.

He is horrified but not surprised to hear that AZTI's market research has found that the ideal fish for a young Basque couple today is boneless and odourless. "If we served a fish here without its head, people would still be offended, because they want to see the whole creature, but yes, that is changing. It is a shame, because there is nothing more tasty and juicy than a turbot cooked on the bone." No doubt AZTI, and Zubikarai, are right that values are changing, yet the wealth of Basque popular gastronomy is still so evident in so many daily transactions that one may be permitted to hope for at least some stabilization.

A Few Snacks in Asteasu

A cold and wet autumn morning in the Guipuzcoan village of Asteasu: a friend and I have an appointment for 10 o'clock and we meet, of course, in a bar, the Iturriondo. Coffee promises a poor antidote to the damp, so we order *caldo,* a broth made from chicken or beef stock which would warm up the dead.

Then we do some business, which takes perhaps ninety minutes, and includes some food shopping because my friend believes the best tomatoes are grown by his neighbours. Each one is examined and approved, some the size of small melons. Then it is time for another *caldo,* in another bar, the Patxine. We are beginning to get peckish now, so we order *pintxos* with a little red wine: sheep's cheese on the first *pintxo,* chorizo on the second. Then a spoonful of lamb stew scooped into a piece of thick bread. My friend groans because he has remembered that he has to call in on his mother-in-law, who is a splendid cook, and since it is still only 1.30 pm, there is no way he will be allowed to leave her house without eating a four-course lunch.

Andrés, a mechanic by trade and a friend of my friend, sees me in the Patxine over the next few days. We chat at the agricultural fair, where the most visited stall is a display of some hundred varieties of local mushrooms, some of them delicious, most of them edible, a few of them toxic. Dozens of people, young and old, pore over them all day long, seeking expert advice from the stallholder. Andrés invites me to spend my last evening researching this book in his *txoko*. My research in the Bardenas, far to the south, detains me longer than I expect, and I arrive back half an hour late. Andrés' face is grim. "The monkfish was *a punto*, baked to perfection, twenty minutes ago," he says. "Who knows what it will taste like now?" A two-litre bottle of excellent Bordeaux, for three of us, is on our space at the refectory-style table. The white flesh of the monkfish peels off the bone, still just juicy enough to melt Andrés' gloom.

He rises from the table to inspect a monstrous chop, so fresh you would not be surprised to find the cow it came from hanging in the field outside. It is thrown on a grid-iron and charred quickly over red coals, then sliced off the bone into inch-wide strips. "In the old days we would have had one each," Andrés says, putting half a kilo on my plate. Apples and sheep's cheese follows, while we attempt, once again, to resolve old conundrums about who the Basque people are, and where they came from. Because of the ETA ceasefire, we even dare to talk about where they may be going. No-one is too hopeful, but no-one is very downbeat either. But we can't tell the future. The only certain thing in life, after all, is a good dinner when it is eaten.

Chapter Seven
Wow, Bilbao!
The Transformation of a Tough City

In the beginning was the Mineral...
Dolores Ibárruri, "La Pasionaria", *El Único Camino*, 1979

Few cities display their history quite as nakedly, quite as brutally, as Bilbao does. The novelist Kate O'Brien, who spent a year here as a governess in the early 1920s, saw it clearly: the commercial capital of the Basque Country had a "pock-marked look, made frantic by the ceaseless all-in wrestling match of greed and misery."

In O'Brien's time, Bilbao's brutality was more obvious than it is today, but its history is still very evident all along its main thoroughfare, the Nervión river, and it has not—yet—been erased by the unprecedented transformations of the last decade. For a century and a half, the Left Bank of the Nervión was dominated by iron mines, blast furnaces, shipyards and muddy slums. Directly opposite, new palaces loudly proclaimed the power of the industrial oligarchy, as if wealth had drained from one side of the river and, magically transmuted, flourished on the other.

The mines and the furnaces closed in the 1990s, leaving a spectacular panorama of rusting industrial ruins. The palaces remain, though their ownership is shifting, and the city's new masters (still mostly masculine) are radically rewriting Bilbao's skyline in an orgy of trophy architecture.

The dramatic transfiguration of the city since the 1980s is epitomized by the daring gamble of the Guggenheim-Bilbao museum, designed by Frank Gehry. The new Bilbao has an uneasy relationship to the old. It remains to be seen whether the city's colossal urban regeneration project, still in process at the time of writing, can genuinely transcend its grim but dynamic heritage, or whether it is only an attempt

Trophy architecture: the Guggenheim Museum in Bilbao, designed by Frank Gehry, has made the city a magnet for tourists, and diminished its association with terrorism. Seen here alongside the Nervión river, with Louise Bourgeois' *Maman* on the walkway in the foreground, it dwarfs the city's old landmarks, like the Jesuit University in Deusto, across the river, and the *casa torre* and farmhouses which stand in the hills beyond.

to divert attention from the greed and misery which have made the city what it is today.

Averting one's eyes from the obvious is a tradition in this city. Despite the visibility of its history, Bilbao has been, and remains, in denial about the origins and consequences of its wealth. It has even been in denial about what used to be most pungently conspicuous in the air itself.

When I moved to Bilbao in 1975, the atmosphere was sulphurous with pollution. The city sits in a basin, "beside the mobile river and between the breasts of the hills", as Kate O'Brien rather lyrically puts it, imagining earlier days than her own. The Nervión sucked the persistent mists down from these steep cleavages. In the 1970s the wet air formed a soup of lung-choking smog as it absorbed the dust from the mines and the fumes from the furnaces and smelters. For days and weeks on end the clouds hugged the broad depression that runs from the old city down along the river to the *Abra*, or opening, where the harbour meets the Bay of Biscay. The water in the river, appropriately known as the "navigable sewer", was as filthy as the air above it. A postcard featuring an aerial view of Bilbao at this time was unusually honest: it showed a great shit-brown stain, much bigger than the whole urban conglomeration, spreading out from the *Abra* into the sea.

Bilbao in the 1970s was said to be the most polluted city in the world, next to Tokyo. The dictatorship set few environmental limits, and even these were breached with impunity. People sometimes keeled over and died in the street, asphyxiated by atmospheric contamination. People who had never lit a cigarette in their lives wheezed as if they smoked sixty a day. But here is the strange thing: if you mentioned this toxic cocktail to a group of *bilbaínos*, they would affect astonishment at the misconceptions entertained by foreigners. They would then inhale deeply, and swear there was nowhere healthier to live on the planet. And this was true of militant leftists just as much as it was of diehard supporters of the regime. In Bilbao muck was brass, and it was indecorous to point out that muck stinks.

The self-deception of the *bilbaínos* was infectious. I often found, especially after a night spent in their excellent company, that the rasping edge on the air was indeed invigorating, like the last hit on a hot joint. Most of these nights were spent *txikiteando*, a custom that involves drinking small glasses of wine, one in each of as many different bars as possible. The days were different. As Franco lay in his death agony, the war between greed and misery was played out on the streets of the city, with tear gas and burning barricades further enriching the atmospheric mix. Bilbao smelled of struggle, or of wealth, depending on which side you took in that battle, and both smells were bracing.

Today, the air beneath the silent mines is fresh, sometimes even sweet, though the Vizcayan *sirimiri* persists. On a clear day the hill-sides—those that held no iron to mine—now stand up sharply in clean green, marking the city's narrow lateral limits at the end of its few broad avenues. But Bilbao's sense of denial is still in play. The city has lived almost exclusively off industry and commerce since it was granted its charter to trade as a *Villa* by Don Diego López de Haro, Lord of Vizcaya, on 15 June 1300. Its entire *raison d'être* has been mercantile, and it has never—until the Guggenheim—wasted either much breath or much money on culture. Despite this, "Bilbao's folklore shamelessly ignores the real motor of its history: the obsessive pursuit of profit," as the acerbic commentator Jon Juaristi puts it.

Apart from the palaces on the Right Bank, wealth in Bilbao was not and is not ostentatious, by Spanish standards. (The Guggenheim project forces a rethink on this question, however, as on many others.) The intensely Anglophile oligarchy took their cue on discretion from London. There are moments when Bilbao's business district, around the Gran Vía, can feel like the Square Mile in the City, with dark three-piece pinstripe suits and rolled umbrellas dominating the pavements.

Conversely, even the poorest of the poor in Bilbao have always had a pride that raised them above their circumstances. Kate O'Brien remembered "the slum suburbs about those furnaces… savage and shameless in poverty, but very gay on Sunday, with harmonicas playing up and down the stations and young men and women, shining and neat, crowding on to the train to go and dance at a *verbena* in Santurce." Mostly, though, gloom predominated. In her memoir *Txoriburu* (1998) the Bilbao writer and illustrator Asun Balzola describes her childhood in the 1940s:

These were years of iron and we lived in Bilbao, a city of iron, always wet, gleaming and black because it was always raining… The green shadows of umbrellas stained the streets and houses were blackened by smoke from the factories... Bilbao was a replica of Coketown, the imaginary industrial town described by Dickens in *Hard Times*.

A City Built on Iron, Wood and Water

Bilbao was endowed at birth with numerous assets. Some of the most important iron deposits in Europe lay right on top of the western hills overlooking the river and its sheltered estuary. The river was navigable for a good eight miles from the *Abra* up to the sheltered site of the original chartered city, now the *casco viejo*, and the old port at El Arenal. That port, which would extend and shift down the river over the centuries, was the gateway for the wool trade between Castile, London and Flanders, and for the Basque manufacturing trade. Meanwhile, the forests which carpeted the hills and their hinterland provided ample charcoal for smelting iron. When the forests were exhausted, coal could be easily imported by sea from Britain, on ships that then exported iron, and later steel, on the return journey. Many other industries, of which shipbuilding was one of the most important, contributed to making Bilbao the Manchester of Iberia.

Iron-mining here probably pre-dates Roman times. Pliny the Elder referred to a "marvellous mountain, entirely made of iron" on the Cantabrian coast. Bilbao's products were familiar enough in Elizabethan England for Shakespeare to twice use its Basque name, *Bilbo*, as a synonym for iron manacles in *The Merry Wives of Windsor*, and to pun with it in *Henry V*. But it was the 1856 invention of the Bessemer furnace, which converted low-phosphorous iron to high-quality steel, that turned Bilbao into an industrial dynamo. Low-phosphorous iron was Bilbao's speciality. The city provided Britain with two-thirds of her iron ore in the late nineteenth century, and supplied twenty per cent of the world's steel in the decades that followed, as profits from ore exports were invested in steel mills along the banks of the Nervión. Immigrant workers from other parts of Iberia, and, to a lesser extent, from the Basque countryside, poured into the mining towns of the Nervión's Left Bank.

"The panorama of the mountains rising above the sea and the Nervión valley, smoking with a hundred chimneys, forms a spectacle that is so stunning as to become unforgettable," the sociologist Max

Weber wrote at the dawn of the twentieth century in a letter to his mother. The western skyline pulsed with the vulcanic glow of smelting for many more decades. Its lurid artificial sunsets reflected hell on earth for the miners. But they represented heaven for the industrial oligarchy in their mansions across the river. This was the new Basque ruling class, most of them natives of the region. The Ybarras, Chavarris, Urquijos and other family dynasties were remarkably successful in forming beneficial partnerships with French, Belgian and especially British enterprises. They made sure that between 60 and 75 per cent of the profits generated in the city stayed in the Basque Country—or at least in Basque banks, through which they were establishing themselves as front-rank players in the new game of Spanish finance capital. By 1929, although Basques constituted a mere three per cent of Spain's population, Basque capital represented 25 per cent of Spanish banking resources, 38 per cent of the investment in shipyards, 40 per cent of the stock in engineering and electrical construction firms, 68 per cent of the funds dedicated to shipping companies, and 62 per cent of the monies invested in steel factories.

The red sky at night (and often by day as well) was also a beacon to those who believed in a different kind of future to that envisaged by the oligarchy. Bertolt Brecht was able to write, with his usual quota of irony, but some sincerity as well: "How beautiful, how beautiful, how beautiful is the moon of Bilbao, the most beautiful city of the continent."

So the red moon rose over the mining towns, giving greater Bilbao a claim to being one of the midwives, if not the mother, of Spanish communism and socialism. And the bright sun of prosperity shone on the green suburbs of Neguri and Algorta, making the city home to an entrepreneurial elite which only Catalonia could rival on the whole peninsula. As we have seen in Chapter Two, the rise of these two social sectors left the Basque middle classes feeling confused and angry, squeezed between an "alien" immigrant proletariat and a "cosmopolitan" oligarchy, neither of which had much regard for the Basque language and Basque traditions. And this new dynamic led Bilbao to produce a third force, Basque nationalism. It is one of the sharper ironies of Basque history that Sabino Arana's PNV, so given to idealizing rural traditions, should have been born, and remains strongest, in the region's greatest city.

The conflicts which followed are often seen in purely negative terms, or as a battle in which victory for one side means defeat for the other. But Bernardo Atxaga sees the turbulent diversity of this period as a sign of potential strength. "The greatness of Bilbao," he says, "and perhaps the only greatness of this land of ours, is precisely the confluence here on this river of so many different currents, of so many different influences." Over the last decade, new tributaries of immigrants from far beyond Iberia have surged into the city and pose new challenges and new opportunities for its sense of identity.

The rich and intimate contrasts of Basque life are still inscribed on Bilbao's skyline. The Guggenheim, emblem of post-modern Bilbao, stands partly on the site of a shipyard owned by Sabino Arana's traditionalist family. The rest of the site was known as La Campa de los Ingleses, successively a cemetery for British subjects, a shanty town, a fairground, and a railway goods yard. The neoclassical façade of the University of Deusto (founded in 1886 as a *commercial* university) is directly across the river, but is now linked to Abandoibarra by the Pedro Arrupe footbridge, which stretches out between the banks like a mechanical crocodile. The Jesuit ideology which launched the university may be in decline, but its school of economic science remains influential in the business world. Immediately above the university, a medieval *casa torre* rises out of the lush woodlands on the green north-western slopes of Artxanda. And there, hardly more than half a mile from the heart of the city, you can also see a *baserri*, the traditional white and red Basque farmhouse, with placidly grazing cattle in fields surrounded by woods of sweet chestnuts. Today, town and country co-exist peacefully in the environs of Bilbao, though pressure for building land is turning the *baserri* into an expensive luxury. Traditional farming is becoming an allotment hobby for wealthy professionals rather than a livelihood for stout peasant farmers. Nonetheless, this visible presence of *rus in urbe* adds a subtle flavour to the city's rich gastronomy, promising that the primary materials on the dining table have been freshly harvested almost next door.

Traditionally, the *baserritarrak* loathed the *kaletarrak* of Bilbao. Three times in the nineteenth century Carlist peasant armies laid siege to the city, causing many deaths and great hardship. The oligarchy, which was a bulwark of Spanish Liberalism, prevailed on the city to hold out, which it did, with periodic assistance from the British navy. Some luck was on also on the Liberals' side. A stray bullet took the life of Tomás Zumalacárregui, the outstanding Carlist general, while he was directing the first siege in 1835. He was standing beside the Basilica of the Virgin of Begoña, patron saint of the city. This church is a brisk ten-minute walk uphill from the *casco viejo*. That is how close things were. (Zumalacárregui's brother, Miguel Ángel, was a leading Liberal, a reminder, more valid than ever today, that it is risky to assume political loyalties on the basis of social or family background in the Basque Country.) Two more Carlist generals were killed during the last and most severe siege, in 1874. Miguel de Unamuno gives a graphic and tragic account of these events in his novel *Paz en la Guerra* (1895).

The confluence of ideological currents made the city a political whirlpool as Bilbao entered the twentieth century. The surging immigrant population forged the Basque left, and engaged in a series of heroic strikes against the appalling conditions imposed by the oligarchy in the mines and factories. These were more than "labour disputes"; they were aptly described as "wars without weapons" by Ramiro Pinilla, author of the sprawling, 7,000-page epic, *Valles Verdes, Colinas Rojas* (2004), which attempts, rather heavy-handedly, to re-imagine the entire history of the Basque Country, and especially of Bilbao and its hinterland.

Meanwhile, the PNV grew in democratic stature as it struggled to create a distinctive space for the Basque middle classes. And when the Civil War broke out, it was the PNV and the left which made common cause to defend the city, while most of the oligarchy sided with Franco's insurgents. Ironically, Bilbao's super-rich were now on the same side as their old Carlist peasant enemies who were advancing from Pamplona with the fascists, or preparing to seize control in nearby towns like Munguia. It was not the already anachronistic Carlists, however, but Nazi airpower and Italian land forces, assisted by an act of treachery by a Basque engineer, that broke the city's "belt of steel" in 1937.

The Republican administration in Madrid had asked the Basque government to sabotage Bilbao's vital industries before they fell into the hands of the enemy. But the PNV made sure that not a single factory was destroyed by the retreating Basque forces. You can regard this stance either as disloyalty to Spanish democracy or as a defence of Basque self-interest. In any case, Franco showed no gratitude. He rewarded the PNV by executing its captured leaders, imprisoning many of its rank and file, and expropriating businesses owned by nationalists. Bilbao was handed back to the oligarchy, to run as it pleased for the next forty years. Franco's autarkist economic policies protected the city's heavy industry from international competition, and it stagnated quite successfully while supplying the internal Spanish market. The trade unions somehow survived the dictator's unrelenting repression, but it took them three decades to begin to rebuild their bargaining power. And neither owners nor unions were able to cope when EU entry exposed the city's antiquated industrial infrastructure to a global market economy in the 1980s.

Ironically, it was the modernizing socialist (PSOE) governments of that period which imposed ruthless industrial restructuring policies from Madrid, against often violent opposition from the remaining workforce. These policies were the death knell of the old Left Bank which had been so crucial in establishing the PSOE in the first place. With the oligarchy also in disarray, the PNV found itself in charge of a city that looked as if it was plunging into terminal decline. Before we examine what happened next, it is worth pausing for a moment to ask a contemporary descendant of that oligarchy, which shaped the city in so many ways, about his relationship with Bilbao, and with the Basque Country.

The main street in the exclusive Bilbao suburb of Las Arenas is named after Antonio Basagoiti's namesake, a great-great grandfather who made a fortune by founding the Banco Hispano-Americano. The family name is very Basque, but many Basque nationalists would dismiss this bright young man as "Spanish" because they see the oligarchy as a foreign body, and more so because he is the president of the Vizcayan section of the Partido Popular (PP), implacable opponents of the PNV.

When I was growing up, people in our family circle felt more *Bilbaíno* than Basque. Bilbao always had a close relationship with Madrid. Euskera was never a differentiating factor here. The city's founding charter, back in 1300, was written in Spanish. Yes, we feel an attachment to our gastronomy, to the sea, to our fiestas, a stronger attachment than exists in Madrid. But Bilbao has always been a plural place, it has been the home of monarchists, republicans, socialists, and yes, of Basque nationalists like Sabino Arana. I have no problem with Basque nationalist aspirations, only with its tendency to monopolize Basque identity through hijacking linguistic and cultural symbols, even Bilbao Athletic football team! I must say I feel much more in common with someone from the Basque coast, or Vizcaya or just from any big city, than I do with a citizen of the south of Navarre, or a citizen of French Basque Country.

From Ruin to Resurrection

By the turn of the last millennium there was nothing but wreckage for half a mile downriver from the Euskalduna bridge. If you walked the Olabeaga docks towards the distant sea at twilight, the air seemed thick with the melancholy atmosphere of urban decay. The stone steps from the quays down to the water were carpeted with thick slime, and the quays themselves were sagging and collapsing. Barges lay on their sides, half-submerged in the sluggish tide. Rust ate sleeplessly at their iron hulls, shoals of mullet weaved through holes in the decks.

On the Zorrotzaure peninsula, just opposite, long-closed factories and warehouses seemed to aspire to the condition of the great stacks of scrap metal piled in their empty yards. The solid bourgeois homes that housed the factory managers and their families were also caving in, except for a capricious villa built in the style of a miniature Rhineland castle. Squatters—*okupas*—had taken it over. Their garish aerosol artwork provided the only splash of colour in the evening's grey-brown palette.

There were thousands of acres of this kind of landscape in central Bilbao alone in the year 2000. Most of the towns that link the centre to the sea along the Nervión also contained vast open museums of industrial archaeology. The biggest Basque urban region seemed to have choked to death on its own waste. Nothing, however, could have been further from the truth.

If you walked in the other direction, under the Euskalduna bridge and upriver, you found an utterly different city. Some of the best—or at least the most fashionable—architects in the world had worked here over the previous twenty years, engaged on one of the most ambitious urban regeneration projects in recent European history. The Abandoibarra district has come to represent urban transformation on a grand scale. "Bilbao's sudden miracle is literally the best illustration [of postmodernism] to date," writes Zulaika. Its experience has been widely cited as an urban model for the twenty-first century, where extravagant building schemes are metaphors for the ambitions of new services and e-industries. The Olabeaba docks and Zorrotzaure peninsula, though still ruinous at the time of writing, are also due for ambitious makeovers, as are historic industrial municipalities closer to the sea, like Barakaldo. Bilbao now aspires to be the European city mostly closely linked to New York, just a mouse-click away across the Atlantic.

This gigantic project's signature building is an up-market franchise from the Big Apple. The Guggenheim has catapulted the city into the top echelon of the art-and-architecture tourist circuit. It is eulogized in the *New York Times* ("a miracle") and *Condé Nast Traveller* ("city-break hotspot"). Kate O'Brien could not write today that Bilbao is a town "where no real tourist ever goes."

The Guggenheim has its local opponents, though they are much fewer now than on the day it opened in 1997. The PNV, which championed it at municipal, provincial and Basque government level, has been attacked for spending scarce resources, ear-marked for the Basque language and Basque culture, on a project which has no indigenous form or content. Worse, their critics say, these champions of Basque self-determination have been paying a very expensive piper while ceding the right to call the tune. Cultural policy for the museum remains firmly in the hands of the Guggenheim's governing body in New York.

There was, and is, something very disconcerting about this massive Basque subsidy of an institution over which the Basques have no control. The absence of Basque art from the museum exacerbates this concern: a country which has made, for its size, a remarkable contribution to modern and contemporary art is represented only by a single work. This is a modest Chillida sculpture, *The Embrace*, which has been shunted out to an obscure patio approachable only from the first-floor toilets. Of course, had Thomas Krens, the Guggenheim's director, fulfilled his ambition to bring Picasso's *Guernica* to Bilbao, there would have been a Basque-related work at the heart of the museum; but that was not to be.

In any case, the permanent collection is undoubtedly a boon to any city. The vast hall dedicated to Richard Serra's *The Matter of Time* offers a generous opportunity to explore the stimulating spaces created by this master of supple canyons of rusting steel, so appropriate to his beloved Bilbao. *Maman*, from Louise Bourgeois's Spider series, is a hideously beautiful presence on the boardwalk between the museum and the river. And overall, the fear expressed by an American critic that the Bilbao space would be a "very expensive parking lot" for works that the foundation owns but does not want to display in New York has not been borne out. It is true that the opening exhibitions left a sour taste, with second- or even third-rate work only partially masked by its attachment to top-drawer names. But that lesson seems to have been learned, and 2006 alone saw first-class works by artists like Anselm Kiefer, Richard Long, Mario Merz and Jannis Kounellis. And the Basques can take some consolation that all this work is being exhibited in a museum in which Euskera is the first language on every caption—a statement about identity which must make some impression on every visitor.

Again and again, however, the verdict on the Guggenheim comes down to the building rather than its contents. A crushed steel rose, a silver volcano in full eruption, a three-prowed ship soaring off the river and into the sky: the museum is many things from many angles. Clad in reflective titanium and glass, it takes on all the rapidly changing tints of a Biscayan sky and casts them back across a city that has long been starved of light. It can make a misty day look magical. Asun Balzola told the *Unesco Courier*: "When you're inside the building, the light and the spirals of the architecture almost make you forget its contents. You would almost be willing to visit it if it was empty." She can hardly believe the degree to which Abandoibarra, where she spent her childhood, has changed: "Bilbao was a grey city... Now it's white, luminous."

Zulaika was the wittiest and most articulate critic of the Guggenheim project. His *Crónica de una seducción* (1997) is a dazzling account of the risky and often outrageous negotiations which brought together a giant US art institution and a small and culturally undistinguished city. Zulaika's book was understandably sceptical about the Guggenheim's enormous costs to the Basques, but since it has opened he has radically, if provisionally, revised that assessment. Quoting figures from the local paper *El Correo*, he calculates that the Guggenheim has cost the Basques $100 each, or $600 per *bilbaíno*. The building, excluding the cost of the site, cost $100 million. The remodelling of its surroundings was another $20 million, the art itself is worth $50 million and annual running costs are $7 million. A regional government was being asked to underwrite a grandiose US project from floor to ceiling. With supreme chutzpah, the Guggenheim, which was in dire financial straits at the time of the deal, and had been trying to flog this project all over the world, demanded an initial down payment of $20 million for the franchise, simply the right use its magic name.

And yet, as Zulaika expresses it: "Bilbao was the city that, by appropriating the monies formerly destined for Basque culture, *went for it.*" Basque language programmes, Basque cinema, Basque theatre, Basque libraries, Basque music, even Basque visual art, all suffered slashing cutbacks. The PNV, with its history of passionate commitment to indigenous life, appeared to be selling its soul. Even Thomas Krens, the Guggenheim plenipotentiary who liked to be described as having "balls of bronze", seemed amazed at how fast and how far his Basque counterparts were prepared to roll over. "Seduction: that's my business," Krens said in an unguarded and wine-lubricated moment. "I am a professional seducer. I don't make money but I gather it in, and I have to do that on the basis of seduction… Seduction consists in making people desire what you desire without your having asked for it… In a way, I am the biggest whore in the world.

"The Basques came to eat out of my hand," Krens continued. "I couldn't believe it." His amazement may have been fuelled by the fact that his project had allegedly already been turned down by, among other cities, Salzburg, Vienna, Madrid and Seville. He told me at the opening that "I would never have put Bilbao on my list of one hundred possible cities. The Basques came to me and asked me how they could change the misconception that they were famous only for terrorism and Jai Alai handball. I told them they should build the greatest building of the century."

And perhaps they have. Certainly, the PNV negotiators saw the Guggenheim as a kind of stimulant to propel the Basque Country into the future: "the country needs a challenge and this was going to be it," they said. A declining Bilbao was not an option. Sabino Arana's party jettisoned the founder's distaste for urban life in his native city, and made the post-modern metropolis its new international flagship. The countryside was fine for Basque nostalgia, but the big city was where the new Basque Country would be made or broken. But who could say if such an unconventional strategy—sparking an economic revival with an art gallery, and a foreign one at that—was going to work? The PNV knew, says Zulaika, that "this was a huge gamble (they likened it to 'playing in a casino'). But this was no time for timid souls. It was the moment for risk-taking, seduction, gambling, believing." Gambling is part of being Basque. The deal was on. "It is a bet for the future," the Basque cultural minister, Karmen Garmendia, said at the opening.

And, as far as anyone can tell so far, the wager has paid off handsomely. Bilbao has been comprehensively re-branded. It is now part of the e-future rather than a relic of the industrial past. It figures in international glossy magazines as a centre of excellence rather than as a nest of terrorists—though ETA killed an *ertzaina* on its doorstep, in an apparent plot to assassinate King Juan Carlos at the opening. The proof of the success of the high-risk Guggenheim strategy is that, big and brash as the museum is, it is now only a part of the story of Bilbao's ongoing reinvention.

Washing the City's Face, Lifting its Citizens' Hearts

Industrial Bilbao used to "wear its ugliness like a badge of honour", in Zulaika's words. In the early 1980s it could still seem like a film set for a fascist Hades, designed by some deeply depressed expressionist. The smog still lay heavy above the streets, the buildings were caked in grime, and the dim and patchy street lighting often revealed shadowy police at every corner. Those were the days of the "Battle of Euskalduna", as workers resisting redundancy at the historic shipyards clashed with riot squads in a violent daily ritual on Deusto bridge.

The US artist Richard Serra responded warmly to this muscular contempt for conventional beauty. "Wow, Bilbao, the Tough City", he famously declared when he first visited the Basque Country in this period. He called his friend Frank Gehry to tell him about it. He made monumental sculptures out of its colossal industrial flotsam, but he was a little ahead of his time. He offered his sculpture *Bilbao* to city officials, for the cost of the material. They rejected it, and it was dumped outside the Museo de Bellas Artes, a fine but distinctly provincial art gallery, until a private collector recognized its value.

"This was the least hospitable city in all of Spain," wrote Jon Juaristi. But it was beginning to change. The PNV took the first steps towards refurbishment around this time. And when Bilbao's face was thoroughly washed, it turned out to have surprisingly attractive features. Dull, indistinguishable blocks of buildings on the river front revealed unexpected individuality, and even elegance, when a century's grime was sandblasted off them. The glass on their *miradores* (bay windows) gleamed again, and the wooden beams and iron balconies that made these houses Basque were gaily repainted in reds, greens, blues, whites and blacks.

The positive comments made by visitors to pre-industrial Bilbao began to be recalled. Wilhelm von Humboldt, the great German linguist whose pioneering studies of Euskera began a worldwide fascination with the enigma of the language, came to the city at the very beginning of the nineteenth century. He wrote that its "white and amiable houses glitter through the verdure of the trees," and judged it "in many respects the most charming [city] of the Basque Country." He also commented on its clean and pleasing paving, and the efficiency of its sewerage system.

As late as the middle of the nineteenth century, that view was being confirmed by travel writers like Henry O'Shea, in his *Guide to Spain and Portugal.* He thought Bilbao pretty insignificant architecturally and historically, but found "remarkably clean" streets, maintained with "with Dutch-like scrupulosity, for we have never seen at Amsterdam or The Hague anything to compare to it."

One would not go quite as far as that, even today, but those lovely glass *miradores,* their frames picked out in fine detail, have a shine about them which is almost inconceivable to anyone who walked the *ribera* (riverside) or the streets of the *casco viejo* before 1995.

It is not just the tourists who are enthusiastic. Fernando Egileor is a *bilbaíno* who spent many years in ETA, and remains an uncompromising advocate of revolutionary socialism and Basque independence. Yet he, too, says that he has been won over by some aspects of the renewal. Having dismissed the art in the Guggenheim as "decadent cosmopolitan garbage", he pauses and allows himself a smile. "But every time I turn a corner and see that building," he admits ruefully, "it lifts my heart."

Jokes on the Path to Spectacular Success

Visitors to Bilbao today may have their hearts lifted before they even glimpse the Guggenheim. The city's cramped airport terminal used to have all the charm of a wet Monday in any declining provincial city anywhere. Now it has been torn down and replaced by a shimmering glass wonder, hung on white elliptical arches, something like the rib cage of a whale. The designer is another star architect, Santiago Calatrava, from Valencia. Loiu airport gives the traveller a curious sense of continued suspension between the earth and sky. The visitor is clearly also being sent a less ethereal message. The curves of the terminal are extravagantly duplicated in the car park opposite. You have arrived, the building is telling us, in the ante-room to a wealthy, dynamic, and innovative economy. Those who are familiar with the history of the region may briefly wonder, however, whether the whale is of the killer variety.

The word *bilbainada* has been coined by the inhabitants to describe the process whereby the city has reinvented itself. A *bilbainada* is one of a series of "exorbitant projects that appear to be so out of synch with the resources at hand that they become jokes, but [they are jokes] along the path to spectacular success. We are fortunate to have the original patent," says Zulaika. Bilbao's extravagant refurbishment becomes a kind of pot-latch, reversing the city's tradition of discretion in the display of wealth.

The short drive from Loiu airport plunges dramatically into the city over the Salve bridge, so called because it was the point on the river from which returning mariners saw the basilica of the Virgin of Begoña, and sang a *Salve Regina* in her honour. Now the bridge is a vantage point for another kind of worship: it offers a spectacular overview of the necklace of *bilbainadas* stretched out along and behind the riverfront Abandoibarra district. The gleaming titanium mass of the Guggenheim just downriver will inevitably catch your eye first, but the delicate and elegant ZubiZuri bridge should also draw your gaze upstream. Its delightful airy curves of cable, concrete and glass conjure up images of an archer's bow drawn from bank to bank, or the skeletal fin of some great sea-creature. The *ZubiZuri* (WhiteBridge) is another brainchild of Santiago Calatrava.

This broad footbridge in turn draws attention to the ample, well-lit walkways that now run alongside the river from the Guggenheim to the town hall. These offer swathes of space for leisurely *paseos* in a zone that was, as recently as the 1980s, almost as gloomy and run-down as the ruinous docklands on the seaward side of the Euskalduna bridge, designed by Javier Manterota. And this imposing sky road, with its giant right-angle softened by a curve in its elbow, is itself a remarkable feat of sinuous engineering, the opposite of the ZubiZuri in terms of scale and aesthetics. It is a statement of power rather than elegance, but not without its own stark beauty.

The quays directly underneath the Euskalduna bridge have been spruced up to house a maritime museum that celebrates the city's rich heritage as a mercantile and fishing port. The sea remains a very significant source of Bilbao's wealth, but as much money was spent on building the Guggenheim as in the construction of a new super-port at the river mouth, a statistic that gives dramatic economic substance to the concept of the *bilbainada*. As we have seen, the Basques spend well above the Spanish average on research and development, with an emphasis on high-end technology. This suggests that the region will voyage further on the internet than on the oceans in the new century.

Standing under this bridge at night, the quayscape to the right is brilliantly lit by a forest of neon trees, reflected in an artificial lake. This display heralds the Euskalduna Jauregui, the Palace of Congresses and Music, a building almost as grandiose as the Guggenheim itself, designed by Federico Soriano and Dolores Palacios. Bilbao has no great tradition in either theatre or classical music, but this complex of giant auditoria with magnificent river views may change that. After all, the city did not have a much tradition of world-beating architecture until very recently.

We Ain't Seen Nothing Yet...

The regeneration of Abandoibarra is still in full swing. More signature buildings will follow, among them another giant conceived by the Argentinian architect Cesar Pelli. At 550 feet, his Torre Iberdrola should tower over every other construction in Bilbao by 2010. Extensive landscaping, including dense tree-planting, is promised as part of the makeover for the whole area, for which Pelli also has overall responsibility.

But it is already clear that this development can go in several directions. There is the joyfully innovative option represented by the Guggenheim, reflecting the city's past as a monstrous metal works, but pointing exuberantly towards the future. Outside the building, the popularity of the "cybernetic fountain" and of Jeff Koons' *Puppy*, composed entirely of flowers, promises playful public spaces on a grand scale. The Euskalduna Jauregui dramatically juxtaposes past and present, with brilliant glass galleries right up against massive façades of deliberately rusted Cor-Ten steel cladding. The design is broadly nautical, in tribute to the ships built at these docks, but the technology in the auditoria, one of which seats more than 2,000 people, is state-of-the-art. The waterfront also pays homage to the past, while playing with the future. Carola, a huge crane from the old docks allegedly named after a beauty the dockers fancied, and other industrial and dockside artefacts, have been preserved. Many of the lighting facilities are modelled on crane-style structures, but the lighting effects create a floating sensation fit for cyber-fantasies.

On the other hand, Robert A. M. Stern's Zubiarte shopping centre, placed between the Guggenheim and the Euskalduna Jauregui in the hope that visitors to either or both will indulge in retail therapy, is vulgar and brash—a Midwestern mall with European cultural pretensions.

Zulaika asked Gehry whether there was a danger that the "tough beauty" of the Guggenheim could not maintain its integrity in a prettified "garden city" context. He says that the architect "hates the very thought... it makes a world of difference whether his building engages in a dialectical image with the recently closed Altos Hornos [smelter], the life blood of thousands of families for centuries, or whether it is assimilated by Abandoibarra's garden city into a sort of Benetton provocative visual shock effect in order to sell the new Bilbao."

No-one can doubt that the new Bilbao is selling very well at present. The question is whether it can be sold with the integrity achieved by Gehry, or will degenerate into a twenty-first-century Legoland. Inevitably the Guggenheim has become a backdrop for pop culture. Paco Rabanne has used the atrium, compared by Gehry to a Gothic cathedral, as a catwalk. Simple Minds have used it as a video location. These are not bad things in themselves, but they hint at the danger that the building itself could become a passing international fashion. Some lines from Bertolt Brecht, written half a century before the Guggenheim was dreamt of, raise the same question:

> Bill's beerhall in Bilbao, Bilbao, Bilbao,
> now they've clean'd it up and made it middle class,
> with potted palms and ice cream,
> very bourgeois, very bourgeois
> just another place to put your ass!

Re-imagining the River
Much of the reinvention of Bilbao has focused on re-imagining the river, turning the citizens towards the historic but long-neglected source of the

city's place in the world. It has aimed at turning an eyesore into a sight for sore eyes, at building bridges where the water had been a wall between rich and poor, at turning a symbol of grinding toil and filthy riches into a gleaming magnet for clean new industries and wealthy tourists. "You are/memory always turning into hope," Unamuno wrote of the Nervión. You needed some kind of faith to see hope in the river in his dark times. Today, the regenerators of the city claim to be giving hope material form and substance.

What makes the Bilbao project really remarkable is the disadvantages it has faced and, so far, overcome. The city's late twentieth-century political and economic climate was been almost as unpropitious to social well-being as its once-polluted atmosphere was to human health. Unemployment soared as the factories closed, reaching sixty per cent among the under-25s. Plans to re-launch Basque industry through nuclear energy fell flat when the almost constructed Lemoiz power plant, twelve miles from the city, was aborted under pressure from ETA attacks. Bilbao's population began to shrink back towards 300,000.

Jon Juaristi, whose literate polemics passionately castigate the PNV, points out that the party actively contributed to the neglect of Bilbao in the early 1980s. It invested more in cities like San Sebastián, which it regarded as more "truly Basque", or Vitoria, which needed boosting as the administrative capital of the region. Ironically, however, while its municipal vote declined elsewhere, the PNV remained very strong in Bilbao. Then disastrous flooding in 1983 massive prompted militant civic demands for reconstruction. The party which had resisted modernity became the unlikely champion of the post-modern urban future.

Among the most futuristic of all the images created by the new Bilbao are the *fosteritos*. These are the big glass carapaces that gather commuters into the cool, clean underworld of the new metro system, created by the British architect Norman Foster (*fosterito* means "little Foster"). Juaristi mocks Basque nationalism's "primitive accumulation... of floating signs, without significance". He asks if the *fosteritos* are "the shells of armadillos, the ribs of dinosaurs, or earthworms?" Such mockery is probably a backhanded compliment—it would be much easier to attack the nationalist administration if it had insisted on re-branding Bilbao with traditional emblems like the *lauburu* or the tree of Gernika. In Zulaika's more sympathetic but still sceptical view, the new Bilbao "appears to be what history requires of Basque society if it is not to remain marginal-ized from modernity's triumphs and failures." And even Juaristi cannot repress a sneaking regard for the "operatic apotheosis" which the nation-alist administration has achieved on Bilbao's riverfront.

Perhaps the real significance of the new metro system is that it works very well, and incidentally offers a rapid tour of the city's shifting land-scapes. It starts in the *casco viejo*. From here you can travel to the heart of the city's business and banking districts, close to the Abandoibarra riverfront. The train will finally carry you to where greater Bilbao opens out to the Bay of Biscay, along the bracing seafront promenades of Getxo, with the palaces of Neguri as a backdrop and new money and old mingling in the sparkling marinas facing the new super-port.

This area is linked to Portugalete on the Left Bank by an engineer-ing marvel of the city's age of iron, the 1893 "hanging bridge" now called the Puente Bizkaia. Inspired by the network of Heath Robinson struc-tures which transported iron from the mines to the river, it was designed by Alberto Palacio. The Guggenheim of its era, it is often compared favourably to the Eiffel Tower, completed four years earlier. Five hundred million people have been carried across the Nervión on this bridge, more than twice as many as have visited its rival in Paris. Only Gehry's museum attracts more visitors in Bilbao today. In July 2006 UNESCO declared it a World Heritage site. You can still make the journey in a cable car, but the vehicle is no longer the Victorian original, rather closer to a space capsule. It offers superb views of the estuary upriver, of the super-port, and the heavily-mined western hills overlooking the Bay of Biscay.

Dark Heart, Dying Mines
To travel to the dark heart that pumped the lifeblood into twentieth-century Bilbao, the local train down the Left Bank offers an intimate view of decaying industrial sites and shiny new projects. Kate O'Brien recalled that this route "through the premises of the most famous foundries—the 'Vizcaya', the 'Altos Hornos', the 'Santa Ana'—where the great fires never went out and where half-naked men moved like unreal creatures through the glare and darkness." Altos Hornos in Barakaldo was a massive steel plant which became as much the symbol of the indus-trial city as the church and bridge of San Antón had been of the medieval

one. Closed in the 1990s, it started to collapse under its own weight. At the last minute one of its famous chimneys was, reluctantly, preserved as an historical heritage site. The new Basque authorities were slow learners when it came to recognizing that this great and grim enterprise represents the city's history too.

Neglect of the recent past is even more evident when you take the junction west and travel away from the river up through the mining valley of Trapagaran to Gallarta, and look for the Museo de la Minería. You might expect that one of Europe's great industrial revolutions would merit a state-of-the-art museum, glittering with high-tech panels expounding the mechanics of Basque mining, and the human culture that created it and endured it. Instead you find a derelict slaughterhouse, turned into an evocative temple of memory by just one man, Carmelo Uriarte, "and half a dozen old pensioners like me".

Uriarte worked all his life in the mines, as had his mother and father before him. "I saw the mines in their heyday," he says. "I remember people arriving from Castile, from Galicia, from Andalusia, filthy and poor, looking for work." Native Basques like his mother took them in as lodgers for a few pesetas extra income. Less lucky immigrants slept in draughty barracks built by the mining companies. Uriarte recalls no problems between the newcomers and native Basques like his own family, commenting only that "the Basques here were mostly the foremen, I don't know, perhaps we are cut out to be in charge."

Despite the poverty and the political repression, there was a vibrant community in these towns and villages during Uriarte's working life, but that was not to last. "In the early 1980s, one mine closed, another was exhausted, then suddenly it was all over, just like that, *pam! pam! pam!* Two hundred mines shut down one after another." The last mine to close was in Gallarta, and this was also the last mine to open, for a brief and profitable life, just as the others were locking up their gates. It left a dramatically altered landscape behind it.

Uriarte walks over to a balsa wood reproduction of the town, the entrance exhibit at the museum. He reaches right inside the model, grasps a handle, and lifts the whole of Gallarta away as if it were a saucepan lid, revealing a gaping black hole underneath. The museum guide, a volunteer, explains: "All the Vizcayan mines were open cast, and they had all been exhausted. Then a company found the best iron remaining was right on the streets of this town. It was cheaper to knock down the town and rebuild it, where we are today, than to dig under it." A glance out of the window confirms her story; nothing in Gallarta, a town founded in the 1890s, is more than fifteen years old. Just across the road from the museum, where the town used to be, there is a gaping hole a thousand feet across, and close to 650 feet deep. Bernardo Atxaga's concept of the instability of the Basque ground once again comes to mind.

The open mine plunges down to the lowest point in Vizcaya open to the sky, eighty feet below sea level. Even after it reached this point, the company kept finding good iron, and kept digging, creating deeper and deeper galleries with chambers "large enough to accommodate Burgos Cathedral." The last mine in the region had become the first underground one. Then, says the guide, "the owners discovered that blacks would work cheaper than we would, and they went to Africa and South America." The mine which moved a whole town sideways closed after just four years, in 1990.

Uriarte, a prodigiously energetic man, found himself made redundant, a condition which did not suit his character. He takes up the story of his museum. "I was a bit of a naturalist, I liked walking, and everywhere I went in these hills I found mining machinery. I thought that all this history should not go to waste, and I started bring things home." He began storing old mining tools under his bed. Unsurprisingly, he ran out of space almost immediately. He then left his finds down at the old slaughterhouse, "which was full of rats and gypsies." The gypsies could hardly believe the wealth that was being deposited on their doorstep. "They stole enough for two more museums," says Uriarte in disgust. He still has skirmishes with them, battling with today's most marginalized group for the relics of yesterday's poverty and wealth.

Gradually, support started to come from the local mayor, and much more recently from Vizcaya's *Diputación* [provincial administration] and the Basque government. You might think that Basque nationalism's traditional distaste for the mines and their immigrant workers was to blame for the initial disregard towards the museum, and there is probably some truth in that. What is much more surprising is that the big trade unions, which suffered their birth pangs and won their first victories in this region, have still not donated a red cent.

Nevertheless, Uriarte's bullish determination is paying off. The slaughterhouse has been more or less secured, though much material is still piled up outside. The archives remain in disarray, collected but not catalogued, and in danger of deterioration. But some people are paid to work in the museum now, and there is even an area with a couple of digital panels. Uriarte never shows them to me. I understand he does not feel that section is "a real museum".

His pride in the displays he has assembled by instinct and hard labour is justified. A prosthetic leg hanging on the wall speaks volumes about the high risk of injury to miners. So does a crude canvas stretcher, with a cover improvised against the inevitable rain. The ore each miner worked was registered by pegs on a primitive wooden abacus. Looking at some of these crude boards, it is easy—to a point—to imagine the misery of trying to fill the quota of little holes day after day, until age, injury or disease ended the deadly routine.

In the nineteenth century the miners started early, in several senses. They worked from sunrise to sunset, six days a week. And a photograph shows children working in the mines in 1883. There is also photographic evidence of a closer association between the Basque mines and Basque agriculture than is generally acknowledged. Peasants brought their oxen, with carved and colourfully decorated yokes, to haul ore to the boats before mining transport became completely mechanized. Some came from as far away as Guipúzcoa.

Another set of images shows revolutionary messages scrawled repeatedly on the rocks: ¡Viva Rusia! and ¡UHP! ("Unite, Proletarian Brothers"). They must both seem almost as archaic to the children visiting the museum as the bison and bears in the Stone-Age murals in the caves of Santimamiñe. And what must the Castilian or Andalusian grandparents of some of these children think when they hear them chattering happily in Euskera, a language mostly lost to this part of Vizcaya for centuries?

One item near the entrance surprises and delights every bilbaíno who visits the museum. This is a poster that links the mines directly to one of the city's great passions: football. Soccer was introduced here by English sailors, who played on the beaches while their ships were unloading. So Bilbao's football team was called "Athletic" (not Atlético, though the name was forcibly hispanized in the Franco period). But there is another apparently foreign word closely associated with the team, which very few natives now understand.

The ritual chant from the city's soccer "cathedral", San Mamés stadium, is *Alirón, Alirón, Athletic Campeón*. It is obvious why the fans want their team to be champions, but what does *Alirón* mean? The Real Academia Española dictionary will tell you that it comes from the Hispanic-Arabic term *al'ilán*, meaning "proclamation". But the mining museum has an explanation from much closer to home. This derives from another import from Britain: mining technicians, who checked the quality of the ore. The miners got a bonus, paltry but critical to their living standards, if they found rock with iron content above seventy per cent. If the technician was English (or Welsh, or Irish), he would write in chalk on such a deposit: "All Iron". Thus *Alirón* became a cry of jubilation for the workers, and eventually made its way onto the city's football pitches, where its origins, like the mines themselves, were rapidly forgotten.

Outside the museum entrance, a slab of limestone bristles like a painted porcupine with colourful manual drills, little more than crowbars. The *barrenadores*, or drillers, practised one of the elite crafts of the mines. Their job was to hammer the drills deep and accurately into the rock to prepare the insertion of explosives. Though this industrial skill is now almost redundant, Uriarte is delighted to report that young men are taking it up again as a competitive sport. It has begun to feature in fiestas alongside such esteemed Basque agricultural competitions as rock-lifting and log-cutting. It was, of course, a familiar skill in small mines and big quarries right across the region. The rift between Basque urban and rural life here has never been quite as wide as conflicting ideologies have painted it, and that fact is, at last, receiving some cultural recognition

The Passion Flower of Revolution

Cultural recognition saved a nearby town, La Arboleda, from the same fate as Gallarta. The most distinctive and historic of all the mining towns, a last-minute heritage preservation order kept the bulldozers at bay from the ore beneath its streets. Its utterly inappropriate name, "the grove", predates the mining period, when all its trees were cut down. Some of them became the town's clapboard wooden houses, unusual in the region. They were built as hostels for the miners. The rather charming examples which survive today, some quite gentrified, belie their origins. Sanitary conditions were appalling, and poor health was exacerbated by the "company store" system which the foreman used to force the workers to eat in nutrition-deficient canteens. Typhoid, typhus and cholera epidemics helped reduce life expectancy to 38 in the last decades of the nineteenth century.

The great strike of 1890 brought military intervention, and even the authoritarian Spanish army officer corps was outraged by what it found. The general in charge of the operation declared the hostels and canteens "unfit for pigs", and forced some reforms on the mine-owners. Thirty-three years later, things had not improved greatly, as Kate O'Brien recalled:

> These villages are awful in their stillness and despair. The crumbling Renaissance church, very filthy inside… the dilapidated girl at the brothel door; boys, pale and stooped, coming up the lane from their shift; a little way off heavily loaded trolleys rattling down the hill. And in the valley the pricking lights of Bilbao, outlines of banks and moving ships, softly sounding horns of Hispano-Suizas.

These conditions bred reformers and revolutionaries who reached the front rank of Spanish politics, including Indalecio Prieto, who would play a key and controversial role in the Republican governments before and during the Civil War. Towering above all her comrades, however, is the figure of Dolores Ibárruri, better known as *La Pasionaria*, the passion flower. She was the communist orator whose *No pasarán* became the rallying cry of the armies of the Republic during the Civil War, and of beleaguered leftist movements internationally ever since.

But it is surprisingly hard to find traces of La Pasionaria in her home territory. She was born in 1895 in Gallarta. Her birthplace, of course, had been erased with most of the old town by the 1980s. Between Gallarta and La Arboleda lies Triano, perhaps the saddest of all the mining villages, a place without much comfort even today. It gives off a hint of what Ibárruri was fighting against. Miners' lamps and miners' tools still hang arbitrarily on the walls of grubby, crumbling houses on the main street, as if the old mines might reopen tomorrow.

The *plaza mayor* in La Arboleda is clean and nondescript today, more like the open empty square of a depopulated Andalusian village than the intimate, bustling centre of a Basque town. It slopes quite sharply away from a podium or bandstand, where Ibárruri first honed her revolutionary rhetoric as a member of the newly born Communist Party of Spain in the 1920s, rhetoric she would use to incendiary effect in the Spanish parliament leading up to the Civil War. Like many survivors of that conflict, Ibárruri's political record is ambiguous. A Bilbao exhibition, three years after her death in 1989, was titled "Passion for Liberty". But she had flourished in exile in Stalin's Moscow, and was an obedient servant of this most repressive ideology. Her late embrace of pluralist democracy was probably more a matter of pragmatic tactics than a change of heart. Yet anyone who wants to understand how such uncompromising revolutionaries are forged should visit these towns and catch a whiff of the grotesque exploitation which put iron in her soul. However, they will not find even a plaque to commemorate her in La Arboleda, not even a photograph in La Sabina, the restaurant where she worked as a waitress. There is a secondary school named in her honour in the new Gallarta, with a bust outside. There is another bust (by Luis Alcalde) in the Bilbao port town of Santurzi, and a minor street named after her in the Ametzola quarter of the city itself. Such modest homage hardly reflects her status as one of the best-known Basques, and certainly the best-known Basque woman, in the world today. It does reflect the fact that neither nationalism nor socialism in today's Basque Country is willing to claim her as one of their own.

Down the hill in La Arboleda's *plaza mayor*, the Socialist Party's club and bar serves "proletarian *pintxos*" (potato and onion) as purely nostalgic items. Around the corner, there was, at least until 2006, a dignified reminder of a world where such humble fare was not optional. To step into the Hermanos Zaragata bar is to take a step back to a time when sausages and black pudding were made daily behind the counter, and there was no entertainment apart from the company of other equally impoverished customers. It seems unlikely to outlast its elderly owners.

The future of the *zona minera* seems to lie in recreation and tourism. Hiking and biking trails have been developed through the hills; parks have been laid out around the dramatic projecting platforms where ore was directly loaded onto ships at sea; waterlogged mining pits have become magnets for anglers. Valleys that echoed to explosive charges and clanking machinery are now silent except for cowbells. A golf course stretches between Triano and La Arboleda. Aitor Uriarte, Carmelo's son, who helps out at the mining museum in his spare time, shares his father's concern that the mining heritage which shaped these hills and the city below them should not be forgotten. "I don't want to see this landscape restored to nature," he says over a steaming bowl of red beans, bacon and pudding in the restaurant where *La Pasionaria* once waited tables. "I want to see the human landscape maintained, the huge changes that were made here left visible and understood by future generations."

Heritage tourism certainly seems to be taking off in the area. There are proposals to open up one or two mines, including Gallarta's vast galleries, for guided tours. Whether there is a market for such visits is another matter. Down towards the coast at Muskiz, the restored forge of El Pobal attracts hundreds of visitors weekly. Dating back to at least the sixteenth century, this water-powered facility smelted iron ore and manufactured everything from swords to ploughshares, and only closed in 1965. It stands on a site associated with witches, and its water comes from a stream named after its mermaids. Yet it is also part of modernity; it is said that a flame was carried from its fire to light the first of the great industrial smelters at Altos Hornos. It has been lovingly restored to the last detail, and at week-ends can be seen in hot and very smoky operation. You can even see the bicycle on which the last owner used to visit the girl he courted in a distant village every weekend for decades, but never married.

This kind of heritage, halfway between craft and industry, rural in setting, reflecting Basque mythology and Basque characteristics like physical strength and business acumen, is enormously popular. It confirms the self-image of Basque nationalism but does not remind us too closely of contemporary conflicts. The Uriartes and their colleagues face a titanic task in their efforts to make the modern mines of Vizcaya equally attractive to the public. Whether or not they, and people like them, succeed will tell us a lot about the capacity of the new order in the Basque Country to cherish all aspects of the history and commerce which made the region what it is today.

Seven Streets

Before moving on from the Bilbao area, let us go right back to the old centre of the city, and linger there a while. The *casco viejo* is a honeycomb of *tapas* bars and hidden temples to Basque gastronomy. The best restaurants are often unobtrusive first-floor rooms with minimal street signage, like the Amboto (currently closed) and Eguiluz. This quarter has not only preserved much of its medieval structure, but has also retained numerous specialist small shops and businesses which exude haunting aromas of the past. This time-shifting sensation intensifies in the early morning. Walk the Calle de la Cruz at 2 a.m., and enjoy the shadow theatre behind the curtained *miradores*, or just feel the warm glow from each of these beautifully crafted window casements, and it is easy to imagine the city of the nineteenth century. Turn a corner and you find yourself staring into the *anteiglesia* behind the Cathedral of Santiago, its back door a glorious field of brass stars on a blue background. These, and scallop shells in relief above a side door, confirm that this is a major staging post on the coastal route of the Camino de Santiago. For a moment even the down-and-outs sleeping in the shelter of its walls might be from five centuries back.

The origin of the city can be traced to the site of the church of San Antón (1433), where a tower originally guarded what may be the earliest bridge over the river. Bridge and church form the centre-piece of Bilbao's coat of arms. The nearby Ribera market was the old *plaza mayor*, as the arcades along the street indicate. The covered market on the riverside today houses a cornucopia of foodstuffs, suffused with tinted light from magnificent stained-glass windows. Shopping as religion, at least when shopping for the dining table, goes back a long way in Bilbao.

An old meander in the Nervión wraps around the area where the city began to develop, from San Antón bridge around to the Arenal. First there were three streets—Goienkale (upper street), Artekalle (middle street) and Barrenkale (lower street). Four more parallel streets were added, making up the *Siete Calles* ("Seven Streets") which became an alternative name for the whole old quarter.

The most frequented part of the *casco viejo* today lies beyond them, between the cathedral which once marked the city limit and the Arenal. This sandy wetland was reclaimed and paved with streets like the Calles Correo and Bidebarrieta. I suspect that these were what Kate O'Brien refers to as "the two long, lively shopping streets of old Bilbao"; she was delighted by "the jewellery, the *turrón*, the astounding corsets and *brassières*." You can still find all these things today, and much more. La Botica

Stained glass and *miradores*: the view from the old Ribera market in Bilbao towards the Siete Calles, the heart of the *casco viejo*.

de la Abuela is a shop dedicated to products based on lavender. At Lau-Lau a huge fillet of cod bubbles lazily all day long in a *cazuela* of golden oil, and you can order an infinite variety of stuffed peppers and croquettes to take home. The *casco viejo* is an Aladdin's cave for collectors, whether your obsession tends towards fantasy comics or philately. There are shops dedicated to exquisite chocolates (though Vitoria is even better, and Bayonne is quite sinfully better again for this commodity). There are emporia for accessories for recreational drugs, and a store devoted to lesbian erotica. One store offers both body-piercing for people, and hairdressing for dogs. Rather more traditionally, Boinas Elósegui offers Basque berets to fit all sizes, in some remarkably extravagant shapes. They are advertised under a marvellous poster of a pink-cheeked, strong-jawed matinee idol who must have turned heads in O'Brien's day.

But where is "the comforting teashop" where she says that "English and Irish exiles huddled and grumbled on wet afternoons"? It might have been the Café Bar Gayarre, with its wonderfully kitsch Andalusian arches and "English velvet" chairs. It is now a tobacco shop but its original fittings have been lovingly restored by its proprietor, Joaquín Perales Lozano, after forty years' neglect. Or it could have been the Café Boulevard facing the Arenal Park, with its echoing wooden floor and receding caverns, each darker, despite the mirrors, and more intimate than the last. Elderly clients here are still brought their newspaper of choice (a fraught matter) without their having to ask. In its innermost chamber a sentence from Unamuno runs around three walls. His words sum up the pleasure of contemplating a golden brandy in its comforting surroundings on a damp afternoon: "What matter if it rains insistently, and, we should admit it, delicately…"

It seems to rain even more often than elsewhere in the rather ugly nearby plaza dedicated to the same writer, at the bottom of the steps which lead up to the basilica of the Virgin of Begoña. A sculpture of Unamuno's head sits awkwardly on a tall column, his sad face gazing towards the new entrance to the metro station, and away from the ethnographic museum behind him. It would not improve his mood to find that, in this city which championed Liberalism, the Carlists have the lion's share of the museum's collection related to the nineteenth-century civil wars. Incredibly, Bilbao's Liberals are not even mentioned in the panel on the first Carlist war, though they then defended the city right in these buildings, under artillery bombardment from the Carlists' positions up the hill at the basilica.

Bearing that kind of bias in mind, the museum is not as melancholy as it used to be, and is worth a visit for its interesting material about Basque agricultural, maritime and domestic life. And in the arcaded cloister at ground level is Mikeldi, a substantial and oddly pleasing sandstone figure from the late Iron Age. Is it a bear, a bison, or a wild boar? A hunting totem or an object of worship, its legs enclosing a solar symbol? No-one knows. Mikeldi is the perfect emblem for the enigma of Basque origins.

The Liberals were better remembered at a fine building in the Calle Bidebarrieta designed by Severino Achúcarro, a prolific Bilbao architect of the late nineteenth century. This was the home of El Sitio, a society dedicated to celebrating Bilbao's resilience against the Carlists. Badly damaged by the 1983 floods, the building has been beautifully restored and now houses the municipal library. A plaque outside commemorates Azorin, pseudonym of José Martínez Ruiz, a close associate of Pío Baroja and coiner of the phrase "Generation of '98". The quotation on the plaque reads: "Bilbao in its greyness makes us think of our empherality, of the maelstrom which sweeps us away... of eternity which has not begun and which will never end."

You might need a pick-me-up after that, and a good place to go is the newest section of the *casco viejo*, the Plaza Nueva, part of the final expansion of the area in the 1850s. It is spacious and pleasant, though without any architectural distinction, and it harbours two of the most irresistible bars for *pintxos* in the whole city, the Victor Montes and the Café Bilbao. Confusingly, there is also a Restaurante Victor, across the plaza, almost as good for food but lacking the art deco elegance of its namesake. Along with delectable bites of squid, artichoke heart or ham, at prices that are still fairly painless, you could sip a glass of the Basque wine, *txakoli*. And the sun may come out, evaporating Azorin's existential gloom. You are on the doorstep of a delightful country, and everything is possible.

The City of Iron Becomes the City of Titanium
The future mapped out for Bilbao has placed it at the apex of an Atlantic Arc, a kind of cultural and commercial bridge linking Santiago de

Compostela in Galicia to Bordeaux in France, whose spans will be high-speed rail links. More ambitiously still, there are those virtual bridges to New York City, and all the other nerve centres of a globalized world.

Bilbao's apparent success is eyed with some anxiety from very different standpoints. The centralist government in Madrid has paid for some of the infrastructure, including the airport, but sometimes fears that the Basques are going too far in building their own links with the outside world. And the whole enterprise is a dramatic challenge to the radicals of ETA who believe that only their pistols and explosives can make the Basque presence felt effectively in Europe and beyond.

Like many ancient European peoples, the inhabitants of the Basque lands, whether Basques or not, once made their presence felt for posterity by constructing the Stone-Age equivalent of *bilbainadas*—the enormous megalithic tombs that still dominate some Pyrenean and Cantabrian landscapes. Long before the new Bilbao was dreamed of, Oteiza claimed the dolmens as prototypes of vanguard art. This time around, the Basques have started with an art gallery, built amidst the graveyards of their more recent industrial past. Time will tell whether they have been guilty of hubris, or have become the architects of a most unlikely urban resurrection.

"It is the hour for the city of iron to become the city of titanium," Zulaika wrote, half mockingly, half in awe, as the opening of the Guggenheim approached. What this shift means is still unfolding, but it is happening right now, and it is very exciting to witness it.

Chapter Eight

From the Music of Labour to Music as a Labour of Love

If it exists in the Basque Country, it exists everywhere.

Juan Mari Beltran

"When a boat is rocking gently on the sea, in my village we call that *kulunka*, but you could just as well say *kilinka,* or *kilin-kala* and so on. Our language is full of these kinds of onomatopoeic expressions," says Txomin Artola, singer-songwriter and poet. This love for onomatopoeia is evident in many elements of Basque music, but perhaps most notably in the *txalaparta*. The rhythmic notes of this strange instrument, echoing through empty stone streets just before dawn, are dramatic and mesmerizing: *Tta-kun, tta-kun, tta-kun, tta-kun, tta-kun, tta-kun; ta-ka, ta-ka, ta-ka, ta-ka, ta-ka, ta-ka...*

These sounds are made by two men hammering vertically with stout sticks on two thick planks of wood, laid horizontally on straw pads on top of stools, boxes, or upturned buckets. The instrument looks like a primitive xylophone. Its musical range is very limited, but it is remarkably expressive. The *txalaparta* can suggest galloping horses, distant thunder, or the pitter-patter of hailstones on glass. It sounds remarkably similar to the challenge call of the capercaillie, a large game bird still found in the Basque forests. *Txalapartaris* can find a variety of tones in the same piece of wood, but their skill is essentially percussive.

This evocative instrument has become an icon of antediluvian Basqueness. The *txalaparta* almost insists that our fantasies take flight to visions of Neolithic Pyreneans pounding on wood outside their caves. Fanciful accounts of its origins abound: it was a signalling system, a proto-Morse code between the deep valleys; it was a warning of approaching enemies; it was a call to war. These images, credible enough in principle, are satirized in Julio Medem's film *The Red Squirrel*, when a

Sound of celebration, sound of cider: there are many speculative stories about the origins of the *txalaparta*, which almost vanished but is now a feature of every Basque fiesta; it seems most likely to have developed out of festivities associated with cider-making.

Basque rock band, with a *txalaparta* for percussion, makes an excruciatingly bad promo video in "Stone-Age" costumes on a barren mountainside.

The musicologist Juan Mari Beltran has been one of the main figures responsible for bringing the *txalaparta* and other dying Basque instruments back to life. His account of its origins, based on the oldest reference he could find, is relatively mundane. Far from pre-dating the Flood, this reference is surprisingly recent, though it does describes the "chalaparta" as a "very ancient Guipuzcoan custom which is still observed today." In an 1882 book on Basque cider-making Severo Aguirre Miramón saw the instrument as an event rather than as just an instrument, as a "manifestation of rejoicing" to celebrate the end of the cider-pressing. He added: "during the 'Chalaparta' jubilation is expressed by uttering certain shouts or strange cries called 'Irrintziac'." The *irrintzi*, an ear-splitting whoop of joy—or war-cry—something like the whinny of a wild horse, is still heard frequently at Basque celebrations today.

When he began researching the *txalaparta* in the 1960s, Beltran found that it was still played by just a few pairs of brothers in the cider-making areas of Lasarte and Astigarraga, and that they indeed used the instrument to celebrate the completion of the year's cider-pressing with neighbours who had helped out in the tradition of *auzolan* (see p.152).

He sees it as a transitional instrument, between those actually used in labour and those used purely to make music. In *The Txalaparta, Forerunners and Variants* (2004) he traces the close relationship between music and labour in the Basque context. The threshing of gorse for winter fodder (*Ote Jotzea*), for example, was performed by several people thumping long sticks with bladed ends (*trabazas*). They developed recognizable rhythms which greatly eased the tedium of the task. One of the labourers he has recorded (the practice has now died out) remembers his father admonishing him, again and again: "Music, music, you must do *Ote Jotzea* with music!"

Then there is music made by work instruments, though not while actually working. Beltran has unearthed another defunct ceremony from the Araitz valley in Navarre. The first phase of building a house was celebrated by the stonemasons striking measuring bars of different lengths with two chisels. This practice went by the wonderfully onomatopoeic title of *ttinbilin-ttanbalan*. Beltran points out that the *txalaparta* is a further step in this process from work-music towards purely recreational performance because, though associated with labour, neither the sticks nor the planks used as instruments were actually employed in cider-pressing.

Beltran started playing in the streets of San Sebastián as a teenager in the 1960s, and rapidly became a pivotal figure in the flourishing revival of folk music and folk dance at that time. He played the *txistu* (Basque flute) like a pied piper, drawing a river of young people into the turbulent sea of Basque cultural politics and political culture. A gentle bear of a man, he has gone through a complex evolution since then. This evolution is graphically demonstrated in the marvellous variety of exhibits in the museum of the Herriko Musikaren Txokoa, the music centre he has developed with Oiartzun town council.

"When we started off, we took out the *txistu* to say we were Basque, not to say that we were musicians," he says. Basque instruments were like surrogate Basque flags, he continues, a demonstration of identity when overtly political demonstrations were suppressed. But even the tunes

Beltran played attracted police batons on more than one occasion. He travelled the Basque Country, south and north, with influential figures like the director of the folk ballet group Argia, Juan Antonio Urbeltz, and the sculptor and ideologue Jorge Oteiza.

Oteiza's contribution to contemporary Basque cultural thought is controversial and contradictory. He was a man of enormous and generous energy who inspired a generation with his assertion, on the solid basis of his own brilliant and internationally acknowledged work, that Basque culture had a rightful place in the vanguard of modernism. But this international perspective seems undermined by his dogmatic insistence on a Basque "essence", rooted in Neolithic culture, which must throw off all corrupting Latin influences. His writing often seems eccentrically exclusive at best, and close to racist at worst.

Yet Beltran, whose own mature analysis seems much more cosmopolitan and inclusive than Oteiza's, remembers his contribution warmly. He travelled with them on every bus trip "and never shut up for a moment, questioning everything we did." From Oteiza he learned that "traditional music is not old music, traditional music is the music you play today, tradition is living, it is different every time you play it."

Saved from Extinction: the *Alboka*
Another old instrument which fascinated Beltran was the *alboka*, a small single fixed reed horn, which is most unusual in having two parallel tubes with three stops on one tube and five on the other. In the 1930s Rodney Gallop found only six *albokaris* in all the Basque Country, and there were fewer when Beltran set out on the trail of the instrument. "They just played at home, they had no social function in fiestas. The *alboka* had really already disappeared from the Basque public world by the nineteenth century," he says. He was baffled that the remaining players were so good: "They were brilliant, they had polyphonic tricks that it really stretched all my ability to learn." Their repertoire, however, was perilously small, perhaps twenty pieces in all with no individual player knowing more than six.

"We learned several things from this," he says. "First we learned that the *alboka* was not a poor or obsolete instrument, there was gold there and we could preserve it and transmit it. Secondly, we had to develop the repertoire ourselves if the *alboka* was to survive. Thirdly, we had to stop thinking of instruments like the *alboka* only as symbols, only as something which represents us as Basques. This is a musical instrument, for musical purposes which go beyond these original motives."

That third point is a principle which Beltran has applied rigorously in the museum. More than 1,000 instruments from five continents are lovingly displayed there. Twenty years ago, the *alboka* might have been presented as an instrument as unique to the Basque Country as its language appears to be. Here it is shown with closely related horns from Madrid, Morocco, and elsewhere.

For a long time it did appear that there was indeed a unique aspect to the *alboka*: all the other horns have five stops on each tube, not three on one and five on the other. Far from seeing this as proof of Basque originality, it spurred Beltran to keep seeking something similar. "If it exists in the Basque Country," he says, "it must exist everywhere." Not quite everywhere, perhaps, but in 2006 he was relieved to find a Turkish instrument, the *tulun*, where two of the five stops on one tube are always blocked with wax.

This stress on universality is a major paradigm shift from the simplistic cultural nationalism of the 1960s, and suggests a new confidence. "Basque folklore has tended to make what is general very particular," he says. While treasuring what is indeed particular about Basque traditions, he now wants see everything Basque in a much broader context.

Beltran is thus at the opposite end of the argument from the purists who saw no place in the Basque sound spectrum for popular instruments of foreign origin. The accordion arrived in the Basque Country with French and Italian railway workers in the late nineteenth century. It rapidly became ubiquitous among folk groups and in fiestas, but for a period some cultural commissars insisted it could not be "Basque". In the 1950s accordion players like Jacinto Rivas (known as Elgeta) and Eleuterio Tapia were considered disreputable, bohemians or even vagabonds, and Elgeta died in the poorhouse. The Tapia family, however, has taken the tradition to new heights in the work of Eleuterio's son Juan and his nephew Joseba. Meanwhile, Kepa Junquera has used the instrument to cross-fertilize Basque airs with jazz and rock styles, and has become the first Basque contemporary musician with a big international following.

Beltran also wants to move beyond a kind of musical sectarianism which has developed within the cultural expression of Basque national-

Alien instrument? Some purists were unable to accept the accordion as Basque, though it is central to popular music in Euskal Herria today, because it was introduced by Italian railway workers in the nineteenth century.

ist politics. The *txistu* tends to be identified as the instrument of the PNV, and the *txalaparta* is linked to Batasuna and rallies for ETA prisoners. Though he has worked personally on the latter, he strongly rejects the allegation that the *txalaparta* has symbolized a call to arms, that it has, in the words of one newspaper correspondent, "become stained with blood."

"No, no, it's festive instrument, always a festive instrument. My concern is to make the public aware of the *musical* qualities of the instrument in every context," he insists. "Historically it was never used for war, and it is not used to arouse warlike feelings now. New generations give it new social and musical functions, of course. And if people see it as a symbol of Basque identity and Basque particularity, fine. But in the first and last place it is always a musical instrument."

Chapter Nine

Obaba in Asteasu: the Basque Village as a Literary Universe

Places are much more than what they seem.

Bernardo Atxaga

The best-known contemporary Basque novelist, Bernardo Atxaga, did not have to leave home to find his literary universe, to which he has given the name "Obaba". Four villages and their hinterlands formed his youthful imagination: Alkiza, Albiztur, Zizurkil and, especially, Asteasu. These villages of what he calls "forgotten Guipúzcoa" are tucked away in the hills under Mount Ernio, but they are only half an hour from San Sebastián. "This is not a territory," he says, "this is a world."

Many of Atxaga's novels are set in this world, which also gave him the title for his most widely read work to date, *Obabakoak* ("The People of Obaba"). The events which take place in his fiction are sometimes fantastic or surreal. His narrators can be snakes or squirrels, eavesdropping and commenting on human conversations. A troubled orphan boy turns into a white wild boar, a creature from a medieval illuminated manuscript. He is hunted down by his peers, and killed by a man who may be his father. But these tales are hardly stranger than the stories which were told, as matters of fact, to the young Atxaga.

This might give the impression that Atxaga is an anthologist of folk culture, a purveyor of backward-looking nostalgia. On the contrary, he is a sophisticated post-modern writer, drawing from influences as diverse as Evelyn Waugh and Jorge Luis Borges. He weaves inter-textual tapestries informed with a gentle but clear-eyed sensibility, at once humorous and melancholic. He takes the world of Obaba simply as his starting point, showing us that a hidden corner of the Basque Country is indeed a world, a universe, much more than it seems.

A farmyard opens directly onto the main street of Asteasu, just a few

Farmhouse on main street, suburban bungalow in the countryside: the interpenetration of urban and rural in Asteasu, and throughout the Basque Country, is ubiquitous, but sharp lines are still drawn between *baserritarrak* and *kaletarrak*.

houses up from the home where Atxaga grew up in the 1950s and early 1960s. There is a crudely built hay barn beyond the yard, still in use in the summer of 2006. Beyond that again is an open field, rising steeply towards a little rounded hilltop. Here stands a brand new house designed to look like a farmhouse, but which is in fact a suburban dwelling, similar to thousands of *neo-baserriak* in the comfortable outskirts of Bilbao or San Sebastián.

Walking in the other direction from the writer's family home, you come quickly—the village is very small—to *Lege-Zarran Enparanza*, the plaza of the Fueros. It has most of the elements you might expect: an eighteenth-century town hall with a portico, two or three equally venerable big houses, and a couple of bars. There are sculptures commemorating native sons, both very influential in their respective traditions: a *bertsolari*, Pedro José Elizegi *Pello Errota* (1840-1919) and the accordion player, Eleuterio Tapia, who died in 1988.

At first sight it appears that one of the typical components of a village centre, the *fronton*, is missing. Instead, a very smart rectangular wooden frontage dominates one side of the plaza. The wood frames a single assembly of big glass windows, all smoked dark grey. This confidently post-modern architectural statement sits surprisingly well in its surroundings, a kind of Guggenheim-effect in miniature. And the nicest surprise is that it is not an office block. It is a gym, where the citizens of Asteasu can exercise while looking out on their central social space, without being seen themselves. And behind the gym there is, in fact, a fully covered-in *frontón* of Olympic proportions. If that were not enough, part of the side of the *frontón* has been converted into a climbing wall with bolted-on handholds and footholds. The young people of Asteasu will be well prepared for the rock faces of the Pyrenees—or for a crevice in the Himalayas, where Atxaga situates a strangely evocative melodrama of adultery and revenge in *Obabakoak*.

Atxaga's novels, and his essays, frequently explore the intimate yet very tricky relationship between town and country, ancient and modern, in Basque culture. An outsider might think the ubiquitous proximity between the two worlds, especially but not only in Guipúzcoa, would mean a blurring of distinctions. If there is a maize field on main street, and a chemical factory is surrounded by cow pasture, if you can take a jacuzzi overlooking a seventeenth-century plaza, have not the urban/rural and old/new boundaries disappeared? Yet many Basques still draw sharp lines, invisible to others, between the *kaletar* (street-dweller) and the *baserritar* (farm-dweller), and the third traditional class of Basque person, the *arrantzale* (fisherman).

Atxaga still sees these lines in his daily life. A relative of his who is from an *arranzale* background recently told him that he would not buy an attractive apartment because the neighbours were *kaletarrak* "and therefore very boring people". But the writer thinks that the key distinction today is not so much between town, countryside and the sea as between "antiquity" and "modernity": "Things changed less here, and in many other places, between the time of Jesus Christ and the coming of television, than they have changed between the coming of television and today." He believes that people like himself, who grew up in the 1960s, are uniquely privileged, because they have a foot in both worlds. Straddling them, however, could be very painful.

David, the protagonist of Atxaga's *Soinujolearen semea* ("The Son of the Accordionist", 2003), says that 1960s Obaba was "the homeland of his childhood and youth". A casual urban visitor to Obaba at that time would no doubt have described the whole place as "the countryside", and would probably also have said that it all its inhabitants were stuck in the past. Yet David lives in a very divided place. His parents send him to school in San Sebastián, where he is thought to be "misanthropic" and sent for psychological assessment because he has so little interest in his classmates. The psychologist attributes his condition to his "attachment to the rural world", and to his "confusion" between "old values" and "modern ones". His father, who is definitely a *kaletar*, reproaches him for spending time in farmhouses and for "not knowing where he belongs." But while David indeed loves his uncle's farmhouse and stables, he has almost no knowledge of rural skills, and envies his friend Lupis, who does.

Paradoxically, it is David's "rural" uncle who will teach him the realities of the world beyond Obaba's borders. His uncle also sparks his awareness of the dark world of Obaba's fascist past, a world which his father wants to keep hidden from him. And it is at his uncle's farmhouse that David will find a link between that past and a possible future. It is here that he first meets members of ETA, which is striving to modernize nationalism with a Marxist gloss, and bring to birth a new Basque Country.

But David, like his uncle, can ultimately find no place in his homeland, even under democracy, and moves to his uncle's ranch in California. His predecessors in Western exile, the nineteenth-century Basque shepherds, lonely mountain men, are famous for their sad and often erotic tree-carvings. Unlike them, he finds great if transient happiness with an American woman. But like the shepherds, he wants to leave his mark, and writes a memoir in the shadow of terminal illness.

In its final pages we find a man reflecting with dismay on developments in the land of his birth. He learns that the erstwhile victims of oppression have themselves become executioners. Critical and independent spirits like his old leftist teacher live in fear of assassination from Basque radicals. In a typical Atxaga touch, however, the version we receive of this memoir is inherently unreliable. It has been edited, and to an extent rewritten, by David's great friend and former ETA comrade, Joseba, a writer who treads a fine line between loyalty and treachery.

Walking the streets of Asteasu in 2006, Atxaga moves rapidly between different worlds, between town and country, ancient and modern, his biography and his fiction. Climbing the steep hill to the church, where he went to infant school, he points to the wall of an agricultural outhouse:

> A few years ago a man I knew was sealing a hole there. He asked me if I knew what it had been used for. "So the cat could get in?" I asked. "No," he said, "it was made to lock up a little boy called Manueltxu. He was bitten by a rabid dog, and turned into a dog himself. When anyone came by, he used to bark and howl. And that went on until he died." "So what was the hole for?" "For his food. His mother came here twice a day and put a plate through the hole, with great care not to get bitten."

Atxaga lets all the ambiguities hang in the air. Was the man who told him the story spinning a line for the benefit of the local writer? Did the man think the boy had really turned into a dog, or was this another way of saying rabies had driven him mad? In an essay, *El Mundo de Obaba*, he tells several similar stories which he gleaned from people in the area. There was a seventh son of a seventh son who had a cross on his tongue and could cure rabies; there was a woman who died, her granddaughter was convinced, with a snake hissing inside her lungs. The question is not whether these stories are true or false; they simply belong to another time, another world. The story of Manueltxu was the starting point for the boy who became the hunted boar in *Obabakoak*. It is the terror and sadness of these stories, rather than their precise "facts", which ring true for him.

Sometimes, however, the outsider can think they have seen something out of this world around about Asteasu, and the locals know it is something perfectly normal. Atxaga recounts one such occurrence with mischievous delight. The roads through the hills around these villages twist back and forth in tortuous hairpins. One dark and misty night, a group of French students went for a walk, and rushed back to their hostel claiming that they had seen a UFO, not once but several times. The locals let them believe it, but knew they had seen the evening bus. Its powerful headlamps often created strange effects in the mist as it negotiated a road that repeatedly vanished and reappeared among the hills.

And then there are those events which, while in no way supernatural, might have been scripted by a magic-realist filmmaker. There are several open fields on the road to the church in Asteasu. Most are obviously agricultural, but Atxaga points out some exotic plants in one of them, which suggest a garden, not a farm. "One of the biggest houses in the village stood here when I was a schoolboy," he says. "And one day it simply disappeared. The whole area is honeycombed by a gypsum mine, and a chamber underneath the house caved in. No-one was killed, but I remember we got off school for the rest of the day."

I am not entirely sure whether he is making this up. But on one of the roundabouts entering the village there is a sculptural group commemorating, in socialist realist style, the mineworkers. Someone has stuck put a small sticker with the ETA symbol, the axe and the serpent, on a muscular buttock.

Truths Wrapped in a Tissue of Fictions

One of the central narratives in *Obabakoak* revolves around a school photograph, taken on the steps of a church. Looking at a blow-up of the picture years later, the narrator realizes that one of the schoolboys is slipping a lizard into another boy's ear. He remembers that his mother told him not to sleep on the grass, because a lizard could get into his brain through his ear. It would shatter his ear-drum, she said, and make him simple-minded. Then he recalls that the lizard-victim in the photo has indeed become both deaf and mentally handicapped. Atxaga plays deftly with the multiple possibilities offered by this scenario. He finally opts for a disturbing conclusion in which the narrator himself falls victim to dementia, possibly lizard-induced, which of course makes the whole story retrospectively unstable.

Approaching the church steps, he casually says "that is where our school photograph was taken." For a moment, it is not clear which world we are in. Sometimes the two worlds overlap directly. Atxaga points across a green valley from the church, to where the walls of a roofless *baserri* are crumbling into the ground. "That is the farmhouse of the family of Joseba Arregui," he says. "They never got over his death." Arregui was a real-life classmate of Atxaga's, who later became an *etarra* and was tortured to death by the Spanish police. Those events are mentioned in an aside which forms part of the school photograph episode in

Life and art, photograph and fiction: Bernardo Atxaga is on the far left of the second standing row in this image from his schooldays. Joseba Arregui, who became a member of ETA and was tortured and killed by the Spanish security forces, is in the centre, above and to the left of the girl with the white jersey and plaits. Arregui also features in the school photograph which is central to the narrative of Atxaga's novel, *Obabakoak*.

Obabakoak , using Arregui's real name. Given the importance of "my father's house" in Basque culture, the sight of a dilapidated farmhouse is unusual anywhere in the region. It is curiously disquieting in these circumstances.

One of the many themes of *Obabakoak* is the relationship between the writer, his work and his life. Atxaga has the narrator of the school photograph episode "confess" that in this instance he will not be behaving like a "writer but solely… as a transcriber" of events he has witnessed. It would be a crass mistake—to a point—to confuse Atxaga with the narrators of the stories he tells. But perhaps Atxaga's position may be like that of Joseba, the writer in *Soinujolearen semea*, who says "I don't know how to speak frankly." Joseba asserts that no human being can tell the truth directly, and that he writes stories because "in some way or other, the truth has to be told."

Atxaga's need to wrap truth in a tissue of fictions, and to set his fictions in real-life contexts, is often playful. But it is far from frivolous. A people whose very existence was officially denied under a forty-year dictatorship, and whose location on the map is still uncertain, needs to find subtle and indirect methods of expressing itself. When Atxaga talks about "the instability of the Basque ground", the phrase resonates from the literal—a land honeycombed with caves, mines, cellars, secret passages—to the political and metaphysical, the shifting definitions of the Basque people, the half-life of Basque superstitions. But, again, there is a personal dimension: I first heard him use the phrase in the context of his own name—or rather names.

Bernardo Atxaga is a literary pseudonym. He started using it in the Franco period, when many of his peers in ETA used *noms de guerre*, and he was writing in Euskera, a practice regarded as suspect by the regime. His real name is Joseba Irazu Garmendia, but he uses the Spanish form, José, on one email address, signs some personal emails "b.a." and uses "Atxaga" as his voicemail sign-off. Since the publication of *Soinujolearen semea*, in many ways the distillation of all his previous work, he has talked about dropping his pen name and returning to the "civil identity" of Joseba Irazu Garmendia.

This multiplicity of names perhaps reflects his commitment to plurality of identity as a key to understanding the Basque Country. He has always written in Euskera, but he translates his work into Spanish (usually with his wife, Asun Garikano). He does not consider Euskera to be the only language of the Basques, but gives full recognition to French and Spanish, and acknowledges other linguistic debts ranging from ecclesiastical Latin to the English of movies and rock music.

Like many of his generation, he felt some sympathy for ETA during the Franco period, and at one point refers to giving "night classes" in economics to people close to the organization. He has never supported violence since the advent of democracy. However, he has swum firmly and bravely against the tide of "anti-terrorist" rhetoric which has swept many Basque intellectuals and artists, including leading former members of ETA, into a knee-jerk reaction against all aspects of Basque ethnicity. He has spoken out against Spanish writers who make sweeping judgements about the Basque Country without any knowledge of it, "dangerous poets seduced by power."

But he is impossible to pigeon-hole. Some of his novels, especially *The Lone Man* and *The Lone Woman*, reveal an intimate understanding of the psychology of individual ETA militants. He is critical of the orthodoxies of both radical and mainstream Basque nationalism. In recent years he has lent his public support to Ezker Batua-Berdeak (United Left-Greens), a small political party unusual in the Basque Country in that it fits into neither Spanish nor Basque nationalist ideological boxes.

Atxaga prefers to think of the Basque Country as an "archipelago" rather than as a country, as a mosaic of many identities rather than a culturally uniform entity. Alternatively, he talks of "the Basque City" rather than of "the Basque People". "The idea of the Basque people is easily romanticized, it suggests unique, essential characteristics. A city is less homogenous, it has density of communication, it is pole of attraction for many people from different backgrounds." His love of the particularities of the landscape, both physical and cultural, is infectious:

> If you look at the Basque Country on a map it looks small, but in reality it is very large because there are so many valleys. And each valley is different. The Liberal armies in the Carlist wars exhausted themselves, simply because they found they were always marching around in circles to come back to the same place.

There are references to high suicide rates due to this phenomenon in a museum in Ormaiztegui dedicated to the Carlist general Tomás Zumalacárregui.

He points out how the maze of valleys and hills has dictated the architectural and social organization of villages here, differently in different periods. "In Asteasu, the church is on top of the hill, and that is where the typical old urban centre was. The main roadways ran along ridges, because it was easier in this country to walk or ride from peak to peak—it was called 'cresting'—than from one valley bottom to another. But the ironworks needed water power, so a second centre usually formed in the valley, from the sixteenth century onwards. The arrival of the train in the nineteenth century definitively brought the commercial heart of the village to the valley floor."

The horizon is rarely far away in this landscape. Atxaga indicates the skyline, perhaps three miles to the north. "The sea is just over those hills. Yet the division is absolute. No-one here would say that they lived near the coast."

Asteasu has recently expanded. A grid of new streets, packed with bijou residences, spreads out behind the town hall. The council wanted to name the biggest street after Atxaga, but he balked at this form of recognition. As a compromise, he asked them to name four other streets after works of four other local writers, but accepted that a street in this new part of town should be called Obaba Kalea. It features bronze plate extracts from *Obabakoak*. To one side of it, an old square has been revamped as a children's playground. Its name, Tranpazulo Plaza, ("Trickery Plaza"), is drawn from local history, not fiction. A sculpture reflecting this history is based on a witty drawing by Mikel Valverde, who illustrates Atxaga's stories for children. It has been sculpted by Tomas Ugartemendia as a relief in slate. Atxaga takes wry pleasure in explaining the background. Basques are often fanatical gamblers, who will bet on a change of wind direction. Many traditional agricultural activities were transformed into competitive sports which attract gamblers, such as rock-lifting and log-cutting and, in this case, hay-mowing. The relief shows two *segalaris* scything furiously, while the spectators exchange bets on the outcome. The real point, however, is that, behind the judge's back, a lot of cheating is going on. On one side, two men are throwing horse-shoes and steel bolts into the path of one competitor, to blunt his scythe. On the other, a man is pouring water onto the grass already cut, which will increase its weight, the factor which determines the outcome of the contest.

Atxaga's nostalgic fondness for such scenes is qualified by other memories of his youth, in which the power of the Catholic Church was still enormous. The Society of Jesus was founded in Loyola, on the other side of Asteasu's dominant mountain, Ernio, by St. Ignatius. The Jesuits were hugely influential in the area. Atxaga remembers some benefits, in that the parish priests were intellectuals with a taste for good music. It was the Franciscans, as the Church's "shock troops", who put the fear of God into the parishioners.

As a boy, he loved the church rituals: "The organ, the Latin, the flowers strewn on the street for Corpus Christi. But as a social force it was, quite simply, horrific. My father told me how his aunt had been expelled from the church's young women's sorority. This meant she was the only girl in the village to walk down the church steps without its conspicuous blue ribbon of membership on a Sunday. Its absence was the mark of a great sin, like Hawthorne's Scarlet Letter in reverse. The only thing she had done was dance a waltz, or some kind of *pasodoble* involving physical contact with a boy, during the fiestas. Other punishments were much harsher. Pregnancies resulted in suicides. One girl in Azpeitia was forced to hide her pregnancy, her clothes asphyxiated her, and she died."

This is the 1930s atmosphere evoked in one section of *Soinujolearen semea*, when a small group of educated liberals in Obaba reflect on their country: "so green outside, so dark within; a black province subject to an equally black religion." They will be shot in the church porch when the fascists take the village in 1936, with active support from many of the Basque-speaking villagers. This bleak image of the heartland of Euskal Herria contrasts sharply with the rural idylls portrayed by traditional Basque nationalism, though it is recognized in histories officially sanctioned by the modern PNV like *El Péndulo Patriótico* (2001).

In any case, Francoism maintained this kind of repressive atmosphere right up to the 1960s, Atxaga says. Then, everything changed: "That was the cutting off point." Many disparate and powerful forces— the emergence of ETA, the arrival of television and rock'n'roll, the creative revival, reinvention almost, of literature in Euskera by poets like Gabriel Aresti—all these things turned the old Basque world upside down. "Quite suddenly, no-one went to church any more. We moved from a very controlled society to a very liberated society overnight, but also…" he hesitates, "to a very trivial society."

For all his pluralism, Atxaga is concerned by the lack of some guiding public ethic in contemporary society. He distrusts the new indulgence of consumerism, the globalization of taste. He fears that we have indeed become, as McLuhan predicted, inhabitants of a global village, but he knows from his own experience that villages can be cruel, ignorant places, much given to malicious gossip—the tabloids—and intolerant of minorities:

> But everything has not been lost here. What I like about the Basque Country, apart from the variety, the sense of what I call the archipelago, is what I perceive as the sense of basic social organization, even though I'm lazy about it myself.

Indeed he is, according to one of his own neighbours in Asteasu, who chides him from the next door balcony as he opens up the family home. "We didn't see you at the fiestas," the man calls out, very friendly but making a point nonetheless. For a second, Atxaga looks like a guilty child who has been caught truanting from school. Then he laughs, happy to be reminded of the values which lie behind the reproach. The price of belonging to a living society is that no-one will hesitate to remind you of your obligations.

More intimate pressure had ensured that he had been to other fiestas nearby in 2006, though he was not admitting that to anyone in Asteasu. "I went to the fiestas of Tolosa, because it's my wife's town and my little girls insisted we go. And what always amazes me at events like this is how many choirs there are, how many dance groups, how many music groups, perhaps thirty in all. And all this has to be organized, rehearsed, prepared. I'm too individualistic to get involved in any of that, but I admire it... Also, everyone goes to the country early in the morning and cuts an ash plant, because the tradition is to carry one all day. It sounds like a small thing, but the social organization, the social network behind all this is amazing."

He talks of this kind of tradition as based on *auzolan*, the Basque rural practice of sharing or exchanging periods of intense labour, like harvesting with neighbours, followed by communal celebration. "This is based on a profound reality," he says, "it is the opposite of all that's trivial. If you don't do something to sustain a sense of animation in your community, life falls away, it collapses."

Atxaga has now moved to Zalduondo, an even smaller village in a very different landscape to that of Asteasu: the *llanada* or flatlands of Álava's cereal country. And he finds that one of his neighbours, because he happens to have a tractor with a snow shovel, always clears everyone else's driveways when it snows. "He even does it for people he doesn't particularly like."

And here, in his new home, Atxaga found a way of participating in the *auzolan* of the local fiestas which dovetails neatly with his profession. Even tiny Zalduondo has its own traditions. One of them is that a kind of scarecrow, called Marquitos, is blamed for all the bad things that happened during the previous year. He is given a necklace of coloured eggs, and hauled off to death by burning. First, though, a prosecutor, in disguise, must give an account of recent events, including births, marriages and deaths, in doggerel. Who better to write the script than the local writer? Since the dominant language of the *llanada* is still Castilian ("though Euskera is growing here"), he did it in Spanish, but with typical pluralism included phrases in Basque, French, English and even, he claims, Chinese.

Putting Euskera on the Literary Map

Atxaga carries his own burden. Being *the* local writer on a larger stage, being the one Basque novelist writing in Euskera whom people outside the Basque Country are likely to have heard of, troubles him. First and foremost, the perception of his solitary eminence is itself a distortion of the reality of the lively literary scene in the Basque language today, and for the last thirty years. Talk to any literate *euskaldun*, and you will find that Atxaga's name is one among many, albeit a distinguished one.

Anyone who thinks the level of literary sophistication Atxaga achieves in Euskera is the exception which proves the rule should seek out the work of writers like Ángel Lertxundi, Ramón Saizarbitoria, Arantxa Urretabizkaya and Joseba Sarrionaindia. Saizarbitoria's *Gorde nazazu lurpean* (Keep Me under the Earth, available in English as *Rosetti's Obsession*) is a collection of five novellas united by the theme of disinterred corpses. His black humour hits multiple targets with painful accuracy. They range from the less-than-heroic record of some *gudaris* (Basque soldiers) in the Civil War to a writer's incapacity to seduce a woman without the text which had done the trick with a previous lover. The bleak parody of erotica with which this story concludes is very shocking, not for its anatomical explicitness, but for its convincing entry into the mind of someone incapable of distinguishing between art and life.

Another of these writers, Sarrionaindia, has taken the confusion of these two categories to extremes. A brilliant essayist, poet and writer of very short "hybrid texts", he was imprisoned in 1980, accused of membership of ETA. Five years later he escaped, hidden in a loudspeaker used by a Basque singer, Imanol, who had been performing for the prisoners. Since then, Sarrionaindia has continued publishing work from underground. His first full-length novel, the acclaimed *Lagun izoztua* (The Frozen Friend) was published in 2001. Its subject? The alienation experienced by *etarras* living in exile.

This Basque generation also includes Sarrionaindia's antithesis, Jon Juaristi, who has swapped youthful militancy in ETA for erudite polemics in favour of Spanish conservative positions. Juaristi, however, now writes mainly in Spanish, and his work is mainly non-fiction. It is Atxaga's unique combination of success in Euskera and in international translation which has given him a "representative" function for all Basque writers today. He has reflected long and often on the condition of literature in Euskera—partly because he gets asked the same questions so many times.

He talks about the dangers of the *estereotiposfera*, the "zone of stereotypes" in which newcomers to the subject are likely to be led astray. The first is that Basque is a "primitive" and "rural" language, a view endorsed, with very little first-hand knowledge, by influential hispanophiles like Gerald Brenan. That notion should have been dispelled, at least in recent decades, by the presence of Euskera in the science and technology departments of Basque universities, but it persists. And from that stereotype there follows the idea that Euskera is a purely oral culture, without a literary tradition or an extensive vocabulary. "Why do you not write," people ask him, "in a less limited language?"

Atxaga's response to this is two-pronged. On the one hand, there *is* a significant literary tradition, which opens with Bernart Dechepare's *Lingua Vasconum Primitiae*, a book of secular, religious and erotic poetry printed in Bordeaux in 1545. Significantly, it includes a hymn to the Basque language itself, which was turned into a popular song by Oskorri, a folk group, in the 1970s.

> Euskara,
> get out onto the street!
> Many people thought
> writing in Basque was impossible.
> Now they recognize
> They were deceiving themselves.

Nearly a century later, the masterpiece of early Basque literature, *Gero* ("Later") appeared. The author of this thesis on the evils of procrastination was another French Basque, Pedro Daquerre Azpilicueta, parish priest of Sara, much better known by his pen name, Axular, and regarded by Atxaga as the Basque Cervantes.

Atxaga points out that these early Basque writers followed a process common to the progenitors of written literature in all modern European cultures, including English and Spanish. They radically adapted oral syntax to make it comprehensible on the page, often taking precedents from the classical languages with which they were familiar.

It is certainly true, however, that the early flowering of Basque literature produced a very sparse and uneven crop in the centuries that followed, indeed until we reach the generation immediately before Atxaga's. This failure to sustain a vibrant literary culture certainly contributed to the anguish which many Basques felt about their language in the nineteenth and twentieth centuries. Fear that the language was dying, coupled with the belief that linguistic and national survival were intimately linked, fuelled a sense of desperation. This is something which the Catalans, with a much greater literary output, never experienced. This desperation was a major factor in driving many Basques towards the espousal of violence against the dictatorship in the 1960s. It was influential, too, in maintaining support for ETA's campaign under democracy. Only total independence, Basque radicals said, could guarantee the survival of Euskera. They portrayed Spanish democracy, despite the autonomy statute, as a façade for "genocide", conceived as the extinction of the language.

Atxaga, while just as passionate about the fate of Euskera, calls for more self-criticism from the Basques themselves. He stresses that the relative weakness of the language, in literature at any rate, cannot all be conveniently attributed to malign exterior forces like Francoism and "Madrid". He points out that Basque institutions did little to support writers like Axular in his own day. In a witty story, "How to Plagiarise", in *Obabakoak*, the narrator's uncle tells of a dream in which he meets Axular on an island which symbolizes the Basque language. Axular is scathing about those who mock the language as primitive, and also about those who use the island of Euskera for political and personal advantage, but do nothing to develop it:

> If as many books had been written in Euskera… as in any other language, it would be as rich and perfect as they are, and if that is not the case, it is the Basque speakers who are to blame, and not the island [the language itself].

The solution the fictional Axular proposes to the narrator is the systematic plagiarism of the classics by Basque writers. This is a doubly ironic point in Atxaga's book in that all the stories in *Obabakoak*—except this one—are indeed adaptations of narratives from the European and Middle Eastern traditions.

Underlying this polemic is a critique of the language policy of traditional Basque nationalism, which regarded Euskera as a "monument" rather than a living language. This critique was developed by another Basque writer, Iñaki Garziarena, who points out that a monument is "hard, impossible to transform, inert". It comes as no great surprise that Garziarena was a pseudonym used to sign all the articles in a review edited by Atxaga and his wife, Asun Garikano, who has translated writers like William Faulkner into Euskera. In this case, the Garziarena turns out to have been Atxaga's own brother, Iñaki Irazu, an accomplished poet who writes in Spanish as Ramón Albisu. "The mania for pseudonyms runs in the family," says Atxaga, which seems an understatement.

Atxaga's attraction to the concept of plagiarism—understood in a very particular sense—is the key to his argument about literature in Euskera. The failures of the past need not impact very negatively on the present, he says, because literary traditions are not contained by linguistic boundaries. So Basque writers today are not dependent on a rich pre-existing canon in poetry, prose and drama in their own language. To explain this view, he invents a "law of literary osmosis":

> This law, not yet written, says the following: If an author knows two languages well, A and B, and language A has a great literary tradition, and language B lacks one, the said author can make use of the formal resources of language A in language B in the time it takes to write a book in that language.

He deduces from this that "there is only one literary language, and that language is universal."

Atxaga is much too creative and playful a thinker to be entirely consistent. The second prong of his argument delivers a killer blow to the *canard* about the literary limitations of Euskera. But it could also undermine a critical argument in favour of Basques writing in that language, rather than in Spanish or French: surely they write in Basque precisely because it is distinctive, because things can be said in it that can be said no other way?

Atxaga is ambiguous on this question. In terms of theoretical linguistics, he rejects it outright, insisting that what can be said in one language can always be said in any other. And yet, almost in the same breath, he identifies being Basque with the Basque language: "I believe that the relationship with Euskera... is the most characteristic thing about our behaviour and our way of life, something which we cannot lose without losing, at least a little, our own selves." More dramatically, in the same essay, he talks about how "lack of recognition kills." This suggests that, without a community of speakers and writers in Euskera who can recognize each other in the fullest linguistic sense, some kind of genocide might indeed occur.

It may be that Atxaga underplays these arguments because, happily, things have moved on a great deal in his lifetime. Two factors have transformed the health and status of the Basque language since the 1960s. One is the creation of Euskera Batua, a Herculean linguistic project which forged Euskera's many disparate dialects into a single written and spoken form. The other is the success of the language revival movement, starting privately under late Francoism with the creation of *ikastolas* (schools which teach through the medium of Euskera), and massively boosted by the public policies of successive Basque autonomous governments since 1980.

No-one could be complacent about the status and prospects of Euskera today. But it is undoubtedly more widely spoken, and much more widely written and read, than was the case when Atxaga was growing up. And the publishing industry is booming, with upwards of 1,500 new books published annually. In these circumstances, he prefers to make the case that he writes in Basque simply because it is natural to write in your first language. Here is his reply to an American journalist who asked him why it was important that the Basque language should survive, if he could write just as well in Spanish: "We want to conserve our language," he said, "but not because it is beautiful or old. The reason is simpler than that. I think it is because it is a language which we know well, and we find it useful in our daily lives." He wanted to add "just like English for you," but lost his nerve.

He has never expressed his passion for his native language as clearly as he does in this poem, specially written for the English version of *Obabakoak* (1992), "We speak":

We speak a strange language. Its verbs,
the structure of its relative clauses,
the words it uses to designate ancient things
—rivers, plants, birds—
have no sisters anywhere on Earth.
A house is *etxe*, a bee *erle*, death *heriotz.*
The sun of the long winters we call *eguzki* or *eki*;
the sun of the sweet, rainy springs is also
—as you'd expect—called *eguzki* or *eki*
(it's a strange language but not that strange).

Born, they say, in the megalithic age,
it survived, this stubborn language, by withdrawing,
by hiding away like a hedgehog in a place,
which, thanks to the traces it left behind there,
the world named the Basque Country or Euskal Herria.
Yet its isolation could never have been absolute
—cat is *katu*, pipe is *pipa*, logic is *lojika*—
rather, as the prince of detectives would have said,
the hedgehog, my dear Watson, crept out of its hiding place
(to visit, above all, Rome and all its progeny).

The language of a tiny nation, so small
you cannot even find it on the map,
it never strolled in the gardens of the Court
or past the marble statues of government buildings;
in four centuries it produced only a hundred books...
the first in 1545; the most important in 1643;
the Calvinist New Testament in 1571;
the complete Catholic Bible around 1860.
Its sleep was long, its bibliography brief
(but in the twentieth century the hedgehog awoke).

Chapter Ten
Serious Fun: Fiestas in Laguardia

Laguardia takes the form of a boat, with its prow to the north and its stern to the south.

Pío Baroja, *El aprendiz de conspirador*, 1913

Laguardia [Biasteri] is a dusty jewel, standing proud on a small hill above the gently undulating vineyards of the Rioja Alavesa. The Ebro river meanders to the south, and its floodplain of calcareous clay nurtures this small region's world-class wine husbandry. A few miles away in the opposite direction, the Sierra de Toloño, part of the Cantabrian Cordillera, rises proud, protecting the vines from biting northern winds.

Wine is so central to life here that the people of Laguardia walk on air: their whole town is honeycombed with cool bodegas beneath their homes and beneath their streets. It is said that every house is connected to at least one other by an underground cellar, and it is certainly quite easy to enter one front door and emerge from another several streets away—with the owners' permissions, of course.

The walls established in the Middle Ages enclose the town in an elegant ellipse. It is perhaps four times longer than it is wide—the shape of a sleek battleship. There are only three long streets, running slightly tipsily between the walls, crisscrossed by a dozen short alleys. It is easy to imagine, walking on cobble stones polished by the centuries, beneath fantastically eroded stone coats of arms, that this is an almost perfectly preserved medieval town.

Laguardia is certainly old, but its bellicose history has ensured that quite a lot of what you see is restoration. Its name refers to its origin as the "guardian" of the old kingdom of Navarre, which periodically included parts of Álava, against marauders from al-Andalus or Castile. Most of its towers and its entire castle have been destroyed, some buildings several times over. Much of this destruction happened as recently as the nineteenth century, when the *tradicionalista* Carlist forces showed no

No boys for the girls: the danzarines in Laguardia's fiestas are all female, though traditionally young boys took part in equal numbers. "Boys here now think this kind of dancing is for gays," says a town councillor.

respect for architectural traditions and wrecked the place. Even the impressive-looking walls are largely recent reconstructions.

But much of the interior did originate in the Middle Ages; and it is not only very lovely, but is also the home of a charming fiesta. Approaching five o'clock on the eve of the feast day of St. John the Baptist, 23 June, a dozen dancers gather beneath the arches of the town hall, in the cramped and narrowly rectangular *plaza mayor*.

This is an intimate fiesta, a town celebrating itself modestly. It stands at the opposite extreme from Pamplona's overexposed *sanfermines*, at its worst a circus for international backpackers, which drives many of the locals out of town. Here in Laguardia, most of the people lining the walls of the plaza have only travelled a few hundred yards to see the show, and are on first name terms with the *danzarines* (dancers) who are about to perform. These are all young teenaged or pre-teen girls, dressed in white layered dresses with red trim and red belts. They each carry something that resembles a miniature kite, also in white and red. They are giggling a lot, a little self-conscious about their costumes.

Hovering on the fringe of the group, and four or five times as shy as the shyest girl, is the *cachimorro*, an adolescent boy dressed in a green and red harlequin costume. One of his stockings is white, the other is black. One of his *alpargatas* is laced in blue, the other in red. He wears a strange hood with a zigzag fringe. He carries a half-stuffed rabbit over his shoulder, suspended on a stick. As the hour approaches, he takes his place in front of the *danzarines*, who have lined up on either side of the plaza. His head is bowed in tense anticipation, his cheeks sucked in with concentration; he waits for the music to begin. As the first note is sounded, he bounds forward, and the girls follow him, springing into a jerky, lively dance.

Their task is to fetch the mayor and one other town councillor, the *regidor síndico*, from their homes and lead them back to the town hall. This only takes a few minutes in each case. (It seems unlikely that you could be elected in Laguardia if your domicile was outside the city walls: it would just take too long to get you to the fiesta.) After a few minutes the dancers return with their charges, who join the other dignitaries present, all of whom are given bouquets of flowers by the *danzarines*.

The *regidor síndico*, or trustee alderman, has a very special role in the fiesta. The role used to go to the youngest member of the council, but now it goes to the youngest member of the ruling party. Since the town council is split six-five in favour of the Spanish nationalists of the Partido Popular, this change causes some resentment among the mainstream Basque nationalists of the PNV. Now that the fiesta has begun everyone is smiling, but the smiles are a little forced.

The alderman's role revolves around Laguardia's municipal flag. This is an elaborate piece of work recalling the town's grander past, with its golden triangles on a white field and its rich pink-red border. The banner is handed down on its wooden staff from the town hall's second-storey balcony. A strikingly tall woman, elegant in an all-white outfit and red kerchief—generic fiesta colours—receives it in the street. She passes it to the alderman. He is not as tall and not nearly as elegant as she is. A large *txapela* is his only concession to festive dress. This traditional beret looks out of place with his sombre grey suit. He nevertheless hoists the flag over his shoulder with good-humoured determination, and marches off after the *danzarines* and the *cachimorro*, who dance their way to the church of St. John the Baptist.

The alderman enters through the chapel of the Virgen del Pilar, an octagonal seventeenth-century addition to the main building, which is at least 400 years older. Standing before the image of the Virgin, the alderman pays homage to her with the flag. This is easier said than done: the flag is some six feet square and made of heavy cloth. Tradition demands that he should make it flow and dance as though it were a river of silk. He must swing it around full circle half a dozen times, undulating it between a horizontal and almost perpendicular position. He then repeats the whole performance in the main body of the church, in front of the image of the patron saint of this part of the fiestas, St. John the Baptist.

The alderman is doing his best, too obviously so for the performance to have much real grace. Nevertheless, the ceremony creates a quiet kind of magic. And when the choir, disembodied in shadowy stone galleries above our heads, bursts into *Panis Angelicus* ("Bread of Angels"), the sound is spine-shiveringly intense.

This whole ritual will be repeated three times over the next 24 hours. On each occasion, both chapel and church will be packed for the "dancing" of the flag, but most people head back out to the bars before the religious service proper begins. On the final occasion, the priest preaches a sermon on John the Baptist's fierce honesty. "He was a man who called a spade a spade, and who did not live in some fairy tale world, but died in the crude reality of a prison, the victim of the whim of a dancer." He speaks of the need for neighbourliness. In a society which is increasingly individualistic and selfish, the priest, like the Baptist before him, sounds like a voice crying in the wilderness.

The Real Gods of the Fiesta

Rituals and religious ceremonies are central to almost every fiesta in the Basque Country, sometimes linked, as in Laguardia, and sometimes occurring separately. The attitude of many citizens to both is ambiguous.

They would be outraged, for reasons they might not be able to fully explain, if these ceremonies did not take place. There can be bitter and even violent reactions, as we shall see in Chapter Thirteen, if traditions are subjected to sudden changes. But local people do not necessarily attend all such events every year. When they do, they may just wander in and out as the mood takes them, arriving late and leaving early, like most of the church congregation in Laguardia. Often they are happy if they have caught five minutes of rituals that are as familiar and natural to them as the local weather.

Ask a Basque what she or he most enjoys about the local fiesta, and two phrases are likely to figure large. One is *la juerga*, which translates from Spanish into Hiberno-English as "the craic"; the other is *gaupasa egin*, the phrase in Euskera for staying up all night. Whoever the nominal patron saint of the town may be, Bacchus and Dionysus are the gods universally revered at fiestas.

The Basque appetite for the *txikiteo* seems limitless, and the culture of fiestas nurtures it copiously. But this endless circuit of bars is not just an excuse for getting drunk. The typical Basque drinks to get merry rather than to get legless. Excessive inebriation is unusual. At least, it used to be: the quantities and toxic combinations consumed by many younger and some older revellers are the topic of much critical comment over the last few years. The *txikiteo* used to be based on small (*txiki*) glasses of wine. Beer is now overtaking wine in popularity, and spirits and recreational drugs may also be thrown into the mix.

The ideal object of the whole fiesta exercise is a kind of joyous sociability. In Laguardia it sometimes seems as though the whole town is engaged in an endlessly extended conversation, as a river of citizens flow from bar to bar, rarely staying for more than one drink in each one, but frequently pausing to chat in the street.

Conversation is not always easy in today's Basque bars, as a visit to the *batzoki* in Laguardia shows. *Batzokis* are clubs run by the PNV but, like similar centres run by other parties, they are open to the public. The walls of this establishment are dominated by sober portraits of all the patriarchs of the party, from the founder, Sabino Arana, to the current *lehendakari* (first minister) Juan José Ibarretxe. What Arana would make of the *batzoki* is anybody's guess, though he would surely approve of the basics: the bar serves decent wine and passable beer, and the kitchen offers excellent *raciones* of succulent Iberian ham, tasty croquettes, and *rabos* ("tails")—tender strips of squid crisped in batter.

The patriarchs might find some of the other iconography a little disturbing. A vividly coloured photograph shows two traditionally dressed Basque dancers, in a traditional context, a clearing in a beech wood surrounded by stone walls. But the image is suffused with surreal and erotic touches which subvert the tradition. The male dancer is frozen at the high point of a kick step, directed towards his female partner in the upper centre of the image, his right leg almost parallel with his chest. She appears to be levitating in response, as though the energy of her partner's gesture is propelling her into the air. Her feet are suspended a few inches above a stone bench. Her bright red skirt swells around white-stockinged legs. Her image is cut off at the waist by the top of the picture frame. To the left, completing a triangular dynamic to balance the dancer on her right, a sheep is suckling a lamb, a touch Buñuel surely would have appreciated.

I sit at a table, and a waitress quickly approaches. She is wearing a T-shirt on which Eve, whose eyes are strategically situated on the waitress's breasts, says to Adam (apropos the apple): *Come y Calle*, "Eat and Shut Up." Happily, the waitress' manners are much better than Eve's, and she helpfully explains obscure items on the menu. But communication is difficult, because Madonna is blasting *Like a Virgin* out of the speakers at maximum decibels, and doing her own black-stockinged high-steps on a huge flat screen on the back wall.

Some old-fashioned elements of decorum are still maintained. Two men take the remaining seats at my table, and greet me with the formal *¡Que aproveche!* This is the Spanish equivalent of "bon appétit!", and lit-

erally means "may you benefit [from your meal]." But any further interaction is rendered impossible by the volume of the MTV. This in turn
forces those who do attempt to converse to shout, thus making conversation even harder for everyone else.

At a nearby table, an extended family comprising at least three generations is tucking into a dozen plates of *raciones*. An old woman sits
beside a little girl. The PNV cherishes family values, and family ties
remain strong in this society despite rapid social change. So this occasion
should be, surely, a moment for sharing family memories of past fiestas,
and a time for a granddaughter to tell her granny her dreams. But they
could not hear each other if they tried. In any case the girl's eyes are fixed
on the screen, on a role model who, for good or ill, and probably both,
has little in common with the Virgen del Pilar.

The problem of noise pollution is almost universal in the Basque
Country, and has been growing for a long time. Basque bars and restaurants were always high-volume places, but the sound effects used to be
human: voices raised in banter, glasses banged down for emphasis, crockery clattered by impatient waiters. Now the noises are electronically
generated, and the chances of communicating with your friends, or
getting to know the opinions of strangers, are greatly diminished.
Another casualty is the singing voice. It used to be commonplace for one
cuadrilla to break into a four-part harmony of a well-loved song, to be
joined and echoed by other groups on the premises. It does still happen,
in the very few bars which, at least occasionally, switch off their infernal
machines. But it is a rare pleasure now, not a normal part of an evening's
drinking.

A Spontaneous Chorus for the Virgin

To hear that sort of singing today, you might have to go to a choral
society or, as I found out in Laguardia, to the porch of a church.

Santa María de los Reyes stands at the other end of the town from
the church of San Juan Bautista. The outer door is unexceptional, but it
opens on a second entrance, which is one of the most sumptuous Gothic
monuments on the Iberian Peninsula.

The inner and original doorway, now protected by the additional
porch, is a richly complex archway. Key events in the life (and afterlife)
of the Virgin Mary are presented in woodcarvings of exuberant virtuos-

ity. More miraculous still is the fact that, due to the early construction of the prophylactic porch, the vibrant colours of the original work have been protected almost intact.

This sudden spectrum creates an overwhelming impact on the eyes of the unsuspecting first-time visitor, expecting to encounter yet another Gothic interior, uplifting but monochrome. It is well worth devoting time to exploring the detail of the archway and tympanum. Freudians may smile at the curiously vaginal form of the Virgin's bodily assumption into heaven; but even the most sceptical are likely to find themselves entranced by the exquisitely tender and human rendering of the annunciation scene, above the lintel to the left.

But back to the singing voice: I was examining these scenes one afternoon, when a couple behind me began to sing:

Salve Regina, Mater misericordiae,
Vita dulcedo et spes nostra salve.

The words are saccharine enough: "Hail holy queen, mother of mercy, Hail our life, our sweetness and our hope." But the unadorned simplicity of the voices, especially when they were enriched by those of another couple, were enough to melt even a heart like mine, conditioned in a Protestant childhood to regard Marian devotion as deeply suspect. The context of the archway helped, of course, making the experience a kind of spontaneous *son et lumière*.

When the singing died away, I turned and asked the couple if they sang in a choir. No, they replied, just for pleasure, and just among friends. But the doorway had inspired them to perform in public. What exactly, I asked, was the music they were singing? One of the most common *Salves*, they replied, the one you would hear most often in church. So there were other versions? This prompted a rendition of a *Salve* typical of the north of Spain, though not especially of the Basque Country. And then one from Andalusia, spiced with *Olés* to the Virgin. And all the time, other people were entering and leaving the church, pausing briefly perhaps to listen, but not evidently surprised by what was happening.

Were they especially religious people, I asked the foursome. "No, we are Catholics but we don't really practise. We just like the music," they said. "We sing songs from *zarzuela* (Spanish light opera) when we play cards," they added.

I told them I had often heard people singing in the bars in Vitoria in the 1970s, everything from rousing (and prohibited) patriotic and leftist songs of struggle to tender love ballads. It turned out that Vitoria was the home city of the foursome. We parted lamenting the lack of spontaneous music in the bars there today. Happily, I have since encountered a movement which is promoting a revival in public choral singing in Euskera. It started in San Sebastián a few years ago, but can now be found across the Basque Country. Look out for groups of people with little yellow song sheets, and prepare to be entertained royally, and for free.

In the sacristy I hear another lament. "The traditions of the fiesta are dying," says Father Antonio baldly. Unconsciously proving his point, the priest absently flicks a switch which sends the recorded sound of bells pealing from his fourteenth-century church across the narrow streets. But surely, I asked him, the flag ceremony retained a strong traditional and religious significance? "Not any more," he says categorically. "We live in a globalized world in which everyone wears the same jeans and listens to the same music. There is no respect for the flag now. They used to rehearse with a stick and piece of cloth to protect the flag itself, it should only be used in the actual ceremony. Now they rehearse with the real thing, and they leave it lying about anywhere."

This remark makes him sound as though he is obsessed with the fetishization of the rituals. In fact it is the loss of the social significance behind them which he wants to draw attention to. "In the old days," he says, "people came to the church on the flag days to discuss their problems. The brotherhoods which organize fiesta events provided mutual support to their members throughout the year. Now they just exist to organize an annual meal."

The erosion of traditions associated with the fiesta is obviously linked to changes in society, and may in any case be coloured by an idealization of the past. But there is hard evidence of the erosion of some of its key ritual elements. Look at the photographs from the 1940s and 1950s, collected by the town's indefatigable amateur archivist, Encarna Martínez. They show *cabezudos*, the "big head" clowns in papier-mâché which scare and delight the children, chasing the *cachimorro*. They no longer appear in this fiesta. And sketches in the town museum show that the harlequin jester's costume used to be much more elaborate than it is today.

There is a more recent change, and a very big one, which can be seen if you just look at the town clock. The performance of the *danzarines* looks so traditional that it is easy to imagine that you are watching a ceremony unchanged since the Middle Ages. But the clock gives the game away. When it strikes certain hours, three key figures from the pageant pop out of its casing. There is the *cachimorro*, and one boy and one girl dancer. Look at the dancers on the street below today, however, and you will find that they are all girls. "Boys here now think this kind of dancing is for gays," says town councillor and cultural delegate for the county, María Jesús Amilibia. "For several years we have not been able to get a single boy involved, except as the *cachimorro*." It was curious that, in the week she made this comment, gay marriage was legalized in Spain.

When Pío Baroja visited Laguardia, he was much taken by its charms. He commented archly that it was odd that one of his great contemporaries, the novelist Benito Pérez Galdós had not paid due deference to the town in his novel *De Oñate a La Granja*. Baroja took the trouble of asking the local judge and doctor to check with the secretary of the town council as to how Galdós had researched the town for his book, and found that he had simply written to the council asking for information. "He writes of [Laguardia] without giving it any significance, as though it did not have any character, because he was never there," Baroja concluded dryly.

As a writer of fiction, Galdós might perhaps be excused this lapse. One wonders what Baroja would have made of the remarkable admission of Rodney Gallop, whose *Book of the Basques* was the first study of the region in English:

> I am hardly competent to write of Álava, for my impressions have been formed exclusively from a railway carriage. I remember only that, as the train left Vitoria, and wound between the mountains towards the Guipuzcoan border, all the Basque ingredients seemed to be there: little villages clustered round grim brown churches; black berets amid the maize fields; oxen ploughing or dragging rude carts with solid wheels, scattered farms crouching under the weight of their broad

The past in the present: a house in the medieval quarter of El Ciego, a village near Laguardia, is protected from night spirits by a dried *eguzki-lore* ("flower of the sun"), and from the dark by an electricity meter. The *eguzki-lore* is not the familiar sunflower, but an alpine stemless thistle. It can still be seen on many Basque doors, and is sometimes painted onto walls. Tradition has it that the Basque goddess Mari gave the *eguzki-lore* to her people so that evil creatures, confusing the plant with the sun, would fear to enter houses which displayed it.

sloping roofs, seen as flecks of white against green hillside or blue mountain slope. It was hard to believe that the spirit of Eskual Herria had fled for ever from these lovely valleys.

Gallop identified that Basque spirit almost exclusively with the language, and justified his omission of Álava from his study on the basis that Euskera was then only spoken in "four or five villages". He would no doubt be surprised today to find that the language is taught throughout the province, and can be heard even the Rioja Alavesa, that part of the province which least fits his "ingredients" for the Basque countryside. By not getting off the train, he missed something very special.

Chapter Eleven

Don't Mention the War: the Dark Side of Basque—and Spanish—Politics

Many of our political nightmares begin by being a dream, a utopia shared...This is also what happened in the case of the Basques.
Bernardo Atxaga, "Basque Spring", *New York Times*, March 2005,
after ETA called a "permanent ceasefire".

It is comforting to imagine that ordinary decent people, like you and me and our circles of friends, have nothing in common with those who are capable of putting a bullet in a stranger's head, or exploding a car bomb on a busy street.

For anyone with their eyes half open, that illusion has been shattered repeatedly in the Basque Country over the last forty years. Political violence by ordinary and otherwise decent people has been an unremitting and corrosive presence in many aspects of contemporary Basque life, with a death toll since 1968 which approaches 1,000. One in six voters in the CAV has consistently backed Batasuna, a party whose relationship to ETA is broadly similar to Sinn Féin's association with the IRA. The Spanish state has made its own criminal contribution to the cycle of killing. Indeed, ETA can be understood, in the first instance, as the off-spring of Francoism's systematic rape of Basque culture, though neither father nor child would acknowledge that paternity. Worse, democratic administrations have sponsored state terrorist groups and protected torturers, under both conservative and centre-left prime ministers, at least until the late 1980s.

Paradoxically, this conflict has not made the Basque Country as dangerous a place to live as you might expect. For most people here, for most of the time, it has long been possible to behave as though this were a

ETA's terrorism: The mutilated corpse of a *guardia civil*, Franciso Álvarez, after a bomb exploded in his car in Ortuella in May 1991. ETA has killed more than 800 people, many of them civilians, and most of them since Spain became a democracy.

normal Western European society. But the shadows of violence, sometimes obvious and more often subtle, are ubiquitous if you keep your eyes open.

Go into one bar for a coffee, and you may very likely find a poster with blurred photographs of dozens of young men and women staring at you from behind the counter, under a slogan like *Presoak kalera* (Free the prisoners). To the pleasant and maternal woman serving you, the ETA convicts and suspects portrayed in the poster are all patriots, unjustly imprisoned for asserting the legitimate rights of the Basque nation. They are the victims in this struggle, she will tell you, despite the fact that the casualty rates run something like 10-1 in ETA's favour.

Victimhood is very much in the eye of the beholder in this country. Go into another bar, on the same street, and you may find that several of the customers are trailed by burly men wearing shades, bad ties and ill-fitting suits. "The Basque Country is a place where 2,000 people need bodyguards," quipped the Madrid-based writer Tom Burns Marañon, "and where two million don't notice them." To those who support

Batasuna, and to too many of those who support the PNV, the victims of ETA are abstractions, regrettable but inevitable "consequences of the Basque conflict". To the people with bodyguards, and to many other Basque citizens, these victims are a constantly present absence. At least the dead may be remembered. The bereaved, and those maimed physically and mentally, live on, invisible to and forgotten by much of Basque society. To those who live in these shadowlands, the young men and women in the poster across the road are not patriots, but terrorists, fanatics or psychopaths.

You can also encounter violence and never realize it. Pay your bill in a fashionable restaurant, and you may have made an inadvertent contribution to ETA. The owner, like hundreds of Basque business people, may have been blackmailed into paying a "revolutionary tax" to the group. Some of those who do not pay up have been shot dead, enough of them to keep the cash flow coming from their more malleable colleagues.

Yet the Basque Country is not Belfast, and it is certainly not Beirut. There are no high walls dividing mutually hostile communities. The fracture in Basque society is ideological, not ethnic. You can find radical supporters of Basque independence and conservatives loyal to Madrid celebrating a birthday around the same family table. On the streets, the casual visitor is unlikely to encounter anything unpleasant, despite intermittent outbreaks of *kale borroka* ("street struggle", though a truer translation might be "political vandalism"). And the level of violence has currently reached its lowest level since the 1960s. There were no fatal attacks by ETA between May 2003 and December 2006, when two unfortunate Ecuadorian immigrants were killed, apparently accidentally, in a big bomb attack on an airport car park in Madrid. The fact that this bombing happened during a "permanent ceasefire" called by ETA in March 2006, and which the group claimed was still in operation after the bombing, added another layer of Orwellian unreality to the situation at the time of finishing this book (early 2007). The threat of violence certainly remains: you may still make out gun-sights painted on the homes of Basque citizens loyal to Spain. And the prisoners remain in jail, held in many cases at cruel distances from their families, in a controversial policy of "dispersion". In the absence of a political resolution, the shadows linger.

What has made ordinary young Basques take up arms, generation after generation, when their counterparts all over Spain were content to resolve deep and painful political differences through democratic channels? Why should one of the most prosperous and vibrant regions in the peninsula, materially and culturally, be home to such a bloody conflict? These are very complex questions, which we will not resolve here in a few paragraphs. But perhaps some pointers might be helpful, some stories which contextualize the references to violence we will encounter wherever we travel in the Basque lands.

ETA was born in 1959. It was conceived out of the frustration of young nationalists with the PNV's passivity towards the dictatorship. Franco's repression of Basque culture was draconian. Most public use of Euskera was prohibited, and parents were not allowed to give their children Basque first names. These laws were enforced by a paramilitary police force, the Guardia Civil, whose members were drawn almost entirely from other parts of Spain, and behaved like an army of occupation. Repression was not necessarily harsher in Bilbao than in Badajoz, but it felt qualitatively different, adding a potent national dimension to the deprivation of civil liberties.

ETA began life as a study group, and radically reinvented Basque nationalist culture over its first decade. The PNV's ambiguity about Basque aspirations was challenged by a clear-cut demand for total independence for all seven provinces. A practical consequence of this was ETA's hostility towards any alliances with democratic Madrid-based parties, and it accused the PNV of being objectively *españolista* for doing deals with the Spanish opposition to Franco. On the other hand, it is often not appreciated that ETA significantly broadened the PNV's narrow definition of nationality. ETA shifted from Sabino Arana's ethnic (and quasi-racist) criteria for Basqueness towards a cultural identity based on the use of Euskera. This opened a door to inclusion for the immigrant population. ETA has been remarkably successful in recruiting young second-generation immigrants to its cause. The latter are undeterred by the organization's vitriolic anti-Spanish rhetoric, and are perhaps impelled to establish their new identity by being, as it were, more Basque than the Basques themselves.

A Fetish for Violence, a Fashion for Revolution

Influenced by the heady turmoil of the 1960s, ETA also rejected the religious and social conservatism of the PNV. It explored a repertoire of Marxist and Third Worldist positions, finally opting for a dogmatic "Marxist-Leninism" which still influences its rhetoric. Indeed, there are few parts of Europe where the symbols and language of revolutionary communism are still so fashionable among the young, though they are often almost ludicrously incongruous with their affluence and lifestyles.

It is easy to form the impression that many young Basques lead a radical chic lifestyle, in which Armani logos co-exist peacefully with calls for armed struggle, both on the same elegant T-shirts. There is some truth, but only some, in this. A Sinn Féin member who knows the Basque Country very well has a telling anecdote about the comfortable background of many (though by no means all) Batasuna supporters. He was witness to a bloody and large-scale street battle in Bilbao in 2001 between Batasuna demonstrators and the Basque autonomous police force, the Ertzainza. He commented to one Batasuna leader that, had this been Belfast and the confrontation equally ferocious, every car and every shop on the street would have been burning by this stage in the riot. The Batasuna leader had the grace to be a little embarrassed. "Well," he replied hesitantly, "I suppose that it is different here, because these are *our* cars, these are *our* shops."

The *izquierda abertzale* may only be flirting with revolutionary socialism, but it would be a grave mistake to underestimate its long and faithful marriage to violence. Action was always more significant than ideology to the ETA leadership. This was an understandable response to a moribund PNV, but it conjured up a fetish for violence which haunts radical Basque nationalism to this day. A relatively innocent dream, in response to the nightmare of dictatorship, became a nightmare in itself.

ETA made its public debut with symbolic but dangerous operations like flying the banned *ikurriña* from church towers, and bombing Francoist monuments. In the mid-1960s the group graduated to an insurrectionary strategy based on a simple but effective concept, the "spiral of action-repression-action". In theory it works like this: the group's armed actions provoke the dictatorship into taking ever harsher and more indiscriminate measures against the general population. This in turn increases ETA's support, making more dramatic and more frequent armed actions possible, generating yet more repression, and thus more support for the revolutionaries. And so on, in grim repetition, until the conditions for a full-scale national liberation war have been created.

This spiral suddenly started to revolve much faster in 1968. A young ETA leader, the poet Francisco Javier Etxebarrieta (known as *Txabi*), killed a *guardia civil*, José Pardines. The next day, Etexebarrieta was shot dead, giving ETA its first victim and its first martyr within 24 hours. Massive attendance at requiem masses for Etxebarrieta showed that ETA had struck a deep chord among the Basque public. Ferocious state repression followed, in which numerous uninvolved people were arrested and tortured. Francoist security forces would be ETA's best recruiting sergeant, responding to its stimuli like Pavlov's dogs.

The dynamic of the spiral accelerated rapidly in the last years of the Franco dictatorship. Events like the mass trial of ETA leaders in Burgos in 1970 and the spectacular assassination of Franco's prime minister and confidante Admiral Luis Carrero Blanco in 1973 gave this small group the highest profile of all the resistance groups in the Spanish state. Most significantly, it had won the passionately committed support of many Basques and the admiration of very many more.

The transition to democracy in the late 1970s was widely expected to remove the rationale for ETA's armed struggle. After all, democracy produced a Basque government, consistently led by Basque nationalists, with extensive powers in areas like education, taxation, health and policing. An amnesty which freed every single ETA prisoner briefly removed another major source of grievance. (Continuing ETA attacks ensured the prisons were soon full again.)

Paradoxically, the hard-core ETA-*militar* faction greatly intensified its violent campaign under democracy. ETA killed 91 people in 1980, almost six times more than it had killed in 1975, the year Franco died.

A tricky question underlies ETA's persistence as an armed group during and since the transition, and this question is often ignored, indeed is almost taboo in Spanish analysis of these developments. The 1978 constitution is generally portrayed in Spain as a brilliant expression of the exemplary and generous consensus negotiated between former Francoists and the democratic parties. It is at least equally arguable, however, that this constitution is a botched compromise, heavily conditioned by the threat of intervention by the army. Nevertheless, it was endorsed by a convincing majority (59 per cent) of the whole Spanish electorate, with a mere five per cent voting against.

But here is the tricky bit: the provinces of Guipúzcoa, Vizcaya and Álava stood out conspicuously against this tide of approval, to an extent that indicates a much deeper Basque alienation from the Spanish transition than is generally acknowledged. The PNV campaigned for "active abstention" in the 1978 referendum. Only 31 per cent of the Basque electorate supported the constitution, the exact obverse of the overall trend. The Basque "No" vote, mostly from ETA supporters, was double the Spanish average. While a decisive majority (75 per cent) of those Basques who *did* go to the polls voted "Yes", the CAV is the only region in the state where fewer—much fewer—than half of the potential voters endorsed the new Spanish order. A fracture had opened up between the Basque Country and the Spanish constitutional consensus which has never entirely closed. In the view of many Basques, the writ of Madrid had been shown to have no legitimate mandate north of the Ebro.

It is true that the PNV, and the Basque people, did appear to accept the constitution retrospectively only a year later. The mainstream nationalists agreed a Statute of Autonomy that was framed within the constitution's limits. They campaigned hard and successfully for a resounding endorsement of the statute from the electorate. They were helped by the fact the "political-military" faction of ETA negotiated its own dissolution in the early 1980s, and its supporters in Euskadiko Ezkerra also backed the autonomy statute. The PNV, however, has always hinted to its supporters that support for the statute was merely a tactical move, a pragmatic stepping stone towards self-determination. In recent years this party has called for a Basque "right to decide" which goes well beyond the bounds of the 1979 statute, though its leaders remain chronically ambiguous on the question of total independence.

Basque nationalist reservations about the legitimacy of Spain's jurisdiction are worthy of respect. They provide a context for understanding ETA's violence, but they do not justify it. Spanish democracy may be flawed, but it offers all the classic liberties the Basques need to pursue a more independent relationship with Madrid by peaceful means. Terrorism is an increasingly abused word, often telling us more about those who use it than about those it is applied to. It seems reasonable, however, to apply it to those who use violence for political goals when

State terrorism: A gendarme looks at the car in which Christophe Matxikote (60), a French Basque farmer, and his niece Catherine Brion (16) were shot by a GAL death squad, sponsored by the Spanish administration, near Bidarrai. Neither victim had any connection with ETA. The GAL killed 27 people between 1983 and 1987. A PSOE minister and a Guardia Civil general are among those convicted of GAL crimes.

they are free to seek these goals through democratic channels. By those criteria, and by its increasing recklessness with civilian lives, ETA had undoubtedly become a terrorist organization by the 1980s.

How can we explain continued support for violence among a significant sector of the Basque population in these circumstances? Part of the answer lies in the constitutional context given above. Another part of the answer, but again only a part, lies in the way the democratic state responded to ETA's terrorism. The security forces used death squads and torture with impunity under the conservative administrations of the transition between 1977 and 1982. The PSOE government elected in that year under the charismatic leadership of the young Felipe González could have been expected to clean things up. His was the first Madrid government with unsullied democratic credentials, and no links to the dictatorship, since 1939. Yet very senior members of his administration made the disastrous mistake of launching a new "dirty war" against ETA from 1983 to 1986. The Grupos Antiterroristas de Liberación (GAL) used classic state terrorist tactics, machine-gunning bars and car-bombing busy streets, killing 27 people, at least nine of them unconnected to ETA, and wounding many more.

The Death Squads of a Democratic State

Why would a democratic party countenance the use of death squads? Well, the PSOE was under extreme pressure when it came to power. The loyalty of the Spanish security forces to democracy was still very shaky at best, as demonstrated by a failed coup d'état a year earlier. ETA was killing more generals than Spain had lost in any conventional war. Each such death made another coup more likely. So a dirty war strategy did provide a kind of safety valve for the angry energies of right-wing officers. And the Socialists faced another dilemma: Paris was unwilling to move against ETA's well-established "sanctuary" in Iparralde, where its exiles planned their attacks in Spain and returned afterwards for rest and relaxation. The core aim of the GAL appears to have been to rupture ETA's impunity in France, and cause so much mayhem in the process that French public opinion would begin to demand the extradition or imprisonment of the numerous ETA suspects on French soil.

This strategy was successful, insofar as France began to collaborate effectively against ETA in 1986, and the GAL then withdrew from the field. Even conceding this point, however, Patxo Unzueta wrote that the GAL was not only an ethical but a practical disaster: "the GAL were... a destabilizing factor in the democratic system and... a catalyst for a new flow of members to ETA, prolonging the problem for at least a generation." Unzueta speaks with a double authority here: he was an ETA leader in the 1970s and is now a senior commentator for *El País*, the newspaper closest to the PSOE.

Certainly, the dirty war was a propaganda gift to ETA, as were the increasingly blatant attempts by Madrid to obstruct media and judicial investigations into the GAL's government connections. It is a credit to Spain's young democracy that these investigations eventually resulted in successful prosecutions. This contrasts sharply with Britain's dismal failure to investigate dirty war episodes in Ireland. A general and an Interior Minister were both convicted on murder and kidnapping charges respectively. Their short stays in jail, however, contrast with the harsh penal policy towards ETA convicts, and the GAL remains a live issue in Basque politics, twenty years after it fired its last shots.

Yet the constitutional question and dirty wars are insufficient to explain ETA's long survival in democratic conditions. There are other questions to be asked: why did the various armed and revolutionary Catalan, Galician and workers' groups never achieve ETA's momentum under the dictatorship, and fade away rapidly after Franco's death? This leads us to very problematic terrain.

This landscape has been well mapped by Zulaika, in a complex book which is as much a literary as an anthropological achievement. In *Basque Violence: Metaphor and Sacrament* (1988), he argues that we must dig for the answers deep in the roots of Basque culture. In an analysis of his own village, Itziar, where four young ETA members carried out a particularly disturbing killing in 1976, he uses analogies from many traditional practices, ranging from card-playing through hunting to spontaneous versifying, to suggest that Basque culture views many issues as having only two sides, *bai* or *ez* (yes or no). This makes many Basques regard negotiation, with all the shades of grey it requires, as equivalent to betrayal. When three of Itziar's ETA members returned from prison after the 1978 amnesty, they were initially greeted as heroes. When they attempted to explain the new and complexly nuanced political strategy of ETA *político-militar*, the villagers were baffled and suspicious: "Well then, are you with Madrid, or are you with us?" was the question they were asked, again and again and again. Zulaika also lays great emphasis on the religious formation of many ETA members of the period, and of the metamorphosis of religious vocation into existentialist and Marxist ideologies of commitment and action. ETA was founded on 31 July 1959, the feast day of St. Ignatius, Basque founder of the Jesuit order. (The huge basilica at his birthplace, Loyola [Loiola], in the foothills of Guipúzcoa, was a kind of seventeenth-century spiritual Guggenheim, and remains a telling monument to the Jesuits' power among the Basques.) Zulaika argues that this connection with St. Ignatius is not coincidental, even though the Jesuits were not nearly as intimately involved with ETA as other sectors of the Basque Catholic Church. He argues that Basque traditions and aesthetics had a deep influence on the Ignatian Spiritual Exercises. These, in turn, have had a decisive influence in reinforcing a Basque cultural tendency to see complex issues in antagonistic black-and-white terms.

The Manichean thinking identified by Zulaika is reflected, with religious overtones, in one of ETA's earliest theoretical documents, written in 1961 by José Antonio Extebarrieta, brother of *Txabi*. "There can be no peace," he wrote, "between good and evil, between truth and falsehood, between justice and oppression, between liberty and tyranny".

This answer, however, begs another question. Etxebarrieta and ETA's other early leaders were not, generally speaking, simplistic thinkers. Some of them were sophisticated intellectuals and accomplished novelists, poets and essayists, among the finest minds of their generation. So why was this *bai/ez* dichotomy so attractive to them? The existentialist writer José Luis Álvarez Emparanza (*Txillardegi*) was perhaps the brightest of them all. He put his finger on the underlying anxiety which motivated ETA. Action was urgent, he wrote, because of the "imminent danger of the disappearance [of the Basques] as a people".

The Italian writer Daniel Conversi, who has also carefully explored this painful and confusing territory, believes that this fear of national extinction, well founded or otherwise, has been fundamental to the violent course taken by ETA. In *The Basques, the Catalans and Spain* (1997), he contrasts the "alternative routes to nationalist mobilisation" taken at either end of the Pyrenees. He suggests that it was the weakness, not the strength, of Basque national culture that led to the emergence of a violent nationalist movement. The Catalan language had a literary tradition comparable with the best in Europe, and was still a means of daily communication for millions in the 1950s. This was a source of great national self-confidence for the Catalans. Their rich and vibrant cultural world gave them a stage on which to experience and play out their sense of national identity even under the dictatorship.

And the Catalans had another advantage over the Basques: their language is relatively easy to learn by casual social contact because of its similarities to Castilian Spanish. This means that immigrants were much more easily assimilated into Catalonia than into Euskal Herria. In short, the Catalan nationalists under the dictatorship experienced their culture as oppressed, but by no means thought of it as verging on extinction.

In contrast, the Basque literary tradition was relatively weak, or at least was so perceived by the Basques themselves until writers like Atxaga challenged this view. And Euskera cannot be learned by osmosis, but only by a long period of study and immersion, far beyond the cultural and financial means of most immigrants. As a result, Basque nationalists had long felt that their culture was not just under siege but in danger of suffering what they have frequently described as a form of genocide. In the Franco period, there was indeed a widespread sense of despair, a *sentimento agónico*, of living on the threshold of extinction as a people. As Conversi puts it, the first generations of ETA believed that "only drastic measures such as mass insurrection could save them from their doom," and this feeling found a broad echo in the Basque population. Conversi concludes that the Basque experience is one where "violent conflicts have been revived by weak identities, and weak identities have been rejuvenated through violent conflict."

This is the background to the insistence by ETA-*militar* (the sole ETA after the mid-1980s) that only an independent state could guarantee the survival of Basque identity. Despite the progress made in the recuperation of Euskera and of Basque culture generally by Basque governments, the radicals continued to regard Spanish democracy and Basque autonomy as mere façades for continued, if subtle, dictatorship. True democracy would only exist through the exercise of self-determination by the seven provinces, without interference by Paris or Madrid. To outsiders, and to most Basques, the genocide scenario looks almost criminally deluded in 2007. Many peoples around the world would envy the Basques the degree of liberty and self-rule they enjoy. Unfortunately, that is not the point. The point is that a substantial Basque minority nurtures this sense of victimhood. The challenge is how they can best be persuaded to recognize the enormous and positive changes which have taken place in Euskal Herria since Franco's death. With the peace process recently initiated by the Spanish Prime Minister, José Luis Rodríguez Zapatero, there were many indications that this has been happening among ETA supporters.

Political support for ETA and its aims has been expressed through Herri Batasuna (People United, later simply "Batasuna"), founded in Lekeitio in 1978. This extraordinary political movement includes rural traditionalists and urban anarchists, and monopolizes the radical expression of many traditional left-wing causes, from environmentalism to feminism. It is often compared to Sinn Féin, but its relationship to ETA is different from Sinn Féin's to the IRA. Because the leadership of ETA has traditionally lived in exile, it has tended to control Batasuna at one remove. ETA's military leaders ensure that there are loyal supporters in the political leadership but they do not usually participate directly in day-to-day politics themselves, as senior IRA figures like Gerry Adams and Martin McGuinness have always done. This has negative consequences in that ETA leaders have little contact with their own social base, while Batasuna leaders appear to accept directives from those who are making the "real sacrifices", whether they agree with them or not.

Socializing the Suffering: a Teenage Intifada

Batasuna has nevertheless been a very effective organization, sustaining the radical vote at around the 15 per cent mark, and dominating the municipal administrations in many small and medium Basque towns. When ETA was close to collapse under police pressure in the early 1990s, Batasuna took on a dynamic of its own. A grim new strategy of "socializing the suffering" was intended to make all of Basque society feel the pain of ETA's prisoners and militants. The tactic of *kale borroka* used teenagers to carry out a campaign of political vandalism, in imitation of the Palestinian *intifada*. Opponents and critics were intimidated by attacks on their offices and homes; buses and ATMs were burned. Meanwhile, a slowly reviving ETA extended its list of "legitimate targets" to local councillors from the PP and PSOE. This campaign succeeded in driving a new and terrible wedge through the heart of a society which, despite its strong internal differences, worked, ate and drank together in remarkable harmony. The stench of fear and loathing in the Basque Country in the mid-1990s was more intense than at any time since the dictatorship. The especially callous killing of the young PP councillor Miguel Ángel Blanco in 1997 sent an unprecedented wave of revulsion surging through the Basque Country and the whole of Spain.

Yet ETA's spiral continued to function in new and perverse directions. The targeting of councillors fostered a kind of "Spanish front" in the Basque Country, with the PP and PSOE viewing Basque nationalism in general as the root cause of ETA's terrorism. Some elements in both parties, but particularly the conservatives, privately saw ETA as an electoral and ideological bonus. The terror campaign allowed them to revive Spanish nationalism, an ideology that had not spoken its name out loud in the Spanish mainstream since Franco's death. ETA had effectively given the Spanish hard right the leverage to mobilize its supporters throughout Spain. The Spanish conservatives set out to discredit demo-cratic nationalism in the Basque Country and also in Catalonia. (Some well-informed observers even detected a sinister symbiosis between ETA and the PP.) The tone of powerful sections of the Spanish media became hysterically anti-Basque, crudely identifying everything from the PNV to Euskera with terrorism, a tendency which regrettably continues unabat-ed and amplified today.

But the conservatives' offensive backfired. The demonization of the PNV radicalized the moderate nationalists. They entered secret talks with ETA that led to an unprecedented ceasefire in 1998. Far from gaining the approval of the Spanish parties, this development was seen in Madrid as a "truce-trap", an underhand manoeuvre to force through a referendum on self-determination. The ceasefire did, however, show that ETA supporters were wearying of violence. Batasuna's vote soared close to twenty per cent when the guns were silent, and slumped to an all-time low when ETA resumed terrorism in 2000.

ETA's renewed terrorism was more vicious, in some respects, than anything which had gone before. PSOE leaders who had built bridges with Basque nationalism, like Juan María Jauregui and Ernest Lluch, were gunned down. Journalists critical of ETA were threatened, making honest debate on the conflict increasingly difficult. José Luis López de la Calle, who had served five years in Franco's jails for trade union activism, was shot in Zarautz for the "crime" of writing newspaper columns excoriating Basque nationalism. In the same town the family of an assassinated PP councillor, José Ignacio Iruretagoyena Larrañaga, were targeted with a bomb at his graveside when they were laying flowers with the Basque PP leadership on the first anniversary of his death. Only the incompetence of the terrorists prevented a massacre. The bomb exploded after the family had left, scattering the bones and body parts of the dead in a macabre and sacrilegious parody of ETA's intentions on the living.

Regarding ETA as a Higher Power

Over the years, I have repeatedly asked members of Batasuna how they could justify attacks like these. These are, I repeat, individuals whose decency and humanity was evident in everything except in their com-plicit silence before such crimes. Their actual words have varied, of course, but essentially there are two responses. One, a mantra familiar from Sinn Féin members in similar circumstances, runs like this: "These deaths, like all deaths, are regrettable, but they are the inevitable result of the Basque conflict, and will no longer happen when the conflict is resolved."

This is disingenuous, of course. ETA is not a force of nature which operates independently of the will of individuals. A conflict has no finger to squeeze a trigger or detonate a bomb. Only individual human beings can do these things. And these individuals must be aware that there are many non-violent alternatives to such actions in the Basque Country today.

The other standard response runs a little deeper, and tells us a little more about the culture which has nurtured terrorism in the Basque context: "I find this killing as repugnant as you do. It upsets me deeply. But ETA always has its reasons."

This view of ETA as a kind of higher power, whose reason goes beyond our own poor reasoning, was encountered by Zulaika in Itziar. In 1976 four youths from the village were found to have been responsible for two ETA kidnappings, one of which resulted in the cold-blooded killing of the victim, a Basque businessman associated with the PNV. Most of the villagers simply could not believe what had happened. For one thing, "they had always imagined ETA as an organization made up of far-off supermen," not local teenagers. For another, they did not believe that ETA would have killed a PNV supporter, so they preferred to think that the boys had been trying to raise money for their own use. It was easier to believe that their neighbours' children were common criminals (a most unlikely possibility in that culture) than that they were members of ETA, and doing something most Basques disapproved of on ETA's orders.

In one way or another, Basque nationalists have been "in denial" about the real nature of ETA for many years. In the 1990s I asked Loren Arkotxa, an amiable ex-ETA member who was then an impressively energetic Batasuna mayor of Ondarroa, a difficult question. What he would do if he learned that ETA was about to kill a PP councillor who had been his childhood friend? "I would do everything in my power to protect him," he told me, and sounded as if he meant it. And what about PP councillors from other villages? "Ah well, I don't know any of them personally," he said as if that justified his apparent indifference to their fates.

The very intimacy of Basque society makes the position of PP supporters even more difficult, says Antonio Basagoiti, the president of the PP in the Vizcaya. "It's normal in the Basque Country to have relatives from one side and the other, I had an uncle in the PNV, another was assassinated for supporting Franco. It's not like Andalusia where politics runs on class lines, the landowners are PP, the farm-workers PSOE. Some of my councillors have had family members in Batasuna, they socialize with them, but that has not given them any security. On the contrary, these are some of the ones who have been shot."

Outside Bilbao, he believes that PP voters are totally integrated in the indigenous traditions of their towns and villages. Indeed, he thinks they are much more part of the fabric of traditional Basque life than Socialist Party voters, because many of them are ethnic Basques and come from Carlist backgrounds. "The Basque nationalists might hate us more than they hate the Socialists, because we assert our Spanishness more than PSOE members here do. But they consider the Socialists second-class citizens because they are of immigrant origin." He pauses, and adds: "They say being ruled by the PSOE would be like being ruled by their servants," taking sardonic pleasure in wielding a political knife which cuts both his rivals with one stroke.

The Carlist background of many PP voters means that they share a conservative and Catholic philosophy with the PNV's social base, he continues. So, in their daily lives, at business, in the gastronomic society, at the pelota court, or in church an average PP voter leads the life of an average Basque. The one thing that distinguishes them is that they cannot distinguish themselves publicly: "They live in fear. A PNV voter can wear party insignia; a PP voter must keep their loyalty, their feeling of being Spanish as well as Basque, a secret. There are villages where we get 4,000 votes, and not one supporter is willing to run for local office." Like Jews under Nazism, he says, they live in dread of being identified. Fourteen PP councillors have been killed by ETA since 1992.

The worlds in which people like Basagoiti—and their opposite numbers in the PSOE—have had to live are, by definition, closed to most visitors to the Basque Country. Their grim experience contradicts the image, faithful in itself, of a warm, hospitable and sociable society which most of these visitors bring home with them. Yet these shadowlands are also a part of the Basque Country. In a conflict situation, and even in its aftermath, visions of society will be distorted by the positions viewers have occupied. Perhaps the fairest assessment of relationships within the Basque community comes from Txema Montero, a former Batasuna MEP who has long rejected violence, and now directs a PNV think-tank:

> Coexistence and pluralism in the Basque Country are much stronger than the Spanish nationalists claim, but they are also much more fragile than we Basque nationalists would like to think.

Basque nationalists in general, Zulaika believes, "always thought we were the victims, and never wanted to recognize that we could also be the executioners." There is, of course, nothing specifically Basque about this. The leaders of the PSOE in the GAL period persistently still deny responsibility for the death squads, and displayed an equally disturbing disregard for the victims of state terrorism.

This century opened with the Basque Country more polarized than ever. When Batasuna refused to condemn ETA's renewed campaign, the Madrid parliament banned the party, with the support of the courts. This step was questioned by many jurists and human rights advocates. It has left many Basques disenfranchised, and a good number of villages and towns are administered by parties which do not have majority support.

Yet enthusiasm for ETA was already collapsing among Batasuna voters, so that there was surprisingly little resistance to these measures. The 9/11 attacks in the US had created a context in which ETA looked irrelevant as well as repugnant. The IRA's progress towards destroying its own arsenal not only added to this changed context, but offered ETA an exit strategy. If a group as prestigious (in ETA's view) as the Irish terrorists could bid farewell to arms without losing face, then ETA might take the same path with its head held high. The Madrid train bombs massacre in March 2004, at a terrible cost, put the final pieces in place that made a peace process possible.

The blatant attempt by the outgoing PP government to blame ETA for these bombings, when all the evidence pointed to Islamists, not only brought the PP into disrepute, it put it out of office. The Spanish electorate swung from the PP to the PSOE in elections held just three days later. Voters were clearly disgusted with a government that was playing politics with—and, many believed, lying about—the worst terrorist attack the country had ever suffered. The new PSOE prime minister, José Luis Rodríguez Zapatero, quickly recognized that the bombings had also massively accelerated disenchantment with violence among ETA supporters. He courageously offered talks to the Basque group, on the strict condition of a permanent end to violence, in May 2005. ETA responded ominously slowly, however, taking nine months to decide to call a ceasefire in March 2006.

It is still too early to say whether the infant Basque peace process, badly damaged by ETA's December 2006 bomb attack, can still grow to maturity. The signs are far from encouraging. The process lacks the bipartisan support that has been a foundation of its Irish equivalent, which indeed was initiated by a Conservative Party under John Major. The PP, most unfortunately, has seen fit to portray any discussions with ETA as a "betrayal of the dead"—though a PP government held just such discussions during the previous ceasefire. There are also worrying indications that not all key ETA members are willing to take the IRA's painful journey towards standing down. It is unclear whether those Batasuna leaders committed to an unarmed strategy have the will or the political capital to tell the militarists that they must no longer claim a privileged role on the Basque stage. Nor is it certain that Zapatero, a much less experienced politician than Tony Blair, has the skills to advance the process under these very adverse conditions.

Everyone who loves the Basque Country hoped against hope that these difficulties could be overcome. Far too many people have been caught up in one or another aspect of this war, far too many maimed, far too many dead, leaving far too many grieving relatives. The only thing which is certain is that there is unlikely to be a better opportunity to resolve the Basque conflict in this generation. The news that ETA was formally ending its ceasefire, received in June 2007, adds terrible poignancy to the words written by Atxaga on the day that ceasefire had come into effect:

Happiness always seems strange, and the more so in our case, with forty years of political violence at our backs.

Chapter Twelve

Bay of Biscay: Whales, Belle Epoque, Decapitated Geese, Sexual Politics

Baionatik Bilbora
itsaso euskara.
The sea is our language
from Bayonne to Bilbao.

Koldo Izagirre, *Baionatik Bilbora*, 1976

Thirty years ago, the lights of dozens of inshore fishing boats streamed home into Hondarribia harbour every single winter evening. They reflected off the water like a field of dancing stars. The flaring and fading pulse of their engines, as they passed almost directly beneath our balcony, was the sound of night falling. After the last of them faded into darkness and the stillness, it was time to head out down the Calle San Pedro, patron saint of fishermen, and drink a glass or two before dinner. The *arrantzales* slowly filled up the bars. They liked unpretentious places like the Itxaropena, aptly or perhaps ironically named after that essential virtue for the fishing trade, hope. The *arrantzales'* faces were as inscrutable as their Euskera was impenetrable. Hondarribia's dialect was regarded as difficult even by the people from the next village west along the coast, Pasai Donibane. The fishermen did not speak much, in any case. Very occasionally, a sandpapery face would crinkle into a quarter-smile under the shadow of a *txapela*, betraying a particularly bountiful catch.

The Itxaropena today is much as it was then, still unscathed by the plague of interior designers which has infested so many Basque bars. But you will not find many *arrantzales* at the counter in the evenings. Some of those you do find may be speaking sub-Saharan African languages

Casket dancer: supported by his colleagues, Asier Uskola performs the *kaxarranka* in Lekeitio's San Pedros fiestas, with the flying buttresses of the town's Gothic Church of the Assumption in the background. The dance originally celebrated the fishing fleet's annual profits, no motive for rejoicing today.

rather than Euskera. The chronic decline of one of the archetypical Basque employments, and the growth in many more comfortable sectors of the economy, makes fishing less and less attractive to local people. In any case, there are not many fish left to catch. Esteban Olaizola, who grew up discussing the fortunes of fishing in these bars, is angry about how things have worked out.

"Our ignorance is audacious," he declares. "What are we doing to the sea?" He answers his own question. "We are abusing it. Businessmen think it is infinite. But it is not. And it is not private property. It is the patrimony of all humanity. In agriculture, we sow the land, and we nurture the crop, and then we harvest something we have produced ourselves, more or less. But in the sea we sow nothing, we nurture nothing, we produce nothing. We just harvest what the sea gives us. But we have forgotten to let the sea do its own producing, so every year there is less to harvest. Ignorance is audacious." Olaizola repeats the phrase again, between contempt and despair. "And look at the results. The cod are gone, and every year the hake are further away from our shores..."

He breaks off suddenly, worried that he might be misunderstood. "I'm not an ecologist, don't think that." Then he reconsiders. "Or, OK, if we are ecologists, it is because ecology is in our interests." In fact, Olaizola is a businessman himself, but he no longer makes a living from the sea. He runs a successful bed-and-breakfast, well located on a hill above his native Hondarribia. There are spectacular sea views from the dining room, across the Txingudi estuary to the curving strands at Hendaye, and up the smooth sweep of the French Basque Coast. At night, the lighthouse at Biarritz can be seen illuminating the sky. But the river of light that used to flood into the harbour with the fishing boats every evening has diminished to a trickle.

Olaizola went to sea when he was 15, was a captain for 18 years, served two four-year terms as president of the *arrantzale kofradia* (fishermen's guild) of Guipúzcoa, and periodically acted as spokesperson for the fishermen of both the CAV's coastal provinces. He comes from a very long tradition. Since the eleventh century, the *kofradias* have regulated fishing practices in the region, establishing which fish may be caught when, and in what quantities per boat. They have generally enjoyed a remarkable degree of independence from the political authorities. The resilience of the *kofradias* in the Basque Country owes something to the persistence of the Basque *fueros* generally. And because the *kofradias* represented both ship-owners and (in more recent times) sailors, they fitted in well with the concept of "corporatist" trade unions during the Franco dictatorship. They were one of the few deeply rooted indigenous institutions to survive that period, and then renovate themselves during the transition to democracy.

Each Basque fishing town has a distinctive building in the port, also known as the *kofradia*, where the guild supervises the auction of the catch and manages its business. The auction used to be conducted around an elaborate wooden device, rather like a roulette table, into which bidders cast their tokens as prices came into their range. You can see one in the *kofradia zaharra* (old guildhall) in Mutriko, which is now both a hostel and a museum. Many of the recent *kofradias* are trophy buildings. In the small but historic town of Getaria the new *kofradia* is an imposing palace of stainless steel, which would not look out of place in a prestige Chicago low-rise office development.

But modernization has come at a price. In recent decades some of the *kofradias* have fought a losing battle against the "curtains of death", the massive ocean floor drag-nets with which factory ships are scooping up the remaining stocks of cod, hake and anchovy.

The *kofradias* were not always so conscious of the need for sustainable exploitation of maritime resources. One of the emblems of office of Olaizola's guild in Hondarribia is a *makila* (ceremonial walking stick) made of whale tusk, a reminder of an ominous precedent for fish stocks today.

The Basque whalers were brave, resourceful and determined men. The Northern Right Whale (*Eubalaena glacialis*) is often known as the Basque Whale (*Balaena viscayensis*) because it was so heavily hunted along the whole of their coast, and far beyond, by the Basques. They learned their whaling skills from the Normans, whose pirate ships plundered their ports, and then hunted whales under the eyes of the temporarily dispossessed Basques, watching from the hills. In 1095 Bayonne obtained the right to sell whale products, and the Basques never looked back—until there were no more whales to hunt. The complex regulations of the *kofradias* were not strong enough to save the Basque Whale.

Whales are prominent in the coats-of-arms of no fewer than thirteen of the Basque ports, from Biarritz to Bermeo. *Atalayas*, or watch towers, still stand above many seaside towns. Look-outs would constantly watch from them for a whale to blow. Once a spout or breach was spotted, small boats would put out to do battle with the monster, while the whalers' families gathered in the *atalaya* to watch (and pray) while a perilous drama unfolded.

The Right Whale was a particularly attractive quarry. Hence its English name—it was the "right whale" to catch. It is hugely rich in blubber and is (relatively) easy to catch. Most importantly, it floats after death, unlike most cetaceans. For small boats like the Basque caravelles, this greatly eased the task of bringing it ashore. By the early sixteenth century, possibly earlier, the Basques had followed the whale to Galicia, to the seas around Britain and Ireland, and then to Newfoundland. All these stocks were in chronic decline as early as the beginning of the seventeenth century. Then the discovery of new whaling grounds around Greenland revived the industry, especially from the French Basque port of St.-Jean-de-Luz.

The many centuries of transatlantic fishing produced a distinctive social by-product. With the men away from home from spring to autumn, women took on significant public responsibilities in the ports and were the unchallenged mistresses of their homes. So, along the coast, a Basque tendency towards matriarchy was accentuated. Victor Hugo observed that in these communities, "the man has the sea, the woman has the harbour." Yet as more recent and less romantic investigation has shown, the position of women in the ports remained constrained by social conventions. These ensured that men were the ultimate arbiters of major decisions, and the public role of women became increasingly limited from the mid-nineteenth century.

But what of the whales? Sadly, no lessons were learned from the early over-fishing, and the Right Whale in the Atlantic was exploited to exhaustion point. It remains very close to extinction today. The last local Basque Whale was taken off Orio in 1901. Curiously, a UNESCO biosphere reserve in Baja California, Mexico, which today provides sanctuary for a related Pacific whale species, is called El Vizcaíno, the Basque. At the mouth of its sister UNESCO biosphere reserve of Urdaibai, in the heart of contemporary Vizcaya, no whales remain to be protected. For the last thirty years and more, fish stocks have been going the way of the whale. Cod, hake, red sea bream, anchovy, all classic staples of the

Basque fleets and Basque tables, are harder to find every year. In recent years, they sometimes cannot be found at all.

Lekeitio: Dancing on a Casket

Lekeitio was once a proud Vizcayan fishing port, whose ships followed the whale and cod as far as Newfoundland. There is no hard evidence for claims that the Basques actually reached the New World before Columbus reached the Caribbean, but they were certainly fishing there from the early sixteenth century. The industry was a source of considerable wealth, which was managed by the *kofradia*. Every year, on St. Peter's Day, the outgoing treasurer of the guild used to hand over the year's takings to his successor, the gold and silver coins safely locked in a coffin-shaped wooden casket. The story goes that one year the profits were so big that the outgoing official leapt onto the casket and danced for joy.

Every year since then, on the Día de San Pedro, the casket has been carried along the quays of Lekeitio. Until quite recently it was borne on the shoulders of sturdy fishermen. Today it is carried by the members of a traditional dance group. Outside the *kofradia*, and later outside the town hall, one of their number executes an energetic and sophisticated dance, the *kaxaranka*, on the narrow surface of the casket, while it is held, rock steady, on his companions' shoulders. Part of the thrill of the spectacle is the possibility that his footwork, or their shoulders, may fail. If this has ever happened, no-one in the town admits it.

This is one of Lekeitio's two fishermen's fiestas—the other involves decapitating geese—and both put the town very high on any list of exotic Basque customs. Both fiestas illustrate the rule that tradition is intimately linked to change. The San Pedro fiesta is old enough to have fallen foul of the Holy Inquisition in its day, and suffered forced alterations in the Franco period. In the early seventeenth century, the dancer used to dress up as the pope or, according to another version, as St. Peter himself. Other fisherman played the parts of other saints. It was said that the ordinary people took the disguise for reality, and beat their breasts before these ordinary mortals in remorse and adoration.

The local bishop suspected a blasphemous satire. Pious citizens blamed the revellers' alleged irreverence for bringing plague and fires to the town. Matters came to blows, and the Inquisition was asked to adjudicate. The proceedings dragged on and on for decades, and ended inconclusively in legal terms. But the Church won in practice. Since those days, the dancer has worn a costume reminiscent of an elegant circus ringmaster or a dandy undertaker: top hat, morning coat with tails and red carnation in the lapel, white trousers, a red sash and an oversized red kerchief.

There have been more recent changes, too. The women of Lekeitio used to do a special dance at sunrise, midday and sunset on the feast of St. John, 24 June, close to the summer solstice. Sniffing out a pagan homage to the sun-god, the authorities suppressed this custom during the Franco dictatorship. It has now resurfaced, to a degree, transferred as a one-off dance on the feast of St. Peter, five days later.

So change is an integral part of tradition, however strong the temptation is to think of such ceremonies as immutable and eternal. The biggest contemporary threat to the Basque fiesta in general today probably comes from consumer culture, which can reduce these very special events to little more than drinking binges in fancy dress.

To see a fiesta at its best, and most intimate, choose one in a small town or village, when the saint's day which kick-starts it falls on a weekday. This is important because it means the fiesta will only be a public holiday in the village itself and so most of the people attending will be locals, who feel some real sense of connection with its rituals. At weekends, the population will be multiplied, sometimes many times over, by people from other areas, in search of another excuse for *juerga* and *gaupasa*.

In 2005 the festival of St. Peter fell mid-week, and the morning's empty streets in Lekeitio made it seem like a Sunday. The only sign of a fiesta at 10 o'clock was a group of *txistularis* playing in an empty plaza. A mother and her young son watched them sleepily from a balcony. The previous night, *cabezudos*, giant-head caricatures of pirates, witches and Moors, had chased squealing children down the streets, whacking them with sheep's bladders filled with water. After that, most of their parents had gone drinking, and now the whole town seemed to be sleeping it off.

By midday, however, the Lekeitianos were out in some numbers to attend the Mass with which the fiesta proper begins. The fifteenth-century Church of the Assumption of the Virgin Mary is, even by the grandiose standards of Basque Gothic architecture, more like an urban cathedral than a parish church in a small town. Its elongated flying buttresses are one of Lekeitio's signature images, and lend the building's bulk a surprisingly light and airy touch. Inside, its enormous polychromatic altar panels are said to be the finest in Vizcaya. They are certainly bigger than any in Spain except those in the cathedrals of Seville and Toledo, and give an indication of the former wealth and status of the town.

Beneath this imposing grandeur, there is a pleasant sense of informal naturalness about the congregation, whose religious practice seems utterly unselfconscious. A fine-looking man in his sixties enters late, dips his hand in holy water, genuflects, and takes a neighbour's elbow as he sits beside him. It is all part of one seamless movement. The parishioners say the responses confidently, and sing with gusto. The whole service is conducted in Euskera.

The Mass concluded, four elderly but robust men bear a statue of St. Peter, the Keys of the Kingdom of Heaven hanging from his wrist, slowly up the quays. They are followed by the clergy, municipal authorities and the general congregation. The crowd now swells rapidly, joined by younger people who had stayed away from the church. Many of the windows display large white hangings, lace trimmed, in honour of St. Peter. Others, inevitably, bear the ubiquitous poster demanding an end to the "dispersion" of ETA prisoners to jails in faraway parts of Spain: *Euskal Presoak, Euskal Herrira*, Basque Prisoners to the Basque Country.

At the quayside the four men pause, and then bring the saint right to the edge for the Kilin-Kala ceremony. This involves rocking him quite rapidly, until he is leaning over sharply towards the water below. They bring him back to vertical, and then rock him again, in a gesture supposed to help fill the nets of the fishing fleet, something that indeed requires miraculous intervention in these times. "He had better bring us luck this year," a disenchanted woman remarked loudly, "otherwise he can go into the water himself." In fact, St. Peter has got a soaking on a couple of occasions. More often than that, the Kilin-Kala has loosened his grip on the Keys of the Kingdom, which have gone flying into the sea.

In the water or out of it, the saint has been able to do little for Lekeitio's fishing industry. Its decline seems irreversible, though the construction fever which turns the narrow streets into obstacle courses might suggest otherwise. But this building boom is due to city-dwellers seeking second homes. It is part of the widespread transformation of the whole Basque coast into a leisure belt. The fishing traditions which gave the coast much of its attractive character are dying.

There were fifteen deep-sea vessels operating from these quays in 1990. In 2005 there were just two. A superstitious Catholic might wonder whether the bad luck is not linked to the fact that some of today's fishermen worship strange gods.

One of the two remaining ships carries an image of Che Guevara on its prow, and the iconic revolutionary also stares resolutely from its flag-pole. Guevara can be found fluttering above a grave in Lekeitio's cemetery, too. The town council was dominated by Batasuna before the party was banned. Huge posters demanding the resignation of the councillors who have replaced them, from the PNV and other nationalist parties, are strategically placed to take advantage of TV coverage of the fiesta. Lekeitio is the birthplace and burial place of Santi Brouard, a much-loved pediatrician, and the most widely respected leader that Herri Batasuna ever produced.

He was assassinated by a GAL death squad as he attended a little girl in his surgery in 1984. This was part of the dirty war waged against ETA which deeply discredited Felipe González's Socialist Party government. Half a million people attended Brouard's funeral. The municipal guide to the town names him as one of half a dozen "illustrious figures" from its entire history. But this entry is not much help to the curious tourist. Brouard's name alone is followed by no biographical note, leaving a curious blank, an echoing silence, on the page.

But let us return to the fiesta. With St. Peter back in the church, bone dry on this occasion, a dance group has assembled outside the old *kofradia* to perform the *kaxarranka*. A window display had been prepared in honour of the saint, including a model boat, and a drapery of black nets which looks more mournful than festive. High up on the wall is a small statue of St. Peter, in a glass-fronted niche specially opened for the occasion. On the ledge in front is a crucifix, again with a votive boat before it, and the façade has been draped with a bunting of small *ikur-riñas*.

The dancer, who bears an uncanny resemblance to a young Daniel Day-Lewis, is assisted up onto the casket. He seems tense as the little band of *txistularis* begin to play their flutes and drums. After his first few steps, selfconsciousness melts into assurance, even authority. His immaculately white-stockinged feet step nimbly along the very edge of the casket, but never falter. Top hat in one hand, flag and baton in the other, he bows to the audience with an elaborate flourish. You might imagine for a moment that this is a courtier greeting a monarch. But there is no hint of servility here, only a very Basque gesture which reflects mutual respect. His bearers hold their expressions stoically, though the pounding on their shoulders must be hard to bear.

The *kaxarranka* ritual is repeated twice, at the new *kofradia* at the harbour mouth, and then again in the plaza outside the town hall. Here it is preceded by the once-banned *Eguzki-dantza*, in honour of a midday sun that is now agreeably warm. Young women in traditional shawls choose their male partners from the general public, perhaps a vestige of matriarchy in a dance tradition where men are now usually the main protagonists.

Afterwards, upstairs in the town hall chamber which overlooks the plaza, Asier Uskola speaks modestly of his role as *dantzari* of the *kaxarranka*. "I am always a little nervous at first, but by the time I get to the plaza it is pure pleasure." Uskola is now 19, and has performed the role for the past three years. Will he do it as long as his predecessor, for three decades? "If I can, yes, if I'm able. But if someone else wants to do it, fine, it does not have to be me," he replies with characteristically Basque modesty. Self-praise and self-advertisement are still frowned on in the Basque Country, an attractive trait in a people not lacking in pride.

He had no direct connection, he says, with the *arrantzale* world, and neither has most of the group who perform with him. "I joined the dance group, and they picked me to do it," he says matter-of-factly. The link to the sea, however, is still there, albeit at one remove. His father was a sailor, but not from Lekeitio itself, from a neighbouring village, not quite on the coast, Mendexa.

Getaria: the Aesthetics of an Egg

The smell of fresh sardines, grilling over charcoal in the street and carried to one's nostrils by a salty sea breeze, is one of the characteristic and delightful smells of a Basque port. It is nowhere more typical than in Getaria, a small town which has given birth to two very big names, the sixteenth-century naval explorer Juan Sebastián de Elcano, and the twentieth-century couturier, Cristóbal Balenciaga.

Oddly enough, it is easier to imagine the old world of Elcano in Getaria than the once brand new but already dated world of Balenciaga. The port and old quarter are cut off from the new town by a busy road, and once you cross it and plunge down the cavernous streets towards the sea, the centuries roll back very quickly. Ancient houses are piled several storeys high, each floor adjusting to the shifts of time, like layers of sedimentary rock in a canyon. One of the streets (you have a choice of just two) goes underneath part of the parish church of San Salvador (c.1200-1420). This building, a marvellous example of early Basque Gothic construction, is remarkable for its asymmetrical structure.

Entering the church, you find yourself in a stone-clad bubble, a generous breathing space whose scale is in total contrast to the dark and semi-subterranean streets outside. The light is dim, yet there is plenty of it. Its sources are so variously angled that it is almost impossible to establish a single unified perspective. Gradually, you realize that this is partly because so much in the building, from the floor to the obscure complex of arches that makes up the roof, is tilted, uneven, askew. But the curious architectonics of the church are due to something much more deliberate, and much more radical, than awkward location and idiosyncratic workmanship. Move right around the building and you will often find elegant curves, but rarely be offered a straight line.

Jorge Oteiza described San Salvador as "a small, sea-faring cathedral". His idea that Basque Gothic churches are stone ships, massive but somehow lightly anchored to the earth, is at its most irresistible here. San Salvador does not aspire to a heavenly sky but seems rather inclined to slip off into the mystery of the sea. Oteiza saw this church as the antithesis of Castilian Gothic, typified by the cathedral of León, with its "regular geometry and rectilinear symmetry, crystalline and French". Instead, this prototypically atypical Basque church is for Oteiza "a distinct creation, simpler and more popular in appearance, much more prodigious and wise, [and] more living" than the dominant architecture of the period in Spain. The secret, he believed, lay in the Basque discovery of "the aesthetics of the egg", a willingness to resolve the organic and elliptical planes of an ovoid interior into a monument of stone. We may take Oteiza's egg with a pinch of salt, but his homage to San Salvador nonetheless captures the essence of its powerful visual impact.

This church has a close association with the confirmation of another circuitous theory. It was here that the first of Getaria's famous sons, Juan Sebastián de Elcano (1476-1526) worshipped as a boy. In 1519, already a most accomplished captain, Elcano joined an expedition led by Ferdinand de Magellan. This Portuguese explorer proposed finding a westward route to access the spices of the Moluccas. The little fleet sailed from Seville under the patronage of the Holy Roman Emperor Charles V (Charles I of Spain). It reached its destination, via the straits which connect the southern Atlantic and Pacific Oceans, and which now bear Magellan's name. But the voyage was fractious, and its Pacific phase marred by many clashes with indigenous peoples, in one of which Magellan was killed. So it was the Basque captain who brought the fleet home to Seville via the Cape of Good Hope. Elcano thus provided the first conclusive practical demonstration that the world is round. Only 18 of the 265 men who had set out on the expedition returned alive. The emperor granted Elcano a coat of arms which includes the globe and the motto *Primus circumdedisti me* (you were the first to sail around me). An alcove in the church reminds us that he had made a vow of devotion to the Virgen de la Antigua, in Seville Cathedral, and honoured it on his return. Perhaps he should have entrusted himself to the Andra Mari of Itziar, only a few miles from his home town, because his luck had run out and he died on his next expedition. Getaria remembers him with a pair of indifferent monuments and a popular ceremony every four years.

Getaria's own luck as a fishing port is now running out, and the identity of the village is changing rapidly. An avalanche of new apartments threatens to choke what little space remains free on either side of the coast road. As drivers approach from the west, they are confronted with a towering building site, hung with massive banners offering buyers "the biggest swimming pool in the world outside your window", pointing towards the Bay of Biscay.

Belle Epoque: Zarautz, Biarritz, San Sebastián
This shift in attitude to the sea, which sees the ocean as a source of pleasure rather than of food, where sailing is a leisure pursuit rather than a risky

pathway to new worlds, was partly pioneered right here on the Basque coast in the nineteenth century. Getaria's nearest neighbour, Zarautz, was described as the "the most aristocratic bathing resort in Guipúzcoa" by Pío Baroja. It is just a half hour's brisk walk away, around a small promontory on a dramatic but busy road. Yet it is a world away in atmosphere. Here there is none of the cramped intimacy of Getaria. Zarautz is spread out along its sweeping beach—the longest in the region—with an elegant promenade and some fine Belle Epoque architecture.

"Où sont les plages d'antan?" quipped Martha Gellhorn in *Travels with Myself and Another* (1987), remembering "beaches with no debris on them except seaweed". In a globe-trotting inventory running from Cuba to Calabria, the only one she mentions individually is "the great beach at Zarautz".

The Bourbon Queen Isabella II chose the Palacio de Narros, on the right as you enter Zarautz from Getaria, as one of her favourite summering places. She was holding court in nearby San Sebastián in 1868 when news reached her that she had been deposed by a series of *pronunciamientos* in the south. As Raymond Carr (*Spain 1808-1975*; 1982) puts it: "with peculiar delicacy San Sebastian waited till the queen was in the train for exile and France" before it, too, pronounced against her. Ironically, Liberal San Sebastián had been the first city to recognize her as queen (at the age of three) 35 years earlier, in defiance of the pretender Don Carlos, Isabella's uncle. This established the firm anti-Carlist position of this quintessential Basque city right at the opening of the first Carlist war.

The Basque coast may fly the flags of revolutionary icons today, but it was a magnet for reactionaries on both sides of the border towards the end of the nineteenth century. Napoleon III's Spanish-born empress, Eugénie de Montijo, spent some of her childhood in Biarritz, and was so impressed that she brought the emperor and half the aristocracy of Europe to holiday there in the 1860s. After she was deposed she liked to summer in Lekeitio, and had a medieval castle refurbished for herself in Gautegiz Arteaga in nearby Urdaibai.

The Hapsburg Queen Regent, María Cristina, made San Sebastián the official summer home of the Spanish Court from 1887, choosing the eclectically styled Miramar Palace as the royal residence. An eye-catching and equally eclectic casino (now the town hall) was built two years later.

The Spanish Basque coast rapidly became as fashionable for European high society as its French counterpart had been under Napoleon III. The hotel which best evokes this period still bears María Cristina's name today. (She is not to be confused with the Bourbon Queen Regent, also María Cristina, who was the mother of Isabella II.) Spain's neutrality during the First World War made the Guipuzcoan capital the last refuge of the Belle Epoque, and a magnet for prestigious arts companies like the Ballets Russes.

Despite his loathing of Basque nationalism, or perhaps simply to demonstrate its crushing defeat, General Franco revived the reactionary social status of San Sebastián after his victory in the Civil War. He spent every August from 1940 to 1975, the year of his death, in the Ayete Palace.

While one of San Sebastián's most elegant theatres, the Victoria Eugenia, is named after the grandmother of the present king of Spain, Juan Carlos II, contemporary political realities mean that the royal family rarely visits the city today.

The Dutch novelist and poet Cees Nooteboom visited San Sebastián in the 1980s. In *Roads to Santiago* (1997) he finds in the city an air of languid, agreeable decline:

> San Sebastian lies on the Bay of Biscay like a somewhat bizarrely painted lady of a certain age reclining on a sofa. She has known better days, murmurs in theatre boxes, royal admirers—all that belongs to the past now, but the traces of former glory are still in evidence… As there is no money to buy anything new, the lamps, the wardrobes and the engravings of the old days are still in use. San Sebastián is a huge storehouse of Art Nouveau and Jugendstil, odd-looking bridges with lamps of the kind you find nowhere nowadays, hotels that, in Brussels, would have been demolished long ago, wrought-iron railings a collector would like to be hanged from.

Those ubiquitous and sinuous railings, the globular lamps on the Kursaal bridge and those charmingly antiquated hotels (María Cristina, Londres) are still there today, but there is plenty of money now to buy new things also. The city's own most extravagant recent purchase is the Kursaal Palace of Congresses. Replacing a private casino-theatre-restaurant complex knocked down in 1973, the new Kursaal stands on the beach at the edge of the *barrio* of Gros, where the Urumea river meets the sea. On the opposite bank sits the Victoria Eugenia theatre, a Belle Epoque jewel. Many do not like this bold juxtaposition, and would agree that "the Kursaal has eaten up the Victoria Eugenia," as a native of San Sebastián declares in Ramón Saizarbitoria's novel *Rosetti's Obsession*. Colloquially known as *los Kubos* (the Cubes), the Kursaal's two glass prisms (one massive, the other just big) were excoriated by many Donostiarras when the project was finished after a very long gestation in 1999. Described rather unflatteringly by their own architect, Rafael Moneo, as "two beached rocks", they remain a little alien in elegant San Sebastián, in often-noted contrast to the integration of the Guggenheim in the urban mêlée of Bilbao. They have a certain space-age magic when illuminated at night, however, and have become an essential part of the city's cultural life, including its world-class film and jazz festivals.

There are few cities in the world so happily situated as San Sebastián. The centre today is focused around the Concha [Kontxa], a sweeping semi-circular bay which incorporates a glorious promenade, a pretty island, an intimate fishing-port and a first-class beach. Two more fine beaches, Ondarreta and Zurriola, lie on its flanks. Three steep hills, with superb coastal views (and one truly appalling statue of Christ), mark the beaches' limits. One of Chillida's most famous and effective sculptures, *The Comb of the Winds*, is anchored to the rocks at Ondarreta, a reminder that Chillida Leku, a delightful park based around his work, is only twenty minutes away, near Hernani.

The city's greatest asset, however, remains its old quarter, a most atmospheric rabbit-warren between the Concha and Zurriola, where the best *pintxos* in the world (with apologies to Bilbao) are to be found in almost every street. There are not many urban pleasures to compare with a sunny (or even a stormy) stroll around the Concha, followed by a glass of *txakoli* and a tiny slice of fried bread crowned with a teaspoonful of scrambled eggs with mushroom and garlic. Or a saucer of breaded roast red pepper stuffed with very fresh crab. Or... But, pleasant as it is to linger here, San Sebastián is already very well known. Let us go back to Lekeitio, which has more secrets to reveal.

Lekeitio II: Decapitating Geese

Waiting to be decapitated, a goose dangles, tied by its feet to a rope strung across Lekeitio harbour. The harbour is full of rowing boats, which are full of people, too full, one might think, for safety. And the people, most of them, are full of drink. Crates of beer and ten-litre wine containers cram what little space is left on the boats' small decks.

One at a time, each crew rows, as fast as possible, underneath the goose. At the critical moment, one crew member must leap from the boat and seize the goose by the head, ideally winding its entire neck into a solid arm-lock. The rope attached to the goose's legs has been fed through a pulley into the hands of a line of burly men, veterans of the local tug-of-war teams. As the contestant grasps the goose, they let his (or her) full weight dangle from the bird for a brief, dramatic instant. Then they jerk hard on the rope, so that the contestant is thrown up about thirty feet above the water. Next they abruptly release the tension, so that man (or woman) and bird plunge right into the sea. This is followed by a sharp tug back, so that the pair are flung high into the air once again, sending an arc of spray across the harbour. Another jerk-stop, another sudden release, and down they go again, out of sight beneath the waves.

If the goose has a good strong neck and good strong legs, and the contestant has a good strong grip, this fly-and-dunk pattern can be repeated many times. Recorded numbers of *alzadas* ("elevations") run into the high thirties. The game should finish with the contestant tearing the head cleanly off the goose (some enthusiasts even sever it with their teeth). Success leaves the pink inner and white outer parts of the goose's neck pumping and jerking, rather obscenely, from its body. Sometimes the whole goose comes off the rope.

You may be wondering why the animal rights movement does not slap a particularly angry picket on this event. The reason is that each goose has been humanely killed long before it is attached to the rope. But this was not always the case. The geese used to be very much alive, and must have experienced great pain and greater fear before they met their end. But it is curious that not many people in the town agree exactly when the use of living geese was prohibited. Most people think it was sometime in the 1980s, somehow linked to the introduction of democracy.

Goose bumps: a contestant in Lekeitio's San Antolines fiestas clings to a hanging carcass as he is flung up out of the sea by a jerking rope. The Basque flag is wrapped around his waist.

But another version puts the prohibition twenty years further back, and attributes to it to a sly manoeuvre by one of Franco's generals. According to this story, this general used to spend his summers in Lekeitio. One day he read that Spain was coming under international criticism for permitting bullfighting. So he approached the *Caudillo* with a novel proposal: why not make a token gesture to world opinion, and ban the live decapitation of San Antolín's birds in Lekeitio? There could be no question of yielding an inch on the sacred principle of the Spanish right to bullfighting, of course. But stopping the Basques from doing what they wanted was practically a principle of Spanish nationalism. Now yet another ban could be dressed up as showing foreigners that the regime was flexible and humane. Killing two birds with one stone, as it were.

Dismemberment is a subtext of the fiesta. Like those of many beloved saints, the relics of the patron, San Antolín, are scattered across many places where he is honoured. "Palencia has most of his remains today," says the mayor. "We only have one finger. I'm not sure which one."

However well or badly he performs, the contestant will be recovered by his crew, many of whom will have plunged from the boat to form a circle around him. Almost all are fully clothed, and the goose-grabber will probably have (illicitly) filled his pockets with sand, to add weight to his gravity battle with the goose's neck. After half a dozen boats have had their chance, the harbour is thick with crew members, splashing and joshing in good spirits. A first-aid launch stands by. But no-one, apparently, has ever been seriously injured, let alone drowned, during this chaotic and inebriated swim-in.

It seems chaotic, but it is all taken very seriously by the judges. They sit scrupulously ticking boxes as each boat makes its pass. They enter marks for a series of criteria, not just the number of *alzadas*. There are points for the neat severing of the head; for the elegance of the oarsmen as well as that of the goose-grabber; for the speed of the boat, and for the imagination with which it has been decked out and the slogan it proclaims. If a contestant loses his grip on the goose without severing its head, the judges must take into account that the job will be easier for the next crew.

For all the meticulousness of the judges, the event they are evaluating bears only the most superficial resemblance to the fiesta as it was practised in living memory. Forty years ago, only eight to ten boats would have participated, and each would have been crewed by only eight men, all local fishermen. The only alcohol they drank would have been a glass or two of the sixteen litres of wine donated by the town council. This was shared among *all* of the participants, *after* the contest. And if there was any tomfoolery on a boat, I was told by two veterans, the men with the rope were instructed to swing the goose high out of reach as that boat passed, as a punishment to the unruly crew. But nostalgia for the purity of that tradition is also rather misplaced.

Even the practice of hanging the goose over the harbour is little more than a hundred years old, and supersedes a custom, drawn from inland towns like nearby Marquina [Markina], and still practised in a few French Basque villages including Sara, Ainhoa and Zuraide. The older form consists of decapitating a goose from horseback in the *plaza mayor*. Once again, we find that tradition in fiestas is anything but stable, that people reinvent their rituals all the time.

Gradually, from the 1960s, local people from non-fishing trades were allowed to participate, and finally people from other towns were also admitted to the contest. Now as many as half the participants may be visitors from Bilbao, the people whose passion for second homes in the port is turning half of Lekeitio into a building site. Today hardly any fishermen participate. "Ninety per cent of the crews are students," says the mayor. "Traditions change. Most of these people have never seen the sea except from a beach."

Why would so many people, in such a modern society, want to decapitate a dead goose? One can imagine that the ritual had some social function, in the past, as a demonstration of maritime dexterity, vaguely linked to a very distant memory of animal sacrifice. Today, the primary urge seems to be simply for participation in a distinctive celebration, a collective affirmation of local particularity, while avoiding any painful and divisive political definition of Basqueness.

True, about half the boats carry some emblem or other of the *izquierda abertzale*. But the whole affair is extraordinarily good-humoured, especially considering the vast quantities of alcohol consumed and the high political tensions in the town. Some boats look like props from *Mad Max*. The *ikurriña*, Catalan, Palestinian and Irish national flags are ubiquitous as ensigns. But the playful use of the pirate's

Jolly Roger probably comes closer to capturing the essence of the event. This is an escape not only from the routine of daily life, but also from the deadly implications of fiercely opposed political loyalties.

Gender Wars: Hondarribia and Irún

There is one issue related to fiestas and tradition, however, which splits up families and friends and generates violent abuse and sometimes thuggery. It is not related to national identity, animal rights or class struggle. It is simply about gender, and it arises only in two places, a few miles apart.

Irún and Hondarribia both lie on the same side of the Txingudi estuary, but have very little in common except similar festive traditions. Each fiesta is focused upon an *alarde*, or military-style parade, to celebrate a victory several hundred years old. Hondarribia, as we have seen earlier, is a small fishing port where Euskera is still widely spoken. It is also an elite holiday destination. Its medieval walled town is among the most beautifully preserved—and restored—in the Basque Country. Irún, in contrast, is a rather seedy border town. Most of its historically and aesthetically significant buildings were destroyed during the Civil War. Many of its residents are fairly recent immigrants from other parts of the state, and Spanish is the dominant language.

The whole of Irún seems to turn red and white for San Marcial's day. The infantry wears red berets, ties and sashes, white trousers and shirts, and navy jackets. The spectators who throng the streets dress almost universally in the same shades. Most shop windows and houses also hang out the saint's bright colours. It is an occasion for a great display of elegance. Red berets are *de rigueur* for both sexes, while women wear anything from erotic red camisoles with matching red-hot lipstick, to starched white blouses. The "general" and his cavalry have the most splendid and elaborate dress uniforms, blue with white piping and bright brass buttons. The corps of engineers, wielding axes, saws and pick-axes, is impressive in rawhide aprons, while the artillery units show off immaculately polished bronze cannon. You need to be careful not to stand too close to the latter. They fire blanks, but they can still do some nasty damage to your nerves, if not your eardrums.

The parade begins at 4 a.m. with musical wake-up calls around the town—almost every company is drawn from a different *barrio*. Two hours later, the companies must be assembled in formal military formation for the *diana*, or reveille. They will then spend most of the morning marching up and down the streets, periodically stopping for refreshment. (The more refreshment, the less discipline.) The shotguns are only supposed to be discharged periodically, and only on the orders of the general. But as the cava and the beer flow ever more freely, guns are often fired at will. The shotguns also only fire blanks. But the stream of torn leaves, fluttering down from the plane trees that line the route, bear witness to the sharp blasts that even shot-less cartridges will produce. Since many people watch the parade from balconies almost directly above the troops, the rarity of eye injuries is close to miraculous. An acrid whiff of gunpowder is the distinctive smell of this fiesta.

Despite the superficially bellicose scenes, this has always been the happiest of days. Even during the Franco period, or in the tense and violent days of the transition, the *alarde* of Irún usually passed off without serious incident. The fact that so many people were involved gave it a very inclusive feel. Some of the companies are almost entirely working-class, while the cavalry is mostly made up of the town's social elite.

There was, however, a fatal flaw. The parade was only inclusive for half the population. Women were only allowed to participate as *cantineras*, young and gorgeous mascots for each company. They represent the role of the women who brought water, wine, and probably other services to the troops in the field. From the late 1970s a few women began to march with their local companies, but always illicitly, always at least superficially disguised as men. Then, in 1996, the fiesta suddenly changed beyond recognition. A group of women sought permission from the organizers to form a mixed-gender company of foot-soldiers.

Permission was refused. The women chose to disregard the rules, and as the *alarde* moved up from the Plaza de Urdanibia to the Plaza San Juan, where the general formally marshals the troops in the early morning, about fifty of them plunged into a gap in the parade and began to march.

The verbal response was immediate, visceral and violent: "lesbians", "whores", "bitches", even "bearded ladies". Physical response quickly followed, as spectators then flung themselves on the marchers, quickly dispersing them. Many of those who took part in this assault were themselves women, setting a pattern for the controversy to come. It was also evident that what has since became known as the *betiko* ("as always") traditionalist faction had support which crossed ideological lines, as did the women who wanted change.

Izabel Alcain, one of the women involved that first day, had a strong track record as a member of the *izquierda abertzale*. She had done time in prison when she was very young in the early 1980s, though she has taken a more nuanced position since then. That early morning she was shocked to find a young man she knew personally, a Batasuna supporter, thumping and kicking her. As he struck her, he screamed repeatedly: "You deserve to be raped, *hija de puta*."

Alcain, a native of Hondarribia and daughter of an *Euskaldun arranzale*, decided to carry the battle to her home town. She applied for permission to form a mixed gender company for the September *alarde*, which is even more elaborate than the equivalent in Irún. Using the evocative background of the town's old quarter, and later the sanctuary church of the Virgin of Guadalupe directly overlooking Txingudi, it is also an extraordinarily beautiful parade. Permission was again refused, and Alcain and her supporters, including a number of men, decided to march anyway. The response in Hondarribia was even more vicious. Assaults did not only occur on the day of the event, bu threats continued throughout the year. A self-employed male relative of Alcain's lost half his local contracts, even though he did not support her actively.

In both towns the battle has been repeated every year, but the circumstances have changed over the last few years. Equality legislation, supported by the Basque government and the Basque ombudsman, has forced the very reluctant town councils to withdraw public funding from the traditionalist parades. They must also protect the right of the mixed gender parades to march. In Irún, the *alarde público* now musters about a quarter of the troops paraded by the traditionalists. It puts on an impressively choreographed show, complete with cavalry and artillery (see image on back cover). A bafflingly complex schedule allows the two marches to use the same routes on the same day without clashing. But the atmosphere is still poisonous.

In 2005 the mixed parade was officially allowed to use the full route in Hondarribia for the first time. This includes the steep and narrow medieval main street. Traditionalist women, many of them trendily dressed teenagers and young mothers with children, masked the whole length of it with black plastic six feet high on either side, like some bizarre parody of Christo "wrapping" Central Park. It was as though they believed that the venerable buildings themselves would be polluted by the passage of a mixed company, and of course it meant that no supporters of the marching women could line the streets. The atmosphere became medieval in more senses than one. *Kanpora! Kanpora! Kanpora!* ("Out! Out! Out!") howled the traditionalists, as if the marchers were witches or carried the plague. Only the presence of riot police in a one-to-one ratio with the mixed company prevented matters turning very nasty indeed. Seeing me taking notes, Arantza Etxebeste, a complete stranger, approached me, close to tears. "I hate conflicts," she said, "I hate wars. Everyone has a right to think differently. But these women are radical, they politicize everything, they ruin things. Please stay and watch the real thing, that is *our* fiesta." The sense that a closely knit community is being torn apart is palpable. But Alcain convincingly denies any desire to politicize the fiesta, and insists that "we can't live with this rancour, we have to learn to live together, to be constructive." She says she is willing to meet the *betikos* at any time, but they will not talk to her.

It is easy to understand attachment to a traditional ritual. It is easy to understand that many people feel that it is inappropriate for women to march when the historical militias were probably mostly male. After all, would it be appropriate for Christ to be played by woman in the Easter processions, or the Virgin Mary to be played by a man? One teenage girl in Hondarribia told me that she felt the participation of women as soldiers destroyed the very special role of the *cantinera*. "To be a *cantinera* is better than being a bride. You can get married several times these days, but you can only be a *cantinera* once." But the same girl confessed that she was deeply ashamed at the "vile abuse" which the women who wanted to march had suffered.

In Lekeitio, in its own way a very traditional town, women now compete in the goose contest, once a strictly male preserve, and there has been no upset at all. No-one so far has suggested, however, that a woman should dance the *kaxarranka*. But one day they probably will, and I do not think Lekeitio will engage in an uncivil local war as a result, though it surely holds its fiestas as dear as Hondarribia does.

What is not easy to understand is why these disagreements should generate such violent and volatile feelings. The traditionalists genuinely believe that something very precious to them is being publicly disrespected. The mixed gender marchers genuinely believe they are being denied a fundamental right.

Do the gender wars in a modern industrial town and a traditional fishing port represent symptoms of some deep malaise in Basque sexual politics, some primeval fear of women's participation in public life? It does not seem so, because the controversy baffles and embarrasses most Basques in most other towns as much as it does outsiders. Perhaps it can be related to the exclusion of women from professional pelota, another public arena, as briefly discussed in Chapter Four?

I simply do not know. The battle over the *alardes* is as big a mystery to me, or bigger, than the origin of the Basques or of their language. It makes me very sad. I prefer to remember Hondarribia for the lights dancing into the harbour in the evenings, and the warm atmosphere in the Itxaropena when the *arrantzales* had had a good day's fishing.

Chapter Thirteen

Navarre: Heartland or Hinterland?

In back of the plateau were the mountains, and everywhere you looked
there were other were mountains, and ahead the road stretched out white
across the plain...

Ernest Hemingway, *The Sun Also Rises*, 1926

It is heresy, in several senses, to say so, but Roncesvalles is often a cold
and disappointing place, even in sunshine. It bears one of the most
evocative names in the Basque Country, with its double resonance from
the *Chanson de Roland* and the Camino de Santiago. Yet its haphazard
scattering of grey-slated ecclesiastical buildings lacks historical atmosphere. Pilgrims on the Camino, however, would probably disagree. This
is their first night's sanctuary after setting out from St.-Jean-Pied-de-Port
[Donibane-Garazi] and scaling a Pyrenean pass. To them it must be a
very special place.

A long tradition associates Roncesvalles with the unprecedented
defeat inflicted on Charlemagne's army, the vanguard of Christian
Europe as an emerging power. The battle certainly occurred somewhere
nearby in these Navarran mountain valleys. As we saw in Chapter Two,
the great Frankish king had just returned safely from a successful fund-
raising raid on Iberian Muslim territories in 778. Basque warriors
ambushed his rearguard, commanded by Hrodland (Roland), Count of
the Marches of Brittany, who died in the humiliating rout that followed.

However, the seminal French poem, the earliest work in the genre of
the *chanson de geste*, was only committed to paper three centuries later,
and the anonymous poet disdained historical accuracy. To attribute
Charlemagne's only military debacle to a bunch of obscure mountain
men did not lend much epic grandeur to the tale. Nor did it boost tenth-
century crusading propaganda. So the anonymous writer claimed the
victors were a multinational Muslim army hundreds of thousands strong.

Church of many mysteries: Santa María de Eunate, one of the most beautiful and enigmatic buildings along the Camino de Santiago. Associated, probably falsely, with the Knights Templar, because of its octagonal shape, its atmosphere can make "agnostics feel a *frisson* of contact with some powerful form of Otherness."

He sees the Saracen power arrayed,
Helmets gleaming with gold inlaid,
Shields and hauberks in serried row,
Spears with pennons that from them flow.
He may not reckon the mighty mass,
So far their numbers his thought surpass.

"The only battle we ever won," Basque nationalists comment wryly today, "and we get written out of the official history."

Some Basque nationalist historians suggest, more on the basis of intuition than of evidence, that the victory over Charlemagne's forces provided the impetus for the political organization of Navarre. As we have seen, this trans-Pyrenean kingdom is the closest the Basques ever came to having a unitary state. Under the kingship of Sancho Garcés (known as *El Grande*, "the Great", 1004-35) Navarre included all the contemporary Basque provinces, and its writ ran, at least on paper, as far as Burgos, Bordeaux and possibly even Barcelona. But it is important to underline again that it is very debatable whether its rulers had any very strong sense of Basque identity, since Sancho considered himself "King of all the Spains". In any case, his kingdom was divided among his sons, whose fratricidal conflicts put an end to Navarre's brief hegemony over Christian Spain. His cultural heritage was more lasting, and many Navarran monasteries remained "a refuge for Hispanic Christendom" for centuries.

But while Navarre certainly played a key role, and sometimes *the* key role, in the "reconquest" of Muslim lands, its early kings had fluid relationships with their Muslim neighbours, to whom they were sometimes related by blood. The remains of one such king lie in the Chapel of St. Augustine under a massive effigy behind the cloisters in Roncesvalles. A stained glass window above the tomb reminds us that Sancho VII (known as *el Fuerte*, "the Strong", 1194-1234) played a leading role in the battle of Las Navas de Tolosa. This was a critical defeat inflicted on the Muslims in Andalusia in 1212. The chains which he is said to have brought back from that battle, and which are possibly linked to the chains which appear on Navarre's contemporary coat of arms, are displayed on a red cushion nearby.

Sancho *el Fuerte*'s history is, in fact, a little more complex than this display of Christian hagiography suggests. He spent an early part of his reign in the service of a Muslim dynasty in North Africa. His absence facilitated Castile's absorption—or conquest—of the provinces of Álava and Guipúzcoa. But Sancho cannot have taken this filching of Basque lands too much to heart, because at Las Navas de Tolosa he was fighting under the general command of Alfonso VIII, king of Castile and León.

Attributing modern political affiliations to medieval monarchs is a risky business. What is significant here is that some contemporary historians, and many ordinary citizens, continue to do so. As we have seen again and again in relation to nationalism, how people read the past depends upon where they stand in the present, and vice versa. Navarre survived as an independent kingdom for another three centuries. It was then incorporated into the Spanish proto-state being forged by the *Reyes Católicos*, Ferdinand of Aragon and Isabella of Castile. Whether that incorporation was a "happy union" or "aggression and conquest" remains a matter of fierce debate in the Basque Country. Which side you take tends to depend on whether your politics are sympathetic to Basque or Spanish nationalism.

Sancho *el Fuerte* left behind him a Navarre reduced to something like its current dimensions, with one important extension. This was Basse Navarre, also known as "Los Ultrapuertos". These lands "beyond the passes" were made up of the northern Pyrenean valleys leading down to St.-Jean-Pied-de-Port and St.-Etienne-de-Baigorry [Baigorri]. An associated tongue of lowland territory stretched north almost to the Adour river, running between the other French Basque provinces of Labourd and Soule.

The trans-Pyrenean character of Navarre was forged, logically enough, by geographical factors. The first great peak of the central Pyrenees, the Pic d'Anie, lies just beyond Navarre's south-eastern boundary with Aragon. From that boundary northwest to the Bay of Biscay, the mountains drop quite rapidly, so that Navarre has a dozen passes, including Bentarte (4,400 feet) above Roncesvalles, which are traversable for much or all of the year. The kingdom thus formed a broad bridge, facing in two directions, towards the future nation states of France and Spain and giving it both a "continental" and "peninsular" character. In architectural terms, Navarre's glorious Romanesque heritage was influenced by southern traditions, particular from Jaca in Aragon, from the time of

Sancho *el Mayor*. But Navarre also became a pioneer of Iberian Gothic through its French connections, especially after Sancho *el Fuerte*'s heirs turned the kingdom around to face the north.

Dynastic accidents influenced the direction of Navarre's orientation at any given period. Sancho *el Fuerte* died childless, and his crown passed to his nephew, son of the French Lord of Champagne and Brie. This led to a period in which the kings of France were also kings of Navarre, extending the power of Paris across the Pyrenees and into the peninsula down to the banks of the Ebro. But Navarre remained a separate kingdom, with its own laws and rights, under this arrangement.

Navarre's independence ended in 1512, when the Duke of Alba won the territory for Ferdinand of Aragon. This was the monarch whose dynamic union with Isabella of Castile had finally expelled the Muslims from Granada and created the basis for the Spain we know today. Again, though, it is important to bear in mind that while Navarre became a viceroyalty of Castile, it still retained its own parliament and laws. The Autonomous Community formed by the province today still uses the rather anachronistic title of "Kingdom of Navarre" in its official proceedings.

The Navarre subjugated by the united crowns of Aragon and Castile still included its "ultrapuertos" component, but not for long. Charles I of Spain found the trans-Pyrenean territories impossible to defend, and abandoned them in 1528. An independent kingdom of Navarre persisted on the northern side of the mountains until its Protestant monarch, Henry III of Navarre, famously declared that "Paris is worth a Mass," and discarded both the new religion and the old throne to become Henry IV of France in 1593. Basse Navarre was formally incorporated into France in 1620.

The bitter and continuing dispute over the place of Navarre in the Iberian jigsaw has produced a particularly polarized atmosphere in the province today, on the Spanish side of the border. Conservatives and Socialists feel loyal to Madrid, while asserting a strong regional *Navarro* identity. Within this identity they give token recognition to Euskera and Basque traditions, at least in the mountain valleys north of Pamplona. Basque nationalists, a twenty per cent minority in the province and split as usual between moderates and radicals, make varying arguments about the Basqueness of Navarre. These range from aspirations to gradual recuperation of its Basque identity to claims that Navarre is an essential part of Euskal Herria, and should therefore accept the result of an eventual seven-province referendum on Basque self-determination, regardless of the balance of forces inside the province itself.

The fact that this claim is read by most Navarros as a deeply offensive attempt at annexation has been belatedly recognized by some Basque nationalists. They have begun to turn their old argument upside down. It is Navarre, as the mother province, which should absorb the other Basque lands, they say, and somehow recreate the glory days of Sancho *el Mayor*. This school of thought has produced elaborate but contentious recent works of historical scholarship, stressing Navarre's medieval prowess and grandeur. This image of a might-have-been modern European state straddling the Pyrenees, shamefully done down by perfidious Spaniards, seems unlikely to seduce contemporary Navarros, but one never knows.

The Camino de Santiago: Piety and Pleasure

If the odds are against a restoration of Sancho *el Mayor*'s territorial dispensation, the revival of an aspect of his cultural legacy should remind us that history can take most unexpected turns. Visit Roncesvalles today, and you can hardly avoid numerous encounters with pilgrims on the Camino de Santiago, one of modern Europe's most striking instances of the resuscitation of a medieval custom. They come on foot, on bicycles, by car and even on horseback. Some are motivated by deep piety, some simply take pleasure in following an historic route, and the majority combine a bit of both. Some wear state-of-the-art hiking gear, while others try to fend off the Basque rain with black plastic sacks. Some are super-fit, others suffer untold mortification due to obesity, inexperience and ill-fitting boots.

The Camino links the eastern and western extremes of northern Iberia in an extraordinary enterprise, in turn linking Iberia to all of Europe, and today to places as distant as Brazil. Curiously, the pilgrims' goal, the city of Santiago de Compostela in Galicia, is, like Roncesvalles, closely attached in the European Christian imagination to the struggle against the Muslims. Happily, however, there is no connection between the recent revival of the Camino and the new crusaders in London, Washington and Madrid.

Sometime in the first half of the ninth century, the tomb of the apostle St. James the Greater (Sant Iago) was proclaimed to lie in this western city. His remains had been discovered, according to one account, by a shepherd guided by a star: hence *Campus Stellae*, the Field of the Star, Compostela. While this story is shrouded in contradictory legends, its symbolic power was immediate and real, attracting pilgrims from across northern Spain almost immediately. The "discovery" also coincides with the legend that St. James appeared at the (probably apocryphal) battle of Clavijo in 844 and slaughtered hundreds of Muslims. Hence his Spanish title *Matamoros*, the Moor-slayer, and his close association with Spanish nationalism and militarism.

The pilgrimage to the tomb of St. James became both a celebration of the Christian faith and an expression of confidence in final victory over the Islamic civilization which had come to dominate the peninsula. It was also, of course, a great source of secular revenue. As Richard Fletcher puts it in *Spain* (2000): "By the twelfth century much of the paraphernalia of international tourism can be discerned, in guide-books and accoutrements, ritual and souvenirs, songs and stories, Basque phrase-lists, exorbitant lodging-houses and fraudulent money-changers."

By this time, Sancho *el Mayor* ruled Navarre and pilgrims were pouring across or around the Pyrenees in considerable numbers. Some came through Irún and followed a coastal route which passed through Zarautz and Bilbao. Others came from St.-Jean-Pied-de-Port through Roncesvalles. Still others started further east, and came through the pass of Somport down to Jaca in Aragon, entered Navarre at Sangüesa and linked up, south of Pamplona, with the main Navarran route through Roncesvalles, known as the *Camino francés*. All these routes survive, but Sancho *el Mayor*, concerned for the security of the pilgrims, is credited with defining the southern section of the *Camino francés* in Navarre, from Pamplona to Logroño in La Rioja. This route passed through places where such major towns as Puente de la Reina and Estella would subsequently be established. The influx of pilgrims was accompanied by a flow of cultural influences, which Sancho and his successors largely welcomed, so that the Navarran section of the Camino has become a treasure trail of Romanesque and Gothic architecture and art. For that and many other reasons, the Camino offers a royal road through the heart of the province.

Burguete to the Ebro: Hemingway's Hotel, a Magical Church, a Borgia's Tomb

The first stop on the route after Roncesvalles, however, reminds us that the Camino is a medieval and contemporary phenomenon, but almost vanished in the twentieth century. Ernest Hemingway stayed regularly in the quiet mountain town of Burguete [Auritz] when he wanted to escape from the madness of the San Fermín fiestas in Pamplona. But Hemingway showed little awareness of the Camino, though he did take some interest in Roncesvalles. Like Jake, the protagonist of *The Sun Also Rises*, he came to fish for trout in the Iraty river. A shabby little hotel, very like the one which overcharged Jake with the princely rate of 12 pesetas a day, is still on the main street.

Burguete and nearby Espinal (Aurizberri) also have close associations with another kind of journey. On the morning of 5 April, 1976, 24 members of ETA, three communists, a Catalan anarchist and a Maoist launched one of the biggest jail breaks of the period. They had dug a tunnel worth of *The Great Escape* out of Segovia prison, and made off in a sanitation lorry. By the middle of the next night they had reached Espinal. They were only a few miles from the French border, and liberty.

But the area was already swarming with *guardias civiles*. An expert in frontier-crossing despatched by ETA to bring the escapees through the mountains never turned up. They wandered in the thick mist and darkness in small groups, crossing and re-crossing the border without realising it. The anarchist, Oriol Solé Sugranes, was shot dead in a confused encounter with the *guardias*. Most of the others, fearing the same fate, gave themselves up to the mayor of Espinal at dawn. Four hid in a summer house and eventually escaped.

The story of the escape received a successful cinematic treatment as a kind of political Western only five years later. *La Fuga de Segovia* (1981) was directed by Imanol Uribe. Several of the minor parts were played by actual escapees, and the producer was a former member of ETA *político-militar*, Ángel Amigo. "I used to shoot with a 9mm Parabellum," he told press conferences at film festivals around the world. "Now I find it more effective to shoot in 35mm."

But let's return to the Camino: pilgrims enter Pamplona where the lovely and delicate Puente de la Magdalena crosses the river Arga. The alders, willows and poplars are so thick here that you may still feel as though you were in the countryside, and not about to enter a modern provincial capital. That impression is soon corrected by the sight of the imposing walls of the Ciudadela, the star-shaped fortress under which the Camino proceeds to what used to be known as the Portal de Francia. It is now called after Tomás Zumalacárregui, the Carlist hero. However, the fact that the Ciudadela now forms a huge public park creates the sense that Pamplona is indeed swathed in another time zone, a sense reinforced by the maze of small paved streets within the gate. These form the Navarrería, the attractive old part which surrounds the Cathedral of Santa María. One should not be put off by its exceptionally ugly neo-classical façade. The Gothic interior and especially the cloisters (1280-1472) show that stone can be woven like a spider's web. This cathedral was built to replace an earlier Romanesque building, which was started late in the eleventh century and collapsed in 1389. The loss this entailed can be gauged by some surviving capitals of some of its pillars, featuring richly ornamented vegetation, which are preserved in Pamplona's Museum of Navarre.

Heading back out onto the city's ring roads, the illusion of antique Pamplona is quickly shattered. Ribbon development clutters most of the periphery. Post-Franco Spain has been Europe's glutton for construction, consuming more concrete than France, Britain and Germany combined in the last decade, and expanding urban areas at the fastest rate in Europe, along with Portugal. Some of this can be explained, if not justi-fied, by the boom in demand from northern Europe for holiday and retirement homes on the *costas*. Navarre has no such excuse, yet it is the most aggressive urbanizer in the state. The province is throwing up fea-tureless suburbs with no regard for their aesthetic impact, and eating up natural spaces fifty per cent faster than the Spanish average. A chroni-cally corrupt PSOE autonomous administration in the 1980s and a proudly philistine PP since then, share the blame. Many Navarrans worry that this proliferation of box-like dwellings, isolated from the tra-ditional network of bars, restaurants and plazas, will impoverish social life within a generation.

Twelve miles to the south is a small building which expresses very different architectural aspirations to Navarre's contemporary developers. Santa María de Eunate is that very rare kind of church which makes even agnostics feel a *frisson* of contact with some powerful Otherness. Its exquisitely simple interior structure seems to direct the visitor straight to the heart of spiritual experience, dispensing with displays of ecclesiastical power, theological orthodoxy and biblical exposition. Its most unusual exterior offers rare aesthetic pleasures.

The church sits in a meadow of sunflowers, near a river lined with poplars with little terraced hills rising beyond it. It has a slightly irregular octagonal structure, perhaps eighty feet across at its widest point. The curved ceiling is vaulted by four simple interlocking arches. Apart from a small sanctuary apse, with altar, candles, Virgin and Child, and a few carved capitals and columns, there is no interior decoration. The structure invites you to find its centre point, and simply sit there.

Outside, the octagonal motif of the church is replicated by a surrounding wall of linked arches, about one-third the height of the main building. These arches are themselves encircled by a third but much lower surrounding wall. The arches constitute one of Eunate's many enigmas. It is natural to assume that they originally supported a roof from each church wall, forming a cloister. But no trace of such roofs can be found on the church. Another hypothesis is that the arches are part of a vanished complex of buildings around the church, leaving an open promenade on its immediate perimeter. While there is a little more evidence for this, the possibility remains that they are simply an aesthetic caprice, built exactly as they are now to give the church a delightful extra dimension.

These architectural mysteries are simple compared to the ones posed by Eunate's origins and first purposes. Since it lies on the Camino de Santiago route from Somport, it was very likely built for pilgrims. Its late Romanesque style, with its disproportionately high walls stretching towards the coming Gothic dream, date it in the second half of the twelfth century, though there is no documentary evidence to confirm this. And beyond that, everything is speculation. Esoteric theories have flourished like mushrooms. Where esoteric possibilities exist, the Knights Templar are never very far behind. Its unusual octagonal structure certainly recalls their Temple of the Holy Sepulchre in Jerusalem. But there is not a shred of evidence to suggest that the Templars built this church, nor for the magic rituals their modern enthusiasts attribute to them.

If you accept the theory that Eunate was once a complex of buildings, then it could have been a hospital for pilgrims established by the

Order of St. John of God, but the documentary evidence for this theory is also thin and ambiguous. Some experts believe it was one of a series of cemeteries for pilgrims, linked to another remarkable small octagonal church which possibly had a similar function. This is the church of the Holy Sepulchre in Torres del Río, one of the last pilgrimage sites before the Camino leaves Navarre. It shares several of Eunate's interior features, but its cramped location inside a small town makes it rather less attractive.

Both churches are also said to have lit beacons in their bell-towers, so that they guided pilgrims like spiritual lighthouses as they made their way south-west at night. It is a seductive image, but again hard evidence is lacking. In any case, historical speculation, well informed or otherwise, pales beside Eunate itself. Sunrise and sunset lend a rosy flare to its sandstone and give the entire church the quality of a beacon, without any man-made flame at all.

One has to pity the pilgrims who miss this site because they stick rigidly to the *Camino francés*, which the route from Somport joins a few miles further down the road, at a monument to the saint, just before entering Puente de la Reina [Gares]. Here the united Camino goes straight down the long and narrow main street, where a church dedicated to Santiago has a high ceiling etched in Gothic tracery.

The real treasure is at the end of the street, however, where the eponymous bridge arches elegantly across the Arga, now considerably broader than when we crossed it at Pamplona. The queen who commissioned it may have been Doña Mayor, wife of Sancho *el Mayor*, or her daughter-in-law, Doña Estefania. Its simplicity marks it as early eleventh-century Romanesque. But this simplicity—six gently curving arches, lightened by large "windows" above each of its pillars—is deceptive. It is a consummate feat of engineering, extracting the maximum effect, in practical and aesthetic terms, from a minimal quantity of cut stone.

I last saw it on a blustery and wet September day. A pilgrim struggled across it, his cape unfurling and billowing until he appeared to be almost airborne. Had the cape not been black plastic, and his girlfriend not been shooting him in digital video, the scene could have taken place nine hundred years ago.

The bridge points towards Estella [Lizarra], tucked away in the suddenly more rugged landscape of south-western Navarre. Like Puente de la Reina, Estella was apparently established specifically to provide for the needs of pilgrims and especially for their security in lands depopulated by the wars against the Muslims. Ironically, for a town which would later acquire a close association with Basque nationalism, its first inhabitants were not Navarrans but privileged settlers of Frankish origin, encouraged to move there by King Sancho Ramírez in 1090. Though their exclusive rights to live and trade there were soon eroded by local pressure, the dominant language remained Provençal for several generations.

Estella rapidly became, in the words Julio Caro Baroja, "the capital of Navarran Romanesque". The Royal Palace, heavily influenced by French Romanesque, is regarded as the finest civil building in this style in the province. The church of San Pedro de la Rúa, with its magnificent portico at the top of a great stone stairway and its exquisite cloister, also stands comparison with any of Navarre's other churches from the period. Dozens of distinguished buildings sprang up to cater to the spiritual and material needs of the pilgrims.

This rich heritage lent a certain romantic grandeur to Estella when it became the setting for the capital and court of the Pretender, Don Carlos de Bourbon, during the last Carlist war in the early 1870s. Estella's brief ascendancy was less due to its architectural merits, however, than to the fact that his forces were incapable of capturing any major cities. Carlos was known as "Don Bobo", "Don Fool", to his disenchanted supporters. Pío Baroja effectively caricatures this rather bizarre historical moment in *Zalacaín el Adventurero*. He portrays the town in the hands of a motley crew of Catholic zealots and bloodthirsty adventurers: "a lot of gentry, a lot of Mass-going, a lot of singing *jotas*, but little food." This contrasts with the uncharacteristically generous assessment of a grumpy monk, Américo Picaud, who wrote a notorious guide to the Camino eight centuries earlier. He railed against most things Basque, and even accused them of bestiality. But in Estella he found "good bread, excellent wine, plenty of meat and fish and every kind of happiness."

To the north of Estella rise the majestic sierras of Urbasa and Andía, southern bastions of the Cantabrian range, where Basque traditions remain strong. The town and its surrounding *merindad*, or county, has tended to cherish these traditions more than is typical south of Pamplona. In 1931, the town was chosen by Basque nationalists for the formal drafting of a statute of autonomy which would have included

Navarre, but which never came into effect. Its supporters suffered savage repression at the outset of the 1936 Civil War, when, in the words of Paul Preston, traditionalist Carlists in Navarre "turned the coup into a popular festival". The slaughter in some Navarran towns may have been as great, *per capita*, as it was in more notorious rightist purges in Badajoz and Málaga. But Basque nationalists again chose Estella as their backdrop in recent years, when moderates and radicals signed a pact there which bears the name of the town, and heralded ETA's 1998 ceasefire.

Beyond Estella, there are three more noteworthy points for pilgrims in Navarre: Los Arcos [Uranzia], Torres del Río (home to the octagonal church of the Holy Sepulchre) and Viana [Biana]. The church of Santa María in the latter town was once the burial place for Cesare Borgia, model for Machiavelli's *The Prince*—and it may be his burial place again. After the collapse of his military career and political ambitions in Italy, Borgia died in the service of the King of Navarre in 1507, battling rebels just outside the town walls. Originally buried within the church, he was expelled to a spot outside the door by a disapproving bishop. At the time of writing, the mayor of Viana is campaigning for his reinstatement within the sanctuary. Shortly after leaving Viana, the Camino crosses the Ebro, departing Navarre for Logroño in the province of La Rioja.

The Heart of Navarre: Olite, Artajona, Ujué, Gallipienzo

We have travelled diagonally across Navarre, from north-east to south-west, without paying a great deal of attention to the natural landscape. Yet the shifts in physical perspectives have been dramatic, and help explain the mutation in dominant political loyalties as we reach Pamplona and points south from Navarre's Pyrenean valleys. But because the Camino stays in the shadow of the Cantabrian mountains, this transformation is not quite as evident as it is if we take another route, starting in Guipúzcoa and approaching Pamplona along the motorway east of the Sierra de Aralar.

For much of this journey the scenery is very like that of the Guipúzcoan mountains, with vivid green valleys dotted with white-and-red farmhouses under the *sierra*. Its rocky escarpments, alpine meadows and sharp peaks form a breathtaking vista from above the village of Aspirotz. Twelve miles later, the road passes between the twin sentinels of the Dos Hermanas, a brief gorge between two sister cliffs that dwarf the juggernauts thundering beneath them.

And, in a few moments, all changes utterly. The mountains sink into the middle distance and the land rolls out like a vast patchwork quilt of cereal fields, devoid of individual dwellings, but punctuated occasionally by isolated villages on small hilltops. This is the *cuenca* or basin of Pamplona, fertile territory easily accessible to colonizers. It has been occupied and moulded successively by the Romans, Visigoths, Muslims, Navarrans and Castilians. Thriving Jewish communities added a further cosmopolitan dimension in medieval times. Whatever arguments there are for a pristine Basque identity further north, they run into very sandy soil on these wheat fields.

Pamplona is the volatile pot into which all these ethnic and cultural sauces are stirred, and where both Basque and Spanish nationalism can become particularly shrill and violent. The further you travel directly south from the Navarran capital, the more the land flattens out to resemble the Castilian *meseta*. Castilian cultural influences become more and more apparent. The Basque tendency to build mansions for the multitudes fades, and the main streets of villages are lined with low-roofed terraces of humbler houses. The light becomes harsh, the sun becomes pitiless and induces a certain Castilian fatality of attitude. The bustling Basque *paseo* gives way to much more sedentary customs. Benches outside front doors face straight onto the street. Old people sit there, stolid and stoic, waiting for nothing in particular.

But we are running a little ahead of ourselves. The *cuenca* of Pamplona is an intermediate stage, merging some of the characteristics of the northern mountains with those of the southern alluvial plain, or Ribera, spreading out north of the Ebro.

Here you find cities like Olite [Erriberri], home to a huge fifteenth-century palace complex chosen by Charles III of Navarre as his royal residence. His court was a scene of great luxury, with lavish decoration, extensive interior gardens and a zoo boasting lions, a giraffe, and African buffalo. The palace stands beside an older castle, vandalized or refurbished, according to your point of view, as a *parador*. This is one of the chain of sumptuous but reasonably priced state hotels set up in the late Franco period by the aforementioned Manuel Fraga. The *paradores* were part of his campaign to promote his ambiguous catchphrase, "Spain is different", to tourists who wanted something more than the *costas* offered.

Despite the impressive scale of these buildings, plus an intact old quarter and two fine churches, the whole of Olite has the air of a Disneyfied tourist park today. But it is a good base to explore the often neglected treasures which lie in the heart of Navarre.

Beyond the architecturally distinguished neighbouring town of Tafalla lies Artajona, a hilltop village crowned by one of the best preserved fortifications in the province. Most of the wall of this kidney-shaped enclosure survives, with nine of the original 14 towers (17 according to some accounts) still standing. The fortress-church of San Saturnino, which stands in the centre, has a chunky rectangular structure which looks impenetrable in its own right.

Viewed as a long shot from the open fields to the north, you can easily see why this complex was selected for filming romantic period pieces like *Robin and Marian* (Richard Lester, 1976). This movie featured Sean Connery as an ageing Robin Hood returning from the Crusades, with Audrey Hepburn as a mature Maid of Sherwood Forest. No doubt some Navarran crusaders returned to these very walls; but it becomes more difficult to imagine them when you go in for a close-up and find that modern houses have been built, higgledy-piggledy, right in the angles between towers and walls inside the complex. The ancient paved roads are rife with grass and weeds, and when I visited there was a strangely pervasive smell of urine. Navarre's conservative government often proves more pious than practical in its concern for preserving traditions. Artajona, like Olite and so many other towns here, is expanding exponentially into the countryside. The Virgin Mary is in danger of being replaced by the construction industry as the patron saint of the province.

A shoddy approach to heritage and urban planning is also evident all around Ujué [Uxue], an astounding medieval village of which lies off the main road from Olite to Sangüesa [Zangoza]. From a distance Ujué is a hill clad in stone, a kind of architectural armadillo. Again, there is a fortress-church on top, Santa María La Real, which is even bigger, at least in proportion, than San Saturnino at Artajona. This building marries an already substantial fourteenth-century Romanesque church with a massive Gothic one. Experts still debate whether Charles II of Navarre intended to replace the earlier building entirely and ran out of money, or whether the rather awkward but undoubtedly monumental fusion is intentional. In any case, his devotion to the church and its image of the Virgin and Child was such that he left instructions for his heart to be placed in a casket in the sanctuary. It is still there today.

Even if you do not know that, the church is a rather eerie place to visit alone on a bleak autumn day. A lovely, open-faced woman sells religious mementos and bags of almonds (a speciality of Ujué) in a poky shop beside the church. She told me she had been spooked there recently as well, though she had never known fear in the building before. Over the previous three days, every time she went in to sweep the aisles she had made out the same young man sitting in the shadows under the Gothic gallery, staring at the sanctuary. He had made me jump like a cat when, thinking I was alone, I accidentally illuminated him with my flash gun. He remained impassive and immobile. In retrospect, it seems odd to me that we both found it sinister that anyone might want to spend so long in a church to which so many pilgrims have walked with bleeding feet. Perhaps we should have been more willing to accept devotion at face value.

At the bottom of the village is a monument to the canonical crowning of the image of the Virgin at a special ceremony in the 1950s. This is how the plaque beside it reads, in part:

> Here
> Converted Into An Altar Close To The Sky, On This Sierra Where The
> Moor Has Never Been Able To Set Foot,
> On The Radiant Morning Of 8 September 1952,
> Amid The Ardent Acclamation Of 30,000 Navarrans Devoted To The
> Mother Of Heaven,
> With The Sound Of Chains Dragged In Penitence
> And Ground Hallowed By The Stigmata Of Bare And Bleeding Feet...
> The Image Of The Virgin Of Ujué Was Canonically Crowned...
> In An Explosion Of Faith Of Proportions So Gigantic That It Cannot
> Be Described

Such expressions of "National Catholicism" were heavily promoted by the dictatorship, but Marian passions flavoured with xenophobia have always run deep in Navarre, and Ujué is one of the focal points of such devotion. In 1043 the people of Tafalla swore to make an annual pilgrimage to Ujué if they were granted victory over the Muslims. They won their battle, and they (and many other towns and villages) still process each year in an overnight walk to the church, wearing the black hood of the penitent and carrying crosses and chains, often barefoot.

Not everyone from Tafalla takes part, of course, nor did everyone in Ujué share this respect for the Mother of God. Isolation had made Ujué something of a refuge for nonconformists; it had a rather contradictory reputation as a haven for "Reds" as well as a religious sanctuary. And in the 1930s the village set the scene for a distinctly left-wing miracle. In 1934 someone knocked over the medieval stone cross which greets pilgrims a mile or so from the village. There was outrage, and four young and radical local trade unionists from the socialist UGT were arrested as the usual suspects. But these there the days of the secular Republic, and they were simply fined for damage to an historical monument. They pleaded not guilty.

Two years later the Civil War broke out, and they were promptly rearrested by the much less understanding new military authorities. Again and again over the next three years, they saw comrades taken out from their cells for summary execution, some of them simply guilty of holding a union card. They expected the same fate daily, but their names were never called. Some judicial bureaucrat had decided that because obscure charges for desecration were still pending against them they could not be executed until they had been tried. This was quite a luxury in those days of arbitrary killings. The war was over by the time their trial took place, and they were let off with life sentences, later commuted. None of them ever confessed, and many in the village believed them innocent. Whoever committed the crime, the fallen cross almost certainly saved the lives of the four Ujué trade unionists.

For many people visiting today, the village itself will be miracle enough. Descending its steep streets is like moving through a stone honeycomb. Vessels that might well have been used by the Romans for pounding corn are casually used as flower pots, even as rubbish bins. The surrounding hills are intensely and sinuously terraced, bearing witness to centuries of skilled agriculture and viniculture, though also to neglect in recent years.

But it comes as a rude shock to find a shocking pink brick frontage built across a street corner that long predates Cervantes. Holiday homes in half a dozen styles are being thrown up untidily around the village's fringes. That a depopulated village (there were 231 inhabitants at the last count) should be repopulated through refurbished second homes is no bad thing, but it does not have to be done like this.

None of this private development, however, can inflict the damage which has been done by the creation of a traditional public space. Halfway up the eastern side of the village, shattering the harmony of its venerable houses, and breaking the harmonious lines they form against the sky, a large *frontón* has been built in glass, concrete and steel. It would be nice to believe that there are enough young people in Ujué to justify its size, but there are not. There is no reason why a contemporary *frontón* should not be built in a medieval village (the daring post-modern sports complex works very well in Asteasu's *plaza mayor*). But it has to be done with taste, talent and a sense of proportion, all of which are lacking here. Someone has scrawled the inevitable *Gora* [Long Live] *ETA* on the seating banks for spectators. It is tempting to think that the group could find no better place to decommission its explosives—under strict supervision, of course.

The panoramic views from Ujué towards the Pyrenees are justly famous. Where the mountains begin to rise there are other well-known architectural treasure troves like the town of Sangüesa and the monastery of Leyre, both on the Camino route which runs down from Somport in Aragon. But you can hardly drive anywhere along the back-roads in between without encountering hidden marvels. I will always be grateful to the friend who told me about Gallipienzo [Galipenzu]. This is a lost village with as dramatic a location as you could find anywhere, and one which offers the guilty pleasures afforded to comfortable travellers by abandonment and ruin.

Tucked away in the terraced hills to the east of Ujué, Gallipienzo clings perilously to a very steep slope. The village overlooks a meander of the Aragon river where it commands a substantial medieval bridge. The eye is immediately drawn upwards, though, to the former parish church of San Pedro which dominates the hilltop. To compensate for the sharp incline, the church is twice as deep at one end as at the other. The buttresses which support its walls are surprisingly slim. At dusk, patchy floodlighting makes them look like rockets imagined by Jules Verne. The outer structure is Gothic, but the deep end of the church encloses a Romanesque crypt, one of only four in the province, the most famous being at Leyre. But it is rarely open. Some of its frescoes are in the Museum of Navarre in Pamplona.

A few windows are lit in the bulky houses at the bottom of the town. A brave little printed sheet has been pinned to ancient wooden doors, appealing to the populace to celebrate a residents' day, the following Saturday. There will be a *degustación de migas*, a peasant staple based on fried breadcrumbs, prepared by "expert cooks" at noon. A championship of *mus*, a card game, will follow at 3 pm. The climax will be a "delicious" *ajoarriero*, a meal based on a sauce made from fried garlic, eggs and ground peppers, in the evening. There will be crafts on sale, and the whole event will be "livened up with good music."

As you ascend the sharp zigzags towards the church, you may wonder how many residents are still around to attend. Sometimes the whole skeleton of a home stands upright, doorless and windowless. Others have already tumbled into piles of masonry. Humus has accumulated, and camomile, thyme and rosemary flourish on the remains of orange tiled roofs. Fig trees have colonized bedrooms and corridors. Floors are thick and mushy with fruit that no-one comes to gather. Black redstarts nest in bathroom crannies. Suddenly, almost at the top, you find three houses which have been tastefully refurbished, in welcome contrast to the mess at Ujué. They show every sign of permanent occupation. A man is weeding a thriving vegetable plot nearby.

Old fortifications out to the west come into view, around a huge rock formation which resembles a giant iguana. And then the church, suddenly head-on over your head, looms like a monolith. It is all locked up, its windows blocked with brick, but it still has tremendous presence. A simple stone cross teeters drunkenly on a collapsing pillar of cut stone in the church precinct. Crag martins nest above the unadorned Gothic portico, a red-billed chough makes its weird call territorially from the rocks to the west. A bench below the church gives a privileged view of the fertile plain towards the Pyrenees. There is another medieval village across the river, with one or two lights flickering, and another beyond that. Senior clerics, powerful noblemen and rich merchants must have passed this way many times. Now it does not even attract tourists.

The only bar on the only exit road is the Trujal, named after the olive presses which once brought some prosperity to Gallipienzo. Perhaps they still do; there is a Mercedes parked outside the door. The barman fills in some details about the village. "There are about thirty people left here, all pensioners. A few still work the land. Families return to give them a hand at harvest time. But there is no youth. There is talk about a plan to build a proper road to the church, so that people could visit the crypt easily and see the views, but we don't know what will happen."

The Bardenas: Badlands Full of Life

Old traditions die hard in Navarre. Descending the narrow Pyrenean valley of Roncal the day before my visit to Gallipienzo, I rounded a corner and my car was plunged abruptly into a white river of sheep, an occasional goat rearing up like a black rock in foaming rapids. The flock flowed all over the road, sometimes creating unlikely tributaries on the near-vertical slopes to the right in search of a tasty mouthful of herbs. As I inched my way through, I asked a shepherd where they were headed. "*Al sur. A las Bardenas Reales. Hacemos la trashumancia.*"

This is a magic word, ringing down many centuries, perhaps across millennia. "Transhumance" does not have the same resonance in English, but in Iberia *la trashumancia* evokes a great bi-annual migration of humans and animals across the peninsula. It probably began as the ice retreated northwards 10,000 years ago. First our hunter-gatherer ancestors followed flocks of antelopes and bison as they sought summer cool in the northern uplands, then winter growth on the southern plains. Thousands of years later, herdsmen and shepherds made the same journey with domesticated beasts. Their favoured routes became institutionalized in the Middle Ages through the *cañadas reales*. These are broad "royal roads" which crisscross the whole country. They still exist in law, and to some degree in fact, today. A controversial ecologist, Jesús Garzón, has revived the practice on a grand scale, leading herds from Extremadura to Asturias. Their passage through Madrid's Puerta del Sol has become a bi-annual TV event. Garzón argues that the migration makes for much healthier animals, and that their meat flavour is enhanced by the diverse plants they browse across hundreds of miles.

Here in Roncal, and neighbouring Salazar, the two last valleys of the

Strange skyline: more like Arizona than a typical Basque landscape, the Bardenas are surprising in many respects. Despite their arid appearance, they provide pasture for thousands of transhumant sheep, and are home to a great wealth of wildlife.

Navarran Pyrenees before Aragon, the *trashumancia* remains a necessity, not a choice. The high meadow grazing up near the French border in areas like Belagua is exhausted by September. The snow which follows would in any case put the grass beyond the reach of the flocks. So the shepherds walk them down for winter pasture to the Bardenas Reales, a journey of about a week.

Each year on 18 September, up to 120,000 sheep are concentrated around the town of Carcastillo. A pistol shot in the early morning is the signal that they can all enter the 100,000-hectare Bardenas, which quickly swallow up the flocks. A fiesta precedes this annual ritual, with a classical concert, a rock concert and, of course, a celebratory meal. Its main ingredient? Breaded fillets of leg of lamb.

"Bardenas" is another rather magical word, of uncertain original meaning. It designates a most unusual Basque landscape which stretches for about thirty miles down Navarre's western border with Aragon, almost to the Ebro, and is fifteen miles across. The Bardenas are often loosely described as "badlands" or "desert". While these terms capture their most spectacular aspects, they do not do justice to the great diversity of this mini-region.

The most distinctive area is the so-called "white Bardena", simply known as La Blanca. This is a central depression where massive erosion has created broad vistas, reminiscent of the Arizona moonscape where Thelma and Louise accelerated into the sunset. Thin layers of sandstone, gypsum and limestone are separated by broad bands of clay. The artistry of water and time has produced infinite variations on a single theme: a series of flat capstones perched like folds of heavyweight puff pastry on narrowing bases of earth which are barely able to support them. The best-known example is the dramatic Castildetierra, whose "head" looks is if it might collapse at any moment. Hundreds of hills around it already have, and as their crowns slide they leave slabs of rock tilted at implausible angles on steep clay slopes. Eccentric and fantastic shapes abound. Sometimes the effect is like a conical wedding cake. Each of a dozen protruding layers of rock will be smaller than the one below, but wider than the thick filling of earth between them. The earth itself is often banded in shades of claret, ochre, red and brown.

The lower zone of the Bardena Blanca is mostly flat or flattish. It became an airforce bombing range in 1951. The arrival of US planes and pilots in that decade symbolized growing Western support for Franco's dictatorship during the Cold War. "Yankees out of the Bardenas" was one of the slogans of the infant eco-left during the transition. But the crystalline silence of the desert is still broken, time and again, by the menacing *whump whump* of aircraft breaching the sound barrier. Every so often, the scream and dull thump of bombing ratchets up the menace level and disturbs the sheep, and every other living being.

The best way to approach the Bardenas is to take the route followed by the flocks, from Carcastillo. This allows you to experience the rich variations of habitat within the area. It comes as a surprise to find that 60 per cent of the Bardenas are actually cultivated, with cereals and prime asparagus fields stretching across the northern "Plano". There is even a certain amount of shrub and low tree cover: Aleppo pine, Kermes oak, Phoenician juniper. In fact, the high level of erosion is not due only to the geological structure and extremes of temperature and rainfall. Many centuries of deforestation, over-cultivation and over-grazing make this as much a cultural as a natural landscape.

El Paso (where else?) and a monumental social-realist statue of a shepherd mark the entry from the Plano, where a much thicker stratum of rock has largely protected the plateau against erosion, to the beginnings of the Bardena Blanca. Cereal fields still abound, but badland bluffs begin to appear on the horizon. Finally you find yourself completely surrounded by weirdly sculpted ridges. Their sides are deeply scored by occasional torrential rainfall, until they look like the folds of a gypsy woman's dress.

You need to be very careful in the Bardenas. Temperatures can soar to 50°C, but the greatest danger is water. A sudden shower will instantly turn the hard dirt roads into soft and highly adhesive plasticine. Even a 4x4 can founder in these conditions, and a saloon car will simply remain where the rains find it until the road dries out, perhaps 48 hours later. If you see clouds building up, it is time to get out. Even walking on a bone dry day, you need to keep a sharp eye out for sudden shifts in the colour of the soil, which may indicate an unpredictable damp patch. Tangle with one of these, and the weight of your boots will treble as you struggle to get out without sinking altogether. It is advisable to stick to marked roads and paths, though it is very tempting to wander deeper into the wilderness. Even here there is a lot more cultivation than you might expect.

Rosemary is plentiful in this area, and tamarisk thrives in the dryer, saltier patches often along dry stream beds. Wildlife is abundant, most obviously birds, though there are many reptiles. Larks, wagtails, wheatears and chats rise constantly from the roadside. If you are a bird-watcher, your progress may be slow indeed. The prized Dupont's lark can be found here, along with a wide range of steppe birds: stone curlew, two species of sandgrouse, red-necked nightjar and little bustard among them. The great bustard has become extinct here, but individuals are returning in recent years, mostly to the Plano.

Look to the skies, and you may be mesmerized by soaring birds of prey. Twenty-four species can be found in the area, vultures, eagles, kites, harriers, buzzards, hawks and falcons. A short-toed eagle hovering in the breeze, gleaming white, its wings arched back to form a right-angle with its barred tail spread broad, can seem to hold time itself in check as it searches intently for snakes on the sandy earth below.

Not everyone is enamoured of the vultures, of course. Miguel

Logroño Amador claimed he had lost three sheep to vultures this year. "I left a ewe and a new born lamb tethered together, and when I came back three hundred vultures were feeding on their remains. They didn't even pay me any attention," he said as he shared his wine and mineral water with me under a juniper in the midday heat.

Naturalists are sceptical about these claims, but there is growing body of anecdotal evidence to substantiate them as the Basque population of Griffon vultures soars. Amador is a local farmer, and had moved his sheep into the Bardenas from a farm near Carcastillo the day before we met. But he knows the shepherds from the Roncal and Salazar. One of them, he says, loses a sheep to a brown bear every year. This sounds a taller story because the bears have practically disappeared in the Basque Pyrenees. He may be telling it as a cautionary tale against a plan, unpopular with the shepherds despite compensation deals, to reintroduce bears, the largest mammal indigenous to the region.

Amador explains that shepherds with a right to graze the Bardenas can pick any spot they like each year. He has chosen the same place as last year because there is plenty of corn stubble, and his 1,500 sheep are resting in the middle of a field. But now another shepherd has driven his flock almost alongside, and there will less for Amador's sheep to eat. "I can't stop him, he is within his rights. We all are very selfish and compete to make a living," he says philosophically. The government of Navarre is currently considering an EU scheme to divide the Bardenas into 86 districts which may, or may not, make the distribution of grazing more fair. Like Urdaibai, the region is a biosphere reserve, which means that the interests of cultivators, grazers and the eco-system should, theoretically all be developed in harmony.

In any case, though their grazing rights run until the end of June, the drought this year means that some shepherds may only find enough grazing for ten days. Then the sheep will be penned near neighbouring towns and fed on winter hay. One of the shepherds from Salazar has been telling the newspapers that he sees a difficult future for "a profession which gives us a very vivid way of life, but also a very slavish one; you have to work every day. Anyway, wool is worth nothing now." José Antonio Ballent still sleeps out in the open with his flock. His 36-year-old son sleeps in their car. Wives and children generally remain in the mountains, though most of the shepherds have second houses around the Bardenas. It is a long separation, but there are longer ones. A sign of the times is that the next shepherd I meet is a Bulgarian immigrant, studying Spanish from a book as the sheep bells echo around him.

South and east of La Blanca lies the "black" Bardena, La Negra. Much less harshly eroded, it is nonetheless scoured with deep river beds, and relatively heavily vegetated, rich in wildlife. To the west lies the flat Ribera, extensively planted in vines, almost indistinguishable from the Castilian *meseta* across the Ebro, where Navarre extends briefly beyond the river towards Zaragoza, capital of Aragon. Here stands the province's second city, Tudela [Tutera], founded by the Muslims. The degree of tolerance offered to Christians and Jews under the dominion of al-Andalus may occasionally be exaggerated, but it was real and stands in stark contrast to the sectarian bigotry of crusading Europe. Tudela, home to the great Jewish poet Yehuda Haleví (1070-1144), was exemplary in its pluralistic culture for four centuries, until it fell in 1119 to Aragon, and then passed to Navarre. It found its natural home in the province, being the last city to fall to the Castilian armies in 1512. Whether it is the southern outpost of Basqueness today, or the northern fringe of Mozarabic Spain, is a matter of political opinion. But all sides in the contemporary Basque conflict could learn a lot from Tudela's 400 years of peaceful co-existence between three great religious ideologies.

Mari's mountain: Mount Amboto is one of a number of Basque peaks closely associated with the Basque goddess Mari, whose name conveniently assimilates to that of the Virgin Mary. The sanctuary church of Arrate is in the foreground.

Chapter Fourteen
Mountain High: Pleasure, Penitence and Pagan Gods

If Mari gives you what you want, she always takes something in return.
Local farmer on the dangers of doing a deal with the goddess on
Mount Amboto

The Basque fascination with mountains was born of geographical necessity, since you cannot travel very far in most directions without having to climb one steep ridge or another. But it has matured into a cultural activity which can take many forms. Some are a pleasure, some are a penance, and most are something in between.

From the great spine of the Pyrenees to the multiple ribs of the Cantabrian Cordillera, hundreds of little sanctuary chapels, each with their special saint or virgin, bear witness to a long tradition of hilltop festivals which are still practised today as *romerías*. These excursions, half pilgrimage, half picnic, were the subjects of idealized Basque iconography for painters like Aurelio Arteta. Two of his *romerías* hang in the Museo de Bellas Artes in Bilbao and contrast strikingly with his starkly realistic, if still stylized, portraits of industrial Bilbao.

Here is Bernardo Atxaga's description of the *romería* from Asteasu to the summit of Ernio, which takes place on every Sunday in September:

The route takes two hours and it is, at least from Asteasu to the inn of Iturrioz, extraordinary: you climb with views over half the province of Guipúzcoa, with the sea in the background. As you approach the open ground of Zelatun, you will hear snatches of music—European *country* music, naturally—and the smells rise from the shepherds' cabins, converted into taverns for the occasion. You can stay there in the fiesta area, but you can also postpone relaxation and push on with the ascent to the summit, gaining there, as your reward, the coloured ribbons: the modern ones, white, green and red, or the traditional ones, violet, pink and pastel green.

Pre-Christian Basques located a shadowy deity called Urtz, Ortz or Ost, linked to thunder and lightning, in the highest peaks or simply in the sky. His best-known female counterpart, Mari, also had (or has) a mountain residence. She, too, has fiery connotations, appearing as a thunderbolt when she is not a white cloud or a girl with long blond hair.

In the twentieth century religious and social hill-walking segued into political militancy. The PNV formed a youth federation of *Mendigoizaleak* (mountaineers), whose excursions merged a Boy Scout ethos with ideological instruction, cultural immersion and acts of devotion to the Virgin Mary. The high altitudes, coupled with memories of the Carlist guerrillas like Santa Cruz, an archetypical mountain man, went to their heads. By the 1930s they were the most radical sector of the nationalist movement, supporting the pro-independence weekly, appropriately titled *Jagi-Jagi* (Up-Up). They evolved, as Marianne Heiberg says, from a "crucial role" in propaganda and recruitment to becoming the "shock troops" of nationalism during the Civil War and the subsequent repression.

Hill-walking, like choirs and gastronomic societies, was an ideal cover for political activism during the Franco period. ETA inherited this tradition from the PNV, adding the spice of a little clandestine arms training. Zulaika (*Basque Violence*, 1988) reports that one of the ETA members in Itziar had a kind of political/military epiphany during a hill-walking trip in the Ataun valley, an area particularly rich in mythological associations. "At dawn, he heard the echoes of the *txalaparta*, which sounded from the peaks of several mountains and, in a state of intense emotion, decided to join ETA."

In Search of Sanctuary

Today, Basques do not need the excuse of a *romería*, pagan deities or political commitment to head for the hills, though there are resonances, faint or strong, from these traditions in most expeditions. *Cuadrillas* by the dozen set off at dawn every weekend morning to points all over the region. Their outings range from leisurely strolls up soft inclines to serious training for the Himalayas on Pyrenean ice-sheets. Just as Basque topography has nurtured exceptionally talented cyclists, so it has created an appetite for conquering Everest, and even young children can be found scaling polystyrene cliffs in local gyms.

The ratio of reward to effort is very high in the Basque mountains, though there is a hard and easy way of getting the visual benefits of most routes. The most famous sanctuary is probably Aranzazu, in Guipúzcoa, to whose Virgin St. Ignatius made his vow of chastity 500 years ago. When the Franciscans rebuilt the sanctuary church in the 1950s, they invited some of the most prestigious and controversial Basque artists to work on it. The order found that there were no half measures when they gave the Basque avant-garde free rein on the building. Nestor Basterretxea painted a series of large images for the crypt, with themes like the threat of nuclear war and the horror of unjust imprisonment, as well as more traditional Franciscan motifs like "our sisters the flowers". His resurrected Christ over the altar, in flaming red, looks like a Bolshevik hero (our Comrade of the Shipyards) rather than the Lamb of God or Christ the King. The original version has Jesus turning his back on the church, but Basterretxea was persuaded to soften his stance. Not so Jorge Oteiza, who sculpted fourteen apostles over the entrance, and when he was asked why there were so many, he retorted: "because no more would fit." When he was told that *baserritarrak* visiting the church said that his apostles looked just like the rocks in their fields, he responded: "how marvellous! Now they can go about their labours saying 'this rock here is Peter!' and 'that one there is James'!" He claims to have started work on the *pietà*, high on the façade above the apostles, on the day a *guardia civil* shot dead ETA's first killer and first martyr, *Txabi* Etxebarrieta. This bald conjoining of religion and nationality, sacrifice and violence, recalls the terrible lines in Yeats:

> Odour of blood when Christ was slain
> Made all Platonic tolerance vain
> And vain all Doric discipline.

In the 1960s, ETA used the huge annual young men's nocturnal pilgrimage from the medieval university town of Oñati, six miles downhill,

Polemical *pietà*: Jorge Oteiza's sculpture was one of several controversial avant-garde works commissioned for the Franciscan sanctuary church of the Virgin of Aranzazu. Oteiza claims he started sculpting this work on the day ETA's first killer and first martyr, *Txabi* Etexebarrieta, was shot dead in 1968, recognizing the potent association of religious and radical nationalist iconography.

as a recruiting opportunity until the Francoist authorities banned it. Drained of political *frisson* and with religious faith in decline, fewer people make the pilgrimage today. But many drive up to the church and then undertake another kind of mission, for while the sanctuary is on a steep ridge, it is still well below the mountain tops. From a hill-walking point of view, it is the climb beyond Aranzazu that offers the real rewards—plus another two sanctuary churches and several dolmens, if you need more spiritual and aesthetic sustenance en route.

Forty minutes of comfortable ascent through cool beech and larch woods lead the walker out onto alpine meadows for which the word sublime might have been coined. This is one of the most popular picnic sites in the country, but the sweeping green slopes are extensive enough to comfortably absorb hundreds of people, at play, it is tempting to think, in the fields of the Lord. As well as the hermitage of Andra Mari, the Virgin Mary, there is a restaurant for those who have not brought their own food. Only in the Basque Country...

And from these sublime fields you can go further, much further. Limestone peaks poke through the meadows at intervals around the perimeter, and the most seductive ones form the crest of the Aizkorri range, a few miles away to the north-east. Arbelaitz, Irule, Aitxuri, Aitzabal and finally Aizkorri itself all offer panoramas of most of Guipúzcoa and the Bay of Biscay from an average of 5,000 feet. For experienced hill-walkers this is a straightforward climb in good weather. And here again, right on the top of Aizkorri, is a sanctuary chapel, this time dedicated to Jesus Christ.

Below Aitxuri, the pagan Mari is said to lurk in a cave, displaced from the summits by Christianity. But her real home is on Amboto. This peak is a broad cone of naked rock which surges out of a magnificent pollarded and mossy beech forest in the Duranguesado range in Vizcaya, bordering on Álava. Many walkers only go as far as the grass grows, under patrols of low-flying griffon vultures, but the rocky ascent is not dangerous if you are careful.

It is a tough climb, though, and an atheist friend of mine was finding it so demanding that he made a promise of devotion to Mari (the pagan one) in return for strength to reach the summit. On the way down his cap was snatched by a sudden blast of wind. He told the whole story to an elderly *baserritar* in the bar on the valley floor a few hours later. "If

Mari gives you what you want, she always takes something in return," said the farmer, and continued matter-of-factly: "You were lucky. She might have taken your life."

Chapter Fifteen

Iparralde: the Basques on the Other Side of the Mountains

Not all the Basques have the same laws and customs, nor do they have the same way of speaking Euskera, because politically speaking they are part of different states.

Pedro de Axular, "Gero", 1643

The French Basque Country is like a fancy but nutritious cake: it has lots of pretty icing on its maritime edge, and becomes richer and more satisfying as you approach its mysterious interior.

The seaside froth of Belle Epoque villas, surfers and chic restaurants has its own charms, as long as you can see past the clutter of souvenir shops. The lure of the coast was first discovered by the Basques themselves, and its towns have a longer history of recreation than you might expect. Ordinary local people made their own amusements here, long before bathing became fashionable for wealthy tourists. Alain Courbin's fascinating analysis of the late "discovery" of the seaside by Europe's leisured classes, *The Lure of the Sea* (1994), shines a surprising light on the stereotypes of social and sexual repression often associated with the rural Basque Country:

> Every year on the last Sunday in September whole families of Basques living in the mountains would come down to paddle in the sea at Biarritz... Early in the seventeenth century, Pierre de Lancre, president of the Bordeaux Parlement, described the surprise expressed by travellers at the sight of "grown girls and young fishermen" who "mingle in the water", then go and "dry off in the Chamber of Love that Venus has put there on purpose, on the seashore."

Dreaming spires: the Gothic Cathedral of St.-Marie in Bayonne.
Building was started when the town was under English rule in the
twelfth century, and was only completed by restorationists
inspired by Viollet-le Duc in the 1800s.

Courbin goes on to cite an early nineteenth-century account by Auguste Bouet:

> Here there is no etiquette and no uncomfortable clothing; the women are barely covered by light dresses in striped cotton, and as for the men, nature alone takes charge of their dress. The atmosphere is full of shouts, songs and untroubled, unbridled pleasure.

The pleasure of at least one couple was so intense, legend has it, that they did not notice the rising tide in the Chamber of Love, a cave-complex beneath the cliffs at Cap St.-Martin. Their passionate drowning gave Romantics their favourite combination of Love-and-Death. The story has enticed many, including Napoleon I and the Empress Josephine, to pay the caves a visit. Josephine apparently lost a shoe there.

Some Basque associations with eroticism are apocryphal. The tight bodice which borrows the national name probably has its origins in an old French corruption of the Italian *basta*. Anaïs Nin seems to have had little reason other than caprice to christen her unlikely sexual athlete in *Delta of Venus* as "the Basque"—he gets no other name.

But for those who believe chocolate to be an aphrodisiac, Bayonne was an early hotspot. Jewish refugees, having been successively expelled from Spain, Navarre and Portugal, were granted privileges to settle across the Adour from Bayonne in St.-Esprit in the seventeenth century. They brought their chocolate-making skills with them, one of the many gifts this remarkable community gave to the town, which now markets the dark stuff as one of its emblematic products. The town's famous ham, an entirely gentile contribution, is another. Bayonne was, as we have seen, famous for whale oil in the Middle Ages, but shifting sandbars abruptly made it a riverside rather than a seaside town in the fifteenth century, and its importance as a port declined. It never developed a significant industrial base, but its arms factories did invent the bayonet, a rather more successful lexical export than Bilbao's *bilbos*.

Bayonne is an appropriate place to start in the French Basque Country. This is not so much because it is notionally the area's capital, but because it gives a strong flavour of Iparralde's charms while featuring some of its kitsch excesses. Approaching Bayonne from the interminable plains of Les Landes to the north, the sudden appearance of a mountain horizon—with Larrun prominent and the Peñas de Haya standing up like a cockscomb—tells you that you are entering another country. Crossing the broad Adour, the slim, slightly asymmetrical twin spires of Bayonne's Gothic cathedral of St.-Marie beckon towards the heart of the town, almost sunk in the congested and anodyne sprawl that merges it with suburban Biarritz and Anglet [Angelu].

The cathedral stands at the top of a hill overlooking Grand Bayonne—not the sprawl, just the bigger part of the old town. A UNESCO World Heritage Site, St.-Marie's design is based on the cathedrals in Reims and Soissons. Building commenced, on a Romanesque site, in the twelfth century, when Bayonne was under English rule after the marriage of Henry II to Eleanor of Aquitaine. Bayonne's heritage, indeed, is thoroughly cosmopolitan, having been colonized by the Romans, Visigoths, Vikings (who probably named it), Franks and Anglo-Normans, plus the aforementioned Jewish infusion. The three impressive sets of ramparts around the town, now parks and museums, bear witness to almost two millennia of frontier tensions which lasted until the Napoleonic wars.

The French became masters of the city at the end of the Hundred Years' War in 1453. It was only in the next century that the cathedral's south tower went up, and the north tower was not added for another four centuries. St-Marie's slender nave is the epitome of Gothic elegance, its stained glass windows gathering in baskets of tinted light. The cloisters are badly damaged, but form a basin of calm among the busy little streets outside.

These streets are a crash (or crass) course in a particular kind of Basqueness. It would be hard to exaggerate the range of cute souvenirs stamped, embroidered, stitched or carved with Basque insignia. Aprons are decorated with the *ikurriña,* napkins with the *lauburu,* blouses are adorned with the accoutrements of pelota. Entire wedding lists are available in Basque-branded china and kitchenware. Wooden plaques illustrate every Basque pastime, often linked to the motto *Zazpiak Bat,* "the Seven [provinces] are One". There are dolls in traditional Basque costumes by the gross, strings of ceramic red peppers, *makilas* (the Basque walking stick, often a sword-stick) by the dozen, pottery models of *baserriak* and carvings of venerable peasants and fisherfolk with exaggerated aquiline noses. The artificiality of many of these items is epitomized in the ubiquitous prints of Martin-Laurent Parrtieu. His trick is to portray young women in coyly salacious poses which contrast with their traditional Basque contexts—a flash of thigh at Mass, a plunging décolletage at the cider press.

Symbols and Substance: Being Basque in Iparralde

"In the 1960s and 1970s," says Filgi Claverie, "the Basques from the Spanish side would come here and say to us: 'You are so lucky, you have the *ikurriña* here.' I would reply, 'Yes, we have it but it has no significance for most of us. You don't have it, but it has a great significance for you. Our culture has been reduced to folklore for tourists, without an essence, without political content. When we sell our image as much as this, we are in danger of selling out our country.'" Claverie is a native of Biarritz, but he has a foot on both sides of the frontier since he directs an international dance festival in Biarritz, and an association for the promotion of dance throughout the CAV in San Sebastián. He is a committed but realistic Basque nationalist, who recognizes that living in different states has impacted deeply on many aspects of life north and south of the Bidasoa.

He believes there is a "fictitious" element in the nation constructed from Paris since the 1789 revolution, but he thinks French nationalists were much more efficient, and much more subtle, in their nation-building than their Spanish counterparts. The centralizing drive of the revolution and Napoleon I came half a century before Madrid even attempted to abolish the Basque *fueros*, and it proved highly effective. But the genius of the French was to finish by education what they had started with terror and politics. Claverie sees the landmark education acts championed by Jules Ferry in the early 1880s as a crushing blow to Euskera, and to Basque identity, in Iparralde. Ferry introduced free, universal and obligatory primary education. Surely this was an admirable social advance? "Yes, of course, except that it went with the imposition of extreme republican values, hostile to Basque religious traditions, and—this is the key point—it made French the sole language of our schools."

Claverie recalls the "totally perverse" way in which children were not only prevented from speaking Euskera during school hours, but were motivated to spy on their schoolmates to stop them speaking it too.

"The teacher would give a stick to the first child who said a word in Euskera in the morning. The child had to carry the stick until he or she heard a classmate speaking Euskera, to whom they could pass it on. The child who had the stick at the end of the day would be punished." So Basque children were made the agents through whom much of a generation lost its native tongue.

Claverie's maternal grandparents, like many thousands of other French Basque *euskaldunak*, did not teach their own language to their children, so that he grew up a second-generation French speaker. When he became curious about learning Euskera at the age of fourteen, his grandfather warned him that speaking it "would only bring you problems," though there was no persecution of the language outside the education system. When he became fluent, however, his grandfather admitted he was delighted. "He thought the world had turned upside down, that he had returned to the world of his own childhood."

Claverie has been deeply involved in the *ikastola* movement since the late 1960s. There are now more than twenty private schools which teach exclusively through the medium of Euskera, and many more bilingual ones, in Iparralde. In some villages, like Sara, every single child learns at least some subjects through Basque. It has been a long battle. There were perceptions that the *ikastolak* were "terrorist training camps" or at least ideologically radical. For a long time they were dependent entirely on fees and donations. Since Lionel Jospin's tenure as education minister in the 1990s, however, these schools have been partly funded by the French educational system on the same basis as private religious schools. This is rather ironic because a new constitutional provision, also dating from the 1990s, controversially declared French to be the only language of the Republic—ostensibly to keep Anglo-Americanization at bay. A court decision based on the new article suggested a different agenda, since it prohibited "bilingual schools which teach regional languages through immersion". This leaves the *ikastolak* "with a sword of Damocles over our heads", says Claverie. In the meantime, the language is just about holding its own. Recent surveys show that, for the first time in a century, the number of *Euskaldunak* in Iparralde has ceased to fall.

If French cultural nationalism was consolidated by education, political nationalism was hugely boosted by the First World War, when French Basque youth was massively absorbed into a great French national cause. (It is interesting that the 1897 *Ramuntcho*, the novel in which Pierre Loti brought a romantic view of Basque folklore to a mass French and international public, pivots on the disastrous personal impact of military service on the fate of his eponymous hero, a *pelotari* of course.)

The war, says Claverie, acted as a "melting pot", making real a French nation which had hitherto been "somewhat fictitious". In the nineteenth century the Basque Pyrenees had been a single entity, united by the web of contraband which was a way of life on both sides of the border. The same network facilitated Basques fleeing military service—in both directions, from the Carlist wars and from the Franco-Prussian war. Many families have ancestors from "the other side" as a result of these clandestine migrations. During the First World War, however, French Basque public opinion began to see draft evasion as treason and Spanish neutrality as lack of solidarity. Smuggling continued to prosper, however. In the Second World War, the Allies used Basque smugglers to spirit airmen out of occupied Europe, a remarkable operation known as the Comet Network, celebrated in *El Camino de la libertad* (2006) by Juan Carlos Jiménez de Aberásturi.

Yet Claverie notes that the distance between French and Spanish Basques was growing wider at this period, to the point that the first waves of refugees from the Spanish Civil War were regarded with as much suspicion as sympathy. The long years of the dictatorship imposed deeper separation, with its closely guarded border. And Claverie agrees that Franco's attempt to impose centralism through repression, contrasting with France's subtlety, had the paradoxical effect of fostering Basque nationalism in Hegoalde to a level completely out of synch with Basque sentiments across the Bidasoa. Economics also widened the political gap throughout the twentieth century. While Spanish Basques could find plenty of work at home, underdevelopment in Iparralde meant that young French Basques were drawn inexorably towards jobs in Pau and in Paris.

Only in the 1960s, with the influence of many ETA refugees living in Iparralde, and growing left nationalist currents among French Basque youth, did a very tentative reconnection begin. It is still very tentative today.

Returning to the theme of symbolic souvenirs, it is striking that, thirty years after the *ikurriña* was legalized in Hegoalde, you can scour the streets of the old part of Bilbao and only find a single shop selling Basque souvenirs. Even in that one shop, they take third place, after suitcases and belts in the window display.

The tourist industry undoubtedly accounts for much of the frippery that lines the streets of Bayonne or clutters St.-Jean-Pied-de-Port, making it the Lourdes of the Camino de Santiago. The much more recently developed tourism on the Spanish side has learned to steer clear of marketing an excess of Basque kitsch from the negative example of its neighbours.

But the Basque obsession with flags, emblems and self-representation is not only for tourist consumption, and is ubiquitous on both sides of the border. The Restaurant Bayonais is a no-nonsense, good-home-cooking place, mainly patronized by locals. But its décor features a clock in the form of a pelota court, *lauburus* on the jugs and cups and primitive farmyard implements on the walls. Well, you might say, this is an old restaurant that sells itself on tradition. Indeed, but the dining room in the Hotel Bergara in the French Basque village of Souraide [Zudaire] is brand new, starkly white and functional and its paintings (for sale) are all from the twenty-first century. What do they portray? One single image incorporates, arranged around a massive *ikurriña*, a whole gamut of Basque icons: fishing boats, dancers, pelota players, farmhouses and mountain peaks. The other paintings are in the same vein. An adjoining room is in mock farmhouse style with heavy beams and an elaborate ox yoke above the door. The hotel's *gâteau basque* arrives at the table surrounded by *lauburus* in dusted chocolate.

You could make similar inventories, again and again and again, on both sides of the Bidasoa. Sometimes the images are specific and appropriate: a bar in Lastur in Guipúzcoa has marvellous old photographs of local people and traditional sports and music. These portraits give a strong flavour of the *genus loci* and its very specific inhabitants. Much more often, however, the images and artefacts in homes and public places are generic. Many a plaque with *zazpiak bat* on the Spanish side of the border was purchased in the souvenir shops in Bayonne. You have to wonder whether such ubiquitous reminders of Basqueness are the sign of a strong sense of identity, or of a weak one which needs constant reinforcement. Undoubtedly, on the Spanish side, these images were especially charged with significance because they became symbols of resistance to Francoist repression. Whatever the source of their energy, they show no sign of losing it after three decades of democracy.

There is much more to Bayonne, of course, than *Basquerie*. If you raise your eyes above the level of the shop windows, Grand Bayonne offers a delightful open exhibition of Basque architectural frontages. Nowhere else is there quite such a concentration of cool white plaster, crisscrossed with horizontal, vertical and diagonal beams in reds, greens, blues or simply dark brown or black. Shutters and eaves are immaculately painted to match. Cast-iron balconies overflow with geraniums. No two buildings are the same; each manages some subtle variation on the basic format, yet they never clash. One of Hemingway's more puzzling lines in *The Sun Also Rises* is Jake's description of Bayonne as "like a very clean Spanish town", a comment which would annoy Basques on both sides of the border. Clean it certainly is, but Spanish? Not at all.

Petit Bayonne: Cosy Streets, Dirty War and a Fine Museum

These frontages form streets that flow down to the Nive, a little river which divides Grand Bayonne from Petit Bayonne just before it joins the Adour. The Nive and its bridges lend a Venetian lightness to the old town. Cross the bridges and you enter a cosy warren of smaller streets, full of bars and restaurants.

This warren was not cosy at all for a few years in the 1980s, when it took on the atmosphere of a very dangerous maze. Petit Bayonne was at that time the nerve centre of the large community of Spanish Basque exiles associated with ETA. The French authorities had been sympathetic enough to these young fighters against a fascist regime, seeing them as a kind of contemporary *Résistance*. They often gave them official status as political refugees. The so-called "French sanctuary" became an essential, indeed a defining, element in ETA's modus operandi. Leaders planned their strategies here, and received payments of "revolutionary taxes" from Basque business people in the smart cafés of Bayonne, Biarritz and St.-Jean-de-Luz. Activists were trained in the interior, took smugglers' routes across the Pyrenees to carry out attacks, and returned for rest and relaxation to the bars of Petit Bayonne. Their families often moved there with them. Some of them even set up successful businesses.

The pragmatic utility of this situation meant that ETA was distinctly cool, perhaps even hostile, to attempts by radical French Basques to develop their own armed organization, Iparretarrak (ETA of the North). Generally speaking, the Spanish Basque militants behaved like model citizens in Iparralde and were popular with the local population.

The advent of democracy in Spain made little impact on French policy towards ETA. This was one of the factors which pushed senior members of Felipe González's PSOE administration towards their fateful decision to use state terror against the terrorists and authorize a three-year dirty war on French soil, carried out by the Grupos Antiterroristas de Liberación (GAL).

In the parking lot off the Rue des Tonneliers in Petit Bayonne, you will see a plaque, and probably freshly re-painted murals, dedicated to Joxean Lasa and Joxe Zabala. These two young (and rather insignificant) members of ETA disappeared from this car park on the night of 15 October 1983. They left behind them only an anorak, hanks of hair, a crushed cigar and their personal papers in a Renault 4. Two years later, their remains were found buried in quicklime in Alicante, 500 miles away. They would not, however, be identified for another decade.

The Spanish courts have since established that they were abducted by members of the Guardia Civil and tortured for several weeks in a specially prepared dungeon in San Sebastián. They were finally driven across Spain in the boot of car, shot and buried. A Guardia Civil general, Enrique Rodríguez Galindo, and a senior Socialist politician, Julen Elgorriaga, were convicted of their murders.

From 1983 to 1986 the streets of Petit Bayonne became the favoured beat for Spanish death squads. Four ETA members were shot dead at the tiny bar counter of the Hotel Monbar on the Rue Pannecau. Two little girls aged five and three were severely wounded in an indiscriminate attack on another bar on the riverside. The mercenaries responsible had been specifically instructed by Spanish police officers "to shoot anyone with beards" and not to be squeamish about bystanders.

Twenty years later, Petit Bayonne looks remarkably like it did then, with many of the same bars still operating. But it has changed a great deal. A combination of the pressure from the GAL and a shift in French policy towards extraditing ETA suspects means that most remaining exiles have long moved elsewhere or are in deep cover. The area remains a hive of French Basque nationalist radical activity, with offices for the newspaper *Enbata* and several political and cultural organizations based here. Yet there is an oddly anodyne feel to many of the bars now, and their iconography, once implacably revolutionary, suggests a desire to please all customers. On the Rue Pannecau a bar advertising *tapas* (the Spanish word rather than the Basque *pintxos*) displays a matador with "España" emblazoned on his cape, right beside an *ikurriña*. A series of very Spanish prints above the bar itself is complemented by very Basque farmhouses and fishing ports on the opposite wall. Whether this is an expression of inclusiveness, or just post-modern eclectic confusion, I could not guess. It would still be a sensitive topic to ask questions about here, and could lead to misunderstandings.

Around the corner, on the lovely northern riverside, stands a building which raises many more questions, and makes a fair effort to answer some of them. Bayonne's Musée Basque has its origins in the Basque folklore vogue of the 1890s, but has been completely restructured and refurbished for its reopening in 2001. It is now the best organized and most comprehensive of several ethnographic museums north and south of the border. It provides a good introduction to many of the themes we have touched on in this book.

The museum's vision has been guided by a refreshingly pluralist approach, epitomized by the quotation from Pedro de Axular which heads this chapter. Here we learn that while Guipúzcoa and Navarre gave us the Jesuits' founding fathers, Bayonne gave shelter and support to their great Catholic opponent, the Dutch theologian Cornelius Otto Jansen. The result was that the town never allowed the order of St. Ignatius to gain a toehold in its territory. The contribution of French Protestantism to Basque literary culture is recognized, and significant space is dedicated to Jewish industry, customs and religious practice. The interpenetration between Basque, Gascon and Béarnaise traditions is evident.

These are aspects of French Basque reality which can hardly be denied, but it is good to see them so fully acknowledged. If Gernika is ever to truly fulfil a role as Basque cultural capital, a similarly pluralist approach is needed in the Casa de Juntas and the Euskal Herria Museo.

The painful clashes between Jacobinism and Basque traditions are registered: massive deportations of "counter-revolutionaries" from villages like Askain, Sara and Itsasu; the forced political marriage with Béarn; the tensions over rural Basque support for their Pyrenean neigh-

bours during the Carlist wars. But these complex events are not presented as unmitigated national disasters, in contrast to the frequently
one-sided presentation of the loss of the *fueros* on the other side of the
mountains. It is rather the visual images and idiosyncrasies that stay in
the mind: the unexpected practicality of the smuggler's outsize umbrella
and sleeping pallet for his rain-sodden "nightwork"; the maize dolls con-
juring a lost sense of childhood; the collection of sheep bells, each with
a slightly different note.

There is a beautifully organized room devoted to pelota, which
includes a *pelotari's* burial memorial, with his sporting equipment carved
on the stone disc. There is a fine range of paintings of French Basque
dances, which are probably the richest in the region. There are also fascinating portrayals of religious processions and of sports, including, very
appropriately, rugby. And there is a small chamber dedicated to a singular Basque funeral tradition: the speech a bereaved person or their
neighbour must make to the family beehive before taking the wax for the
ritual funeral candles, which are wound like a cord around a small
wooden board. It runs like this: "Good morning, dear bees, good
morning noble queen. I have sad news for you: your master is dead.
From now on it is my turn to look after you. But first you must pay the
wax you owe to the deceased…"

In his book on Basque funeral rites, José Miguel de Barandiarán
points out that it was believed that the bees would die if this is not done.
Other farm animals are similarly threatened by a human death, and must
also be informed verbally, having first been obliged to stand up if they
are lying down.

Biarritz and St.-Jean-de-Luz: Faded Glories, Pleasing Melancholy

Grand and Petit Bayonne make up a compact and easily managed whole,
but Biarritz stretches out languidly around several majestic beaches, with
no obvious beginning, middle or end. Its mansions strive to recall the
glory days of Napoleon III and Empress Eugénie, who turned the fishing
village into a very fashionable elite resort during the Second Empire. A
little later, Edward, Prince of Wales, spent two months a year here, dividing his time between gambling and gastronomic indulgence while
waiting for Queen Victoria to die. The town thrived as a tourist venue
with the advent of the Belle Epoque.

Pleasures of the *plage*: the languid beaches of Biarritz were enjoyed by local Basques long before they were sought out by Belle Epoque tourists. Seventeenth-century travellers expressed surprise at "grown girls and young fishermen" who "mingle in the water."

But Biarritz has not been in this league since the First World War, when elite tourism migrated to the French and Italian Rivieras, and it shows its faded age. Nevertheless, it accommodates its two very different sets of contemporary clients—French retirees and international surfers—comfortably enough. Even when they crowd the beaches there is still a sense of open space along the promenades. Just avoid looking inland from the *grande plage*, where a clumsy stack of white egg-box apartments clutter the urban skyline. The Art Deco splendour of the Casino, and especially of the Gare du Midi, now a theatre hosting international dance and music festivals, should put the egg-box architects to shame.

There is a pleasingly melancholy beauty about the rapidly eroding natural sculptures formed by sandstone formations around the Rocher de la Vierge, with its promontory bridge designed by Gustave Eiffel, while a tall white lighthouse stands as monument to pristine simplicity at the other end of the beach.

To the south, the little ports of Bidart and Guéthary are spotless and rather sterile at first sight. The dominance of smart but characterless neo-

Basque architecture gives a toy-town feel to much of the coastal development. Yet I was happy to find my preconceptions challenged one evening in the very ordinary restaurant at the Hotel Elissaldia in Bidart. Five middle-aged men came to sit at a nearby table. One took out a guitar, and without a by-your-leave they began singing traditional Basque songs in harmony. They fell silent for the more important business of eating, and then sang again between each course, loudly enough to infuse the place with atmosphere, quietly enough that everyone else could easily continue their conversations if they wished. Their singing was first-class (French Basques are said to support their church choirs very well, and it shows). French was the language these diners conversed in, but they sang comfortably in Euskera from little yellow song sheets, familiar from the revival movement south of the border.

Across that border, however, such a scene in a café or restaurant is still unlikely. The volume of piped music, TV and radio in most restaurants would rule out such spontaneous performances, so the revivalists are generally restricted to the streets. The Basques may be one nation, but their tolerance for noise pollution varies enormously from south to north.

A little hill above the cliffs at Bidart offers panoramic southerly views at sunset, the whole coast softly sinking into Biscay on a clear night, with the Pyrenean foothills rising and falling and rising again as they climb away inland. The one enclosed bay to the south before the Bidasoa is hidden away on this sightline, but it shelters the loveliest towns on the coast, St.-Jean-de-Luz, and its twin Ciboure [Ziburu].

Cardinal Mazarin chose St.-Jean-de-Luz as his base to negotiate the Treaty of the Pyrenees, which settled all outstanding territorial issues between France and Spain after the Thirty Years' War, in 1659. The negotiations and the signing took place on the Isle of Pheasants on the Bidasoa, a neutral space on this border river, in a scene marvellously described by Simon Schama in *Landscape and Memory* (1996). The peace was sealed by the marriage between Louis XIV and the Spanish Infanta María Teresa, and the Basque port was also chosen as the venue for their wedding, one of the biggest royal nuptial blow-outs in European history. The town, establishing its pre-eminent gastronomic tradition, did the couple proud. In gratitude, the king licensed the sea captains of St.-Jean-de-Luz as corsairs, a trade in legalized wartime piracy at which they proved most adept. Commercial vessels from rival nations, especially Britain, came to regard the whole Basque coast as a "nest of vipers". Corsairs from San Sebastián and Hondarribia had been serving the Spanish monarchy equally well in the previous century.

St-Jean-de-Luz thus long predates Biarritz as a holiday venue for the super-rich, but the town has retained an active fishing fleet and a refreshing sense of having an existence independent of tourism, despite the proliferation of fashionable—and excellent—restaurants. In many ways it combines the best aspects of the French Basque coast (elegant beauty) and the Spanish Basque coast (the salty buzz of a tough trade proudly conducted). Despite its bright and shiny marina, the old streets of Ciboure have an even more down-to-earth atmosphere. The composer Maurice Ravel was born here to a Basque mother and Swiss father in 1875, and returned annually for holidays to their Dutch-style house on the quay which now bears his name. The influence of Basque folk music on some of his work is evident, for example his Trio for violin, cello and piano (1914). But it is rather harder to spot in his best known work, *Bolero*, which he composed while in Ciboure in 1928.

Sokoa sits at the southern mouth of the bay, and this is where the famous Corniche Basque really begins. It is only about five miles from here to Hendaye and the border, and many people think it among the prettiest walks in the world. The sea and mountain views are certainly spectacular, but, like the huge floral displays on Hendaye's roundabouts, the route is too pretty in places for some tastes, and much too close to a busy road for much of the time to be truly relaxing. It is perhaps time to move inland.

Biriatou and Sara: Calvinist Catholics and the Evils of Procrastination

You do not have to go far to find a very different world. Less than five miles up the Bidasoa from Hendaye, Biriatou perches above the river with superb views of the other side of the border. So superb, in fact, that French Basques flocked here in August 1936 to watch General Mola's troops advance on Irún, a battle which produced some of the bloodiest fighting on the Basque front. War as spectacle long predates television.

Biriatou is the first village on the first foothill of the Pyrenees, Xoldokogaina, and it is a representative preview of its neighbours further inland. As in Guipúzcoan villages, only more so, there is almost always a clearly identifiable nucleus of church, *frontón*, square and town hall. On the French side, the longer history of tourism generally adds a cosy hotel or two to this cluster. Biriatou is so small that its hotels provide the only bars, but the bar/citizen ratio is much lower on the French side in any case. Most of the private dwellings are dispersed, in Biriatou's case almost invisibly, into the hinterland. This village is the starting point for a maze of trails into and around the mountains. Not so long ago, these were busy thoroughfares for smugglers, now transformed into *Grandes Routes*, with myriad diversions and variations, for hikers. The ruins of red-brick sentry boxes at intervals along the Spanish side of the river are reminders of what the smugglers had to contend with.

One of Biriatou's countless smuggling anecdotes concerns an innovative entrepreneur in the 1950s, who tried to punt a battery-operated jukebox across the Bidasoa. The story goes that the bump of impact switched on the machine as he reached the far bank, so that he found himself serenading the *guardias civiles* with *Love Me Tender*. (Or perhaps it was *Jailhouse Rock*.) Some versions of this story have the *guardias* fleeing in terror from the disembodied and satanic music, others have them emptying their submachine guns into its flashing display case until the music died.

Biriatou's church is worth a visit, not because of any significant work of art but because of what it says about cultural differences between northern and southern Basques. You can even smell the contrast; open the door and the strong hint of wax and wood polish says "Protestant" out loud, at least to an Irish nose. The whole atmosphere of the interior is quite distinct from that of similar churches just a few miles across the river. Both sides are Catholic, both sides are Basque, but the simplicity here is striking. There are almost always plain wooden galleries, at two or even three levels, running around the sides and back of the churches. This lends them a practical and participatory feel, as if they were meeting houses as much as places of worship. The remote Gothic grandeur and overpowering Baroque excess, so cherished on the Spanish side even in small villages, is either altogether absent, as in Biriatou, or greatly attenuated. Calvinism's brief ascendancy in Basse-Navarre obviously made a deep impact.

Many aspects of ordinary French Basque life are distinctive, too, though of course these also reflect French national cultural generally.

People go to bed much earlier, and they entertain in their homes, while Hegoalde socializes in the street. French Basques speak much more softly, and crockery and cutlery are not treated as percussion instruments. If you have a coffee in Valcarlos, the last village after Roncesvalles on the Spanish side of the border, and then stop for another in Arnéguy, the first on the French side, the blanket of silence in the latter can seem abnormal, even disturbing, after a couple of weeks in the south. And then it may seem a blessed relief.

Sara is barely ten miles further into the mountains, but if you come at it from St.-Jean-de-Luz much of the way is still dominated by suburbia. After Askain, with its pleasing three-arched "Roman" bridge (built at the end of the sixteenth century), you find yourself in green countryside with softly rounded hills, a softer version of Guipúzcoa.

A scattering of prosperous farmhouses, many of them three or four centuries old, begins to converge on the roadside, almost imperceptibly coalescing into the streets of Sara. The village is built on hills, and two steep slopes lead down to its modest market square, which flows directly into an exceptionally broad and deep *frontón*, appropriate for the long-range and complex modes of pelota known as *laxoa* and *rebote*, which may be the oldest forms of the game. The configuration of square and *frontón* give Sara one of the most pleasing central spaces in any Basque village (when the *frontón* is not abused as a car park). The long irregular banks of seats for spectators double as a vantage point to take in the façades of some of the finest vernacular architecture of the whole region. The smart and antiseptic symmetry of coastal neo-Basque styles here finds its authentic originals, stubbornly beautiful in their irregularity. No beam is quite straight, no stone is plumbed quite true, but the whole configuration always *works*. Their age alone tells us that, but these building also speak of a time when the home building catered for almost every need a family could have, from stabling animals on the first floor to pressing cider in the attic, from eating around great tables to watching the neighbours impassively from spacious balconies.

Families, as we have seen, were often named after houses, and Sara's most famous adoptive son, Pedro de Axular (1556-1644), who wrote *Gero* while parish priest of the village, took his name from a farmhouse just across the contentious border in newly Spanish Navarre, near Urdax. When he was appointed, he asked Henry IV for French citizenship.

Henry, who of course had started out as king of Basse Navarre, told him that no Navarran needed to be naturalized in his own country. A jealous French Basque priest challenged this gift of a prime parish to a "foreigner", but Axular had the ear of the bishop as well as the monarch. He stayed where he was, a very popular, very learned and very literate clergyman.

Sara is one of the nerve centres of the Basque Country, one of the historical and living arguments for its essential unity. It links St.-Jean-de-Luz with Vera de Bidasoa and Etxelar of the Cinco Villas, and with the Baztan valley. A common Pyrenean identity binds the peoples of these valleys, though less so than in earlier times. A border ethos then prevailed, where smuggling was regarded as legitimate business, and families would move fluidly from one side to the other to avoid war or political or religious persecution.

Sara's *plaza mayor* is discreetly overlooked by Axular's church, a fine building with a plaque to the writer on an exterior wall. Beside it is a tribute to José Miguel de Barandiarán. There is a stout but handsome square bell-tower, its steep, dark-grey slated roof hinting at the style of the deeper Basque interior in Soule. Above the tower clock there is a Basque version of a grim Latin motto:

Oren guziek dute
gizona kolpatzen
azkenekoak du
hobirat egortzen

"All hours strike blows at men," the saying goes, "the last one kills." This seems particularly appropriate to Axular's church because the theme of his classic work, whose title translates literally as "After", runs on similar lines. He warns that the sinner's soul risks damnation by postponing the embrace of God's grace until another and more convenient day. *Non duzu gero horren segurantza?* he demands severely. "Where do you get this certainty about having an 'afterwards'? Don't you know the old saying that there is nothing so certain as your death, and nothing so uncertain as the hour in which it will occur?"

It sounds like daunting stuff, but he writes punchily, and it is more engaging than you might imagine. Axular was a robust, witty and subtle

Time and the bell: the church of St.-Martin in Sara, where the sixteenth century Basque writer Pedro de Axular was parish priest. His classic work, *Gero*, warns of the dangers of procrastination, and the Basque proverb on the bell-tower warns of inevitability of death.

theologian. What makes this work really significant, however, is that he showed, once and for all, that Euskera was a fully appropriate vehicle for complex arguments in fluent literary style, fully capable of transmitting the most subtle expressions of Christian culture. As we have seen, Atxaga sees him as the Cervantes of Euskera. His English equivalents might be the authors of the *Book of Common Prayer* or the St. James Bible. The tragedy is that Euskera never found its John Milton. Incidentally, it is surely ironic that death waited 88 long years to cut down the rector of Sara, and Axular only completed his masterpiece at 87. Procrastination, evidently, was a vice close to home.

Another man who made his last hour count is celebrated beside the *frontón*. A relief carved in stone commemorates Victor Ithurria (1914-44), "noble *pelotari* and hero of the Free French Forces". Ithurria is portrayed in double profile, each one shadowing the other. As a *pelotari*, his open hand strikes a ball. As a soldier, his fist is poised to hurl a hand grenade. There is perhaps no more striking illustration of the integration of Basque traditions with the glories of French national history. In the nearby cemetery the tributes on the cenotaph to the many local boys fallen *pour la France* are written in Euskera, a scene repeated frequently in French Basque villages.

During Sara's fiestas in September, the main *frontón* (and several others) displays a wealth of traditional activities besides the inevitable pelota. Geese (dead) are decapitated by horse-riders, *joaldunak* bang their great bells off their backs, a tug-of-war is trumped as *force basque* by a competition for lifting and carrying wooden farm carts. Euskera is spoken by almost everyone. Compared to what lies further inland, however, even lovely Sara—and more especially nearby "classic" Basque villages like Ainhoa and Espelette [Ezpeleta]—still feel just a little as though they are wearing their *Euskaldun* faces with one eye on the tourists.

Bidarrai to Baigorri: Under the Mountains' Skirts

If you follow the Nive towards St.-Jean-Pied-de-Port, nipping in and out under the skirts of the Pyrenees as you go, you may feel as though you are receding into an infinite series of golden-green valleys, each one more medieval than the one before. Itsasu enchanted Simone de Beauvoir in *The Prime of Life* (1960). Her hotel room there had direct access to a tree house, where Jean-Paul Sartre spent the day writing while she "ran around the surrounding hills. I walked through the bracken with my eyes full of sun and the pink of the plum trees." Sartre had a soft spot for the Basques and wrote an influential polemic supporting the ETA defendants in Franco's notorious show trial at Burgos in 1970. It was a passionate piece, but oddly lacking in intellectual rigour, taking on board nationalist myths as historical fact.

In 1963 a group of young Basque nationalists from both sides of the border had planted an acorn from the Gernika oak right outside the treehouse hotel in Itsasu. They put up a stone monument setting out their programme in two stages. The French Basque provinces should first be given the status of a stand-alone *déparetment*, and then all the seven provinces should be united under politically and culturally autonomous institutions. The oak tree has flourished, but Paris still refuses even the first demand. Mitterrand reneged on a 1982 election promise to set up a Basque *département*, and the area remains subsumed in the Pyrenées Atlantiques, with its capital outside the Basque Country in Pau.

A frighteningly narrow road runs along the west bank of the Nive to Bidarrai, which is set on a hill amidst breathtaking rolling pastoral valleys. This village has an oddly elongated structure. The essential central elements follow the ridge of the hill in a straight line, deconstructed as it were, and oddly exposed. The line starts with a Romanesque church perched on the edge of a vertiginous meadow. Its main entrance makes up one side of the plaza, which is formed by just three other houses and a hotel. At the other end of the ridge, the Herriko Etxea stands in rather abandoned isolation. But between plaza and town hall lies a *frontón*, which must be one of the most beautifully situated sports grounds in the world. Framed by high green or purple horizons, depending on the time of day, it gives the perspective from almost every angle that the *pelotaris* are playing against the skyline, if not against the sky.

This is prime country for *fromage de brebis*, and sheep are sprinkled like salt on every green hillside. Just a few miles further on, though, they have competition, as the sun-facing sides of the rounded hills are braided into vineyards, producing the very palatable Irouléguy wines. Baigorri holds some of the biggest bodegas, which are modest enough. With its lovely irregular bridge over the Nive and the exquisite painted wooden ceiling panels in its main church, this dispersed little town stands at the foot of the Aldudes valley. Here Iparralde plunges deep into the mountains and preserves as strong a sense of Basqueness as you will find anyway. An archaic international arrangement, dating from the partition of the two Navarres, still allows a handful of French Basque farmers to live on land owned by Madrid in the high Aldudes. Paris still pays the rent.

Aldudes was the home ground of Perkain, the first *pelotari* whose name is known to history. This is not just because he was a brilliant player, though he must have been all of that. Like many French Basques he despised the 1789 revolution, and took refuge across the border in the Baztan valley as the Terror took hold on Iparralde. But then one of his neighbours in Aldudes challenged him to a pelota match, and he was honour-bound to return. The game was in full swing when he was spotted by a gendarme, who moved to arrest him. With the speed, agility, strength and cunning of the champion that he was, Perkain calmly turned in mid-play and slapped the ball from his palm into the gendarme's head. The unfortunate policeman died. Perkain beat a hasty retreat up the mountains. Or so the legend has it. Pelota is still played everywhere in this part of the country. One evening I parked in an empty corner near the church in Baigorri. Before I could get out of the car, a boy who could not have been more than six years old was at my window. He told me very politely but very firmly to park elsewhere. Could I not see that this corner was a *frontón*? He wanted to play with his father, who was just coming home from work. They were still playing when I left, an hour later, at sunset.

At the End of the Basque World: Saint Engrace, Larrau, Migrating Raptors and a Tribute of Three Cows

Let us leave the charm (and the clutter) of St.-Jean-Pied-de-Port to the pilgrims starting their Camino towards Roncesvalles. There is still a whole region of Iparralde to explore, tucked into the south-eastern valleys of the tiny and depopulated province of Soule [Zuberoa or Xiberoa in Euskera]. Though this area is easily accessible today, Basques from other regions still talk about it as "the end of the world". If the world ends as beautifully as this, there is little to fear from Armageddon. But there is certainly a stunted and hungry look about the sparse oak woods as you head across the small barrier of the Col d'Osquich to Mauléon [Maule Lextarre], the lonesome provincial capital, famous only for its *espadrilles*. The Souletin architecture, with its great grey slate roofs, makes the massive houses look like knights in chain mail. It is a cold, hard style after the cosy red slate, white plaster and multi-coloured fascia of the rest of Euskal Herria, more Béarnaise, in fact, than Basque. The stark *bastide* that overlooks Mauléon, built by Edward I of England, looks grim despite the squeaky clean (and surely anachronistic) *ikurriña* which flutters and snaps over it today. It is easy here to imagine the harsh repression of the 1661 peasants' revolt led by the priest named Matalas, who was held in its dungeons after defeat of his armed campaign for "the land to the people".

Head along the Saison river towards the mountains, and the slightly guilty pleasures of empty landscapes and silent villages multiply. Until Tardets the valley is broad and flat-bottomed, with gravel beaches thrown up by lazy meanders. And then there is a hard choice.

To the south-east runs the valley of St.-Engrace, to the north-west the road to the model Souletin village of Larrau. Let us head for the latter first. The road to Larrau runs through a lush valley, copiously wooded. Then, approaching the village, escarpments rise again, bare slopes of velvet greens with generous blazes of gorse blossom. The cold in the village is a foretaste of the high Pyrenees, its stark lines of slate and dark stone a very puritan pleasure. This is a place for clearing the mind, not indulging the senses. The bulk of the Pic d'Orhy, seen in some legends as the mother mountain of the Basque Country, looms majestically above the village.

A minor road snakes from Larrau north across the foothills to St.-Jean-Pied-de-Port, bisecting the ancient forest of Irati which straddles the border. After about ten miles, just on the first margins of the forest, the Col d'Orgambideska offers one of the great spectacles of European bird-watching every autumn. Big migrants—raptors, storks and cranes—pour over the ridge in exceptional numbers. A ten-minute diversion from my car yielded two dozen black storks, perhaps forty honey buzzards and three short-toed eagles spiralling up and down the thermals. By an odd coincidence, there is another spectacular birding spot in the corresponding foothills directly across the spine of the Pyrenees in Navarre. Again there are many big raptors, but in the Hoz de Arbayun they appear almost subterranean compared to the soaring migrants at the Col. This gorge has still be thoroughly explored, but from a high roadside vantage point you can peer down into it. On a good day, it is possible to make out three species of nesting vulture: the common griffon, the much rarer Egyptian, and the bizarre lammergeier or bone-breaker, which is threatened with extinction.

But what if we had taken the route to St.-Engrace? The sharp limestone flanks of this valley are pierced by dramatic gorges, the most spectacular being Kakoeta, only explored in the last century. It is no great challenge to hikers today. Boardwalks and solar-powered alarm points protect tourists all the way to the cascading torrents and weirdly sculpted caves at its headwaters. Nevertheless, the sensation of walking several miles through a narrow canyon several hundred feet deep is not to be scoffed at. For the adventurous, there are half a dozen less publicised gorges in the valley, where you make your own luck.

St.-Engrace itself is the last village before the border, and is pitiably poor, its road only metalled at the end of the last century. Yet it has a little twelfth-century church which is a gem of Basque architecture. Feast your eyes on the painted pillars and the stories told by their polychromatic capitals. A Christian in the jaws of a lion, centaurs hunting with bows and arrows, the dalliance of Solomon and Sheba, the Nativity, the Wise Men on horseback following the star: these are like frames from movies in the medieval imagination. Then step outside and wonder how the church has not yet tumbled down the hill after nine centuries of slippage.

Going up towards the border, the land empties. Beech gives way to gorse, gorse to grass, grass to rock and scree with a scattering of obstinate conifers. The sky opens up, and the crests of the Pyrenees echo each other to infinity in both directions. The great cone of the Pic D'Anie, just beyond the Basque border with Aragon and Béarn, dominates the landscape, sadly scarred with ski-lifts and cable cars. If you persist, the road twists back into Navarre, into the glorious valley of Belagua, "beautiful water", a high mountain pasture that would not be out of place in Yosemite.

Right on the border here is a very special spot, the rock of St. Martin. Each year on 13 July, the people of Baretous, in Iparralde, and of Isaba, which lies in the Roncal valley below Belagua, come together for the ceremony of the Three Cows. They have been doing this for 600 years. Tradition requires the mayor of Baretous to bring a tribute of three fine heifers in acknowledgement of the use of commonage belonging to Isaba. During the San Fermín fiestas in Pamplona in 2005, I ran into the mayors of Lesaka and Arantza, and they kindly invited me to join them for the ceremony the following day. I could hardly go in better company, I thought, and that was true in every aspect—except navigation. To their intense embarrassment, they missed a junction en route to the Roncal valley, and we proceeded to drive in circles, or rather spiralling hairpin bends, for the next hour. The sure-footed smuggler's internal GPS was not part of these men's make-up. So much for the tightly bound network of Pyrenean mountain men and women. We were all a little carsick by the time we got to the rock of St. Martin, and found to our chagrin that we had missed the ceremony altogether. The cows had already been herded down towards Belagua.

Never mind, said the mayors, come with us quickly. I was rushed to a shepherds' hut doubling as a theatrical changing room. The mayor of Isaba, a shy but obliging man, was persuaded by his colleagues to change back into medieval costume, which he had just shed, for the benefit of my camera.

And then, of course, since this was a Basque ceremony, it was followed by a meal in which about 500 citizens from both villages enjoyed a copious lunch in a marquee astride the border. Perhaps we had not missed the real ceremony after all, I thought, watching these hardy aquiline Pyrenean faces, as they ate, drank, joked and argued amiably. Gay marriage was the topic of the day, and the mayor of Arantza, a man of advanced years and sprightly mind, defended the extension of this old institution forcefully. I was very lucky, I thought, very privileged, to find myself once again in a commensal parliament of transnational Basques.

Back to the source: the Xorroxin falls, origin of the Bidasoa river, which divides—or unites—Iparralde and Hegoalde, hidden deep in the green Pyrenean valley of Baztan.

The Reality of Magic, the Magic of Reality

For much of this book, I have tried to counter "exotic" and "primitive" stereotypes about the Basque Country. But I hope I have also conveyed some small hint of its unique enchantment. Perhaps I might be allowed to conclude with some personal stories about places where its magic has touched me most.

Itziar was the first Basque village I ever saw. As I have written elsewhere, I hitched from San Sebastián to Bilbao on my very first day in Euskal Herria, in the autumn of 1975. I knew (who didn't?) that these were momentous times. Franco lay dying, still signing death warrants as if the execution of his enemies might somehow further postpone his own wretched and lingering departure. A great wave of democracy was poised, waiting to break over Spain. No-one could have imagined then the impact that that wave would have on the Basque Country, but that did not stop me trying. Nevertheless, my overheated political brain suddenly went quiet when I was stuck between lifts on the old main road, which ran between Itziar and the sea.

I thought the great Gothic church above me was like a stone ship anchored to the steep green hillside. I thought that this was an original thought until I found years later that it was a commonplace in Basque writing, and well developed by Jorge Oteiza.

That day, other images seduced me: a brace of oxen, their chunky wooden yoke blazing with wool decorations in primary colours, and the wiry man in blue overalls and a black beret urging them on; the tang of freshly cut grass and bracken; and the sound of sheep bells. Itziar became my image of a Basque pastoral Eden. Yet I was reluctant to return. Perhaps I feared that the industrial estate on the far side of the church had sucked the magic out of the landscape.

So, though I drove past the village many times, it was several years before I turned off the road and took the S-bends up the hill. It was an exceptionally bright June day, and the white *baserriak* gleamed like another country, more North African than Basque. And it was Sunday lunchtime, so not a soul was stirring outside the family homes. But it was not silent. From one of these centennial farmsteads, someone was playing Pink Floyd's *I Wish You Were Here* at full volume. Oddly, it did not seem inappropriate to the unnatural heat of the day. Wandering off through the woods which dipped up and down towards Lastur, I saw a little bull, a very little bull. I thought it was funny when it started tossing its head aggressively, but I stopped laughing when it charged. I climbed a tree very fast. It gave me a glance of bored contempt, and abruptly dashed off again.

Afterwards, I wondered if the whole day had been a dream, some bizarre intersection with nostalgia for student psychedelia and a child-hood fear of cattle. Itziar remained as remote and desirable as ever.

More than a decade later, I began reading Joseba Zulaika's *Violencia Vasca*. I was amazed and thrilled and disturbed to find that Itziar, of all places, was the object of a masterpiece of anthropological fieldwork. It contained stranger, more wonderful and more terrible things than my fantasies could have dreamed up. The caves of Urtiaga and Ekain still guarded their mysteries and their masterpieces in its hinterland. Zulaika's mother had seen Mari of Amboto flying like a ball of fire through the sky. This Mari had apparently co-existed peacefully enough for centuries with her Christian rival (or successor?), the Virgin Mary, who appeared to a local girl where the great stone church stands today. The supernatural was fading in Zulaika's youth, but as an adult he could still interview someone who saw a witch sitting beside his tape-recorder in a *baserri*, in broad day-light. The social world was equally strange. Zulaika's *cuadrilla* included a young ETA commando which no-one knew about. They shocked their village by killing a kidnapped Basque businessman. The first nationalist to be held by ETA, he had happily cooked his captors the best of meals while captive in one of those sprawling *baserriak*. The village and its sur-rounds encompassed both a rich tradition of *bertsolarismo*, and a disco where the callow sex-and-drugs lifestyle of late twentieth-century youth was much the same as in Manchester or Madrid. There were brave and futile attempts to save local agriculture through co-ops, which could not compete with the jobs on offer at the industrial estate.

Fast forward another decade, and Zulaika, whom I had never met, invited me to launch my book on ETA and the GAL at the Basque Center in the University of Reno, Nevada, where he was then director. I told him of my dream day in Itziar. He could explain it all. His brother Xalbador, who has sadly since died, was a big Pink Floyd fan, and always played their music very loud. And Lastur, it turns out, is famous for its puny but pugnacious bulls.

Five years later, Zulaika took me back to Lastur, where another brother, Bixente, has struggled to bring an empty hamlet back to life. A pair of water mills on a little stream above the village have been loving restored. So have the scattering of houses, now an extended restaurant and *hostal*, which enclose two sides of an earth arena. Here Lastur's little bulls again do battle with youths in the Basque style on Saturday afternoons. These *encierros* or enclosures date back to the celebratory round-up of cattle from the commons into winter quarters in the village. A kind of burlesque bull-fighting, in which the animals are taunted but rarely harmed physically, they are enormously popular today with stag parties from nearby towns. The resurrection of Lastur is a commercial enterprise, but Bixente jealously guards the authenticity of the rituals. He knows the intimate history behind every old photograph in the bar: the bohemian-tragic life of the *trikitilaris*, or itinerant accordion players; the brilliant but alcoholic healer who lost his own daughters to typhus; the rock-lifter whose record has never been broken. Leading *bertsolaris* come to sing at the communal meals, champion rock-lifters and lumber cutters perform at fiestas. Lastur is the kind of place where Basques go today to stay in touch with their traditional culture, without self-consciousness, or nationalist rhetoric, or too many gawping foreigners.

That same week, Txomin Artola, took me to Xorroxin, the waterfall at the source of the Bidasoa river. Artola is a gently poetic singer-songwriter, part of the generation including Mikel Laboa, Imanol and Benito Lertxundi. Their songs were light in the darkness of the late Franco period and its grim Basque aftermath. Artola has never been directly attracted to politics, but the song that brings us on this journey is a reminder that even rivers are political here. Artola has only been on one demonstration in his life, a protest against the pollution of the Bidasoa, the river which divides (or unites) Iparralde and Hegoalde. This demonstration took the form of a mass cycle from Xorroxin to Hondarribia, which was then his home, where the river reaches the sea. After the protest, he wrote *Bidasoa*, a ballad which laments the fish which no longer spawned there, and wonders why "strangers" guard the river's bridges, though people who speak the same language live on either bank. He ends the song with words that can never be entirely innocent in this country: the source of the river is *Nafarroan, Euskal Herrian*—in Navarre, in the land of the Basques.

Our walk takes us from the village of Gorostapalo, on the flanks of the Baztan valley, through alder woods, hazels and willows to the falls. The new-born river cascades over rocks thick and green with moss, exposing the gleaming roots of nearby trees, and fills the air with soft mist after smashing exuberantly into the small basin at the bottom. A sign says "No Fishing", and that is good news. Reduced pollution has brought back the salmon and the trout. Some things do get better in this lovely country. On our way back, though, we talk a little about the families of ETA members killed in the conflict, and about the families of ETA's Basque victims, sometimes themselves former members of the organization that has been such a privileged and tragic actor on the Basque stage during all the years of our friendship. We talk about losses which neither of us any longer believes can be redeemed by any kind of resolution, lives utterly wasted, passionately but uselessly.

Yet we are not completely cast down by this knowledge. Something seems to be beginning anew in the fragile peace process, then only a few months old, though this may be an illusion. Nevertheless, the morning is grey turning radiant silver, and the sorcery of the Pyrenean landscape is irresistible. We climb back a cobbled lane back up towards Gorostapalo, drinking in the green and pleasant rotundity of the Baztan hills. A red kite, all russet and ermine, tilts and jinks above an oak tree right above us, before sliding out of sight. I start to tell Txomin about the coincidence of hearing Zulaika's brother play Pink Floyd, years before I had met him or even read him. At that moment we are passing a *baserri*, and a lullaby in Euskera comes into earshot from within. We both pause, riveted. There is no doubt, the singer on the disk is Amaia Zubieta, accompanied by Txomin, in a short-lived band called Haizea, which was formed the year we met, 1978. A woman with long hair and a rainbow poncho comes out and greets us in Euskera, carrying a half-drunk bottle of wine. Txomin asks her what the music is. She doesn't know, she says, it's from a compilation. He tells her, and we all laugh, wondering if Bernardo Atxaga has written the script for yet another magical but very real Basque day.

Further Reading

Atxaga, Bernardo, *Obabakoak*. London: Vintage, 1994.

Atxaga, Bernardo, *El Hijo del Acordeonista*. Madrid: Punto de Lectura, 2006.

Atxaga, Bernardo, *The Lone Man*. London: Harvill Press, 1996.

Atxaga, Bernardo, *The Lone Woman*. London: Harvill Press, 1999.

Atxaga, Bernardo, *Two Brothers*. London: Harvill Press, 2001.

Atxaga, Bernardo, "The Basque Spring", *New York Times,* 29 March 2006.

Atxaga, Bernardo, "La Canción", *El País,* 8 April 2006.

Atxaga, Bernardo, "Alphabet de la culture basque", in *Nations Basques*, Paris: Autrement, 1994.

Atxaga, Bernardo, "El Mundo de Obaba", *El País*, 4 September 2004.

Axular, Pedro de, *Gero*. San Sebastián: Juan Flors, 1964.

Balzola, Asun, *Txoriburu*. Barcelona: Destino, 1998.

Baroja, Pío, *El País Vasco*. Barcelona: Destino, 1953.

Baroja, Pío, *Zalacaín el Aventurero*. Barcelona: Planeta, 1961.

Baroja, Pío, *Fantasías Vascas*. Madrid, Espasa-Calpe, 1969

Baroja, Pío, *La Leyenda de Jaun de Alzate*. Madrid: Espasa-Calpe, 1972.

Barandiarán, José Miguel de, *Estelas funerarias del País Vasco*. San Sebastián: Txertoa, 1980.

Barandiarán, José Miguel de, *Diccionario de mitología vasca*. San Sebastián: Txertoa, 1984.

Beltran, Juan Mari, *The Txalaparta, Forerunners and Variants*. Oiartzun: Herri Musikaren Txokoa, 2004.

Caro Baroja, Julio, *Los Baroja*. Madrid: Taurus, 1972.

Carr, Raymond (ed.), *Spain: a History*. Oxford: Oxford University Press, 2000.

Collins, Roger, *The Basques*. Oxford: Blackwell, 1990, 2nd edn.

Conversi, Daniele, *The Basques, the Catalans, and Spain*. London: Hurst and Co., 1997.

Courbin, Alain, *The Lure of the Sea*. London: Penguin, 1994.

Elorza, Antonio (ed.), *La Historia de ETA*. Madrid: Temas de Hoy, 2000.

Etcheverry-Ainchart, Peio and Hurel, Alexandre (eds.), *Dictionnaire thématique de culture et civilisation basques*. Bayonne: Pimientos, 2001.

Etxegoien, Juan Carlos: *Orhipean–The Country of Basque*. Pamplona: Pamiela, 2001.

Fraser, Ronald, *Blood of Spain.* London: Pimlico, 1994.

Gallop, Rodney, *A Book of the Basques.* London: Macmillan, 1930.

González Abrisketa, Olatz, *Pelota Vasca.* Bilbao: Muelle de Urbitarte, 2005.

Hernández, Ricardo and Caño, Alfonso, *Urdaibai.* Bilbao: BBK, 1999.

Heiberg, Marianne, *The Making of the Basque Nation.* Cambridge: Cambridge University Press, 1989.

Hemingway, Ernest, *Fiesta: the Sun also Rises.* London: Arrow, 1994.

Henningsen, Gustav, *The Witches' Advocate: Basque Witchcraft and the Spanish Inquisition.* Reno: University of Nevada Press, 1980.

Humboldt, W., *Los Vascos.* San Sebastián: Auñamendi, 2002.

Ibárruri, Dolores, *El Único Camino.* Barcelona: Brughera, 1979.

Itsas Memoria 3, *Revistas de Estudios Marítimas del País Vasco, Museo Naval.* San Sebastián, 2003

Juaristi, Jon, "Bilbao, la metamorfosis de una ciudad", *El País Semanal,* 1 June 1997.

Juaristi, Jon, *El Bucle Melancólico.* Madrid: Espasa-Calpe, 1997.

Jiménez de Aberásturi, Juan Carlos, *El camino de la libertad.* Hernán: 2006.

Kurlansky, Mark, *The Basque History of the* World. London: Jonathan Cape, 1999.

Lertxundi, Anjel, *Perfect Happiness.* Reno: University of Nevada Press, 2006.

Loti, Pierre, *Ramuntcho–A Tale of the Pyrenees.* London: Harrap, 1961.

MacClancy, Jeremy, "Biological Basques, Sociologically Speaking", in *Social and Biological Aspects of Ethnicity,* ed. Malcolm Chapman. Oxford: Oxford University Press, 1993.

Nooteboom, Cees, *Roads to Santiago.* London: Harvill Press, 1997.

O'Brien, Kate, *Farewell Spain.* London: Virago Press, 1985.

Olaziregi, M. J., *An Anthology of Basque Short Stories.* Reno: University of Nevada Press, 2004.

Preston, Paul, *A Concise History of the Spanish Civil War.* London: Fontana Press, 1996.

Ramos, José María Diaz, *Zona Minera de las Encartaciones.* Bilbao: Haizelan Multimedia, 2003.

Rankin, Nicholas, *Telegram from Guernica.* London: Faber & Faber, 2003.

Saizarbitoria, Ramón, *Rosetti's Obsession.* Reno: University of Nevada Press, 2005.

Sarrionaindia, Joseba, No soy de aquí. Hondarribia: Argitaletxe, 2002.

Unamuno, Miguel de, *Paz en la Guerra.* Madrid: Alianza Editorial, 1988.

Woodworth, Paddy, *Dirty War, Clean Hands: ETA, the GAL and Spanish Democracy.* New Haven: Yale University Press, 2003.

Woodworth, Paddy, "Why Do They Kill?", *World Policy Journal*, vol. XVIII, no. 1.

Zulaika, Joseba, *Basque Violence: Metaphor and Sacrament.* Reno: University of Nevada Press, 1988.

Zulaika, Joseba, *Del Cromañon al Carnaval.* Tolosa: Erein, 2000.

Zulaika, Joseba, "'Miracle in Bilbao': Basques in the Casino of Globalism". In W. Douglass, C. Urza, L. White, and J. Zulaika, eds., *Basque Cultural Studies* (Basque Studies Program Occasional Papers Series, no.5) Reno: Basque Studies Program, 2000.

Zulaika, Joseba, "Tough Beauty: Bilbao as Ruin, Architecture and Allegory". In Joan Ramon Resina, ed., *Iberian Cities* (New York and London: Routledge), pp.1-17.

Zulaika, Joseba, "Postindustrial Bilbao: the Reinvention of a New City". *Basque Studies Program Newsletter*, 57:3-9. 1998.

Guide Books

Facaros, Dana and Pauls, Michael, *Bilbao and the Basque Lands.* London: Cadogan, 2001.

Losada, Maremi (ed.), *Bilbao Step by Step.* Getxo: De Paso, 1999.

Masnik, Yasna, *The Basque Country*, Hachette Vacances, 2002.

Cultural and Literary Websites

http://www.basqueliterature.com/katalogoak/Euskaratik
http://www.transcript-review.org/section.cfm?id=264&lan=en
http://basque.unr.edu/

Note: I have occasionally drawn on my own articles, published in *The Irish Times* and *The World Policy Journal*, especially in Chapter Seven, "Wow, Bilbao" and Chapter Eleven, "Don't Mention the War".

Except where otherwise stated, all translations are my own. The translation of Bernardo Atxaga's "We Speak" in Chapter Nine is by kind permission of the author, and the translator, Margaret Jull Costa. Lines from "The Song of Roland" on p. 215 from a translation by John O'Hagan:

http://www.fordham.edu/halsall/basis/roland-ohag.html

Glossary

Note: words from Euskera, the Basque language, are italicized. Other words are from Spanish.

Abertzale	lit. patriot (izquierda *abertzale* refers to the radical Basque left, including ETA and Batasuna)
Alarde	ceremonial military-style parade
Alboka	wind instrument
Arrantzale	fisherman
Auzolan	a mutual aid tradition among neighbours in the Basque countryside
Atalaya	watchtower
Barrio	quarter (area) of town or city
Baserri	Basque farmhouse (*baserritar:* farmer or farm-dweller)
Bertsolari	verse-maker, composer of spontaneous oral poetry; *bertsolarismo* is the practice of oral composition)
Bilbaíno	citizen of Bilbao
Borroka	struggle (*kale borroka* is "street struggle", a strategy of political vandalism or "youth intifada" practised by young members of the izquierda *abertzale*)
Cabezudos	"giant heads", large papier-mâché carnival or fiesta masks
Casa torre	tower house, fortified dwelling of medieval nobility
Casco viejo	old quarter of city
Cuadrilla	close-knit group of friends from childhood onwards
Cuenca	watershed
Danzari	male traditional dancers
Danzarine	female traditional dancers

Dultzaina	wind instrument
Diputación	provincial administration
Españolista	pejorative term for Basque person or party whose national loyalty is to Spain rather than the Basque Country
Etarra	member of ETA
Erdera	any language other than Euskera
Ertzaintza	Basque autonomous police force, controlled by the CAV; an individual police officer is an *ertzaina*
Etxea	house
Euskaldun	speaker of *Euskera*, originally indicated any Basque person
Euskera	the Basque language
Fuero	charter of local rights or privileges
Gaupasa egin	to stay up all night
Gora!	"Long live!"
Hegoalde	the Spanish Basque Country, literally "the southern part"
Herriko etxea	town hall ("the house of the people")
Hordago	ultimatum, especially in card games
Ikastola	school where the medium of instruction is *Euskera*
Ikurriña	Basque national flag
Iparralde	the French Basque Country (literally "the Northern side")
Izquierda *abertzale*	see *abertzale*
Jaiak	fiestas, games
Juerga	a good time, "craic"
Kale borroka	see *borroka*
Kaletar	lit. street-dweller, townie.
Kaxarranka	dance on casket in Leketio fiestas
Kofradia	guild, as in fisherman's guild
Lauburu	"four-headed" Basque symbol, possible of solar origin, resembles a curved swastika, or the fan symbol on a car dashboard
Lehendakari	first minister of the CAV

Llanada	plains, flatlands
Makila	stick, usually a ceremonial walking stick, often with a concealed blade or sword
Pilota	Basque handball. The Spanish "pelota" is often used by Basque speakers, however, and to complicate matters this is often used with the Basque suffix –ari to indicate a pelota player, *pelotari*
Plaza mayor	main square
Pintxo	Basque adaptation of Spanish "pincho", a bar snack
Ribera	river plain, especially applied to the south of Navarre in Basque context
Romería	excursion and picnic associated with fiesta, usually to a sanctuary church
Sirimiri	the soft, persistent and drenching Basque mist or light rain
Txapela	Basque beret. *Boina* is also used.
Txikiteo	drinking "small ones", originally glasses of wine in different bars. This has morphed into a Spanish verb, txikitear, to go drinking.
Txalaparta	musical instrument resembling a very large wooden zylophone
Txistu	a small flute, usually played with the right hand while standing or walking, while the left-hand plays a drum. The player is a *txistulari*
Zarzuela	Spanish musical art form, between opera and music hall
Zazpiak bat	"the seven are one", a Basque nationalist slogan referring to the seven Basque provinces

Acronyms and Organizations

Batasuna	the main political party of the izquierda *abertzale*, alleged to be the political wing of

	ETA. Known as Herri Batasuna, Popular Unity, when it was founded in 1978
CAV	Communidad Autónoma Vasca, the Basque Autonomous Community, made up of the provinces of Vizcaya, Álava and Guipúzcoa.
ETA	*Euskadi Ta Askatasuna*, Basque Homeland and Liberty, the terrorist organization which fights for "Basque independence and socialism". Founded in 1959, it split in 1974 into ETA *político-militar* (ETA-pm) and ETA *militar* (ETA-m). ETA-pm dissolved itself in the early 1980s, and many of its leading members became outspoken critics of Basque nationalism in general. Today's ETA is descended from ETA-m and dissident members of ETA-pm.
PNV	Partido Nacionalista Vasco/*Eusko Alderdi Jeltzaleari*, the Basque Nationalist Party. The mainstream democratic expression of Basque nationalism, which has led all governments of the CAV since it was established in 1980.
PP	Partido Popular, the main Spanish nationalist and conservative party, radically opposed to Basque nationalism
PSOE	Partido Socialista Obrero Español, the main Spanish centre-left party, which has a friendlier but still deeply problematic relationship with Basque nationalism. Usually the second-most-voted party among Basques in the CAV, rivals the PP for leadership in Navarre.

Index of Names & Organizations

Index of Places & Landmarks